UNDER REPRESENTATION

T0386117

Under Representation

The Racial Regime of Aesthetics

David Lloyd

FORDHAM UNIVERSITY PRESS

New York 2019

Fordham University Press gratefully acknowledges financial assistance and support provided for the publication of this book by the University of California, Riverside.

Copyright © 2019 Fordham University Press

All rights reserved. No part of this publication may be reproduced, stored in a retrieval system, or transmitted in any form or by any means—electronic, mechanical, photocopy, recording, or any other—except for brief quotations in printed reviews, without the prior permission of the publisher.

Fordham University Press has no responsibility for the persistence or accuracy of URLs for external or third-party Internet websites referred to in this publication and does not guarantee that any content on such websites is, or will remain, accurate or appropriate.

Fordham University Press also publishes its books in a variety of electronic formats. Some content that appears in print may not be available in electronic books.

Visit us online at www.fordhampress.com.

Library of Congress Cataloging-in-Publication Data available online at https://catalog.loc.gov.

Printed in the United States of America

21 20 19   5 4 3 2 1
First edition

CONTENTS

PREFACE

There are books whose unfolding, from a handful of ill-formed questions to the work that finally appears, takes so many years that their chapters begin to resemble fragments of a memoir. They map out the shifting perspectives and learning processes that the passage of time hopefully entails. *Under Representation* is one of those books. The initial framing of its arguments stemmed from the "culture wars" of the late 1980s, out of a need to account for the seemingly unyielding racism of the so-called liberal institutions. How could institutions whose missions promised democratic inclusivity and enlightened inquiry remain in practice so resistant to the project of racial desegregation? To approach that question was, in the context of the intellectual left's then-pressing concern with ideology and institutions, to inquire into the political formation of subjects that educational institutions were charged with producing. Coming to such questions from research into Irish nationalism and anticolonialism, where the role of culture in the shaping of political subjects was so prominent, I found myself pursuing them into the terrain of aesthetic philosophy, the foundation of the humanities disciplines that were most troubled by the culture wars. Those circumstantial conjunctions would become the enduring matrix of a set of questions about aesthetics, race, and politics that continued to engage me on a track that ran parallel to my ongoing work on Ireland and postcolonialism.

They were not questions that lost their urgency. In the insurgent optimism of the late 1980s, it would have been hard to envisage the retrenchment that was about to take place in the wake of the Cold War: the defunding of the university and its consequent privatization and corporatization; the rise of neoliberal economics globally, harnessed to a political foreclosure of alternatives to brutal regimes of austerity and expropriation of public goods, from welfare to education; and the rollback of the small gains of affirmative action in the name of postracial rubrics like "excellence and diversity." All those factors stalled the transformative aims that had been at stake in the culture wars, above all the democratization of the university through its radical diversification. Though the institutions still spoke the language of inclusion and representation, their actual capacity to continue to segregate and to restrict access to the educational commons was borne out in the ever-more stratified demography of both the university and society. Merely to maintain and defend some of the gains of the post–civil rights decades seemed struggle enough. And the language of rights and representation that was still the idiom necessary to any defensive agenda came to seem as inadequate to the actual political situation as the invocation of universality and the human in the face of the increasing relegation of so many to disposability under the neoliberal dispensation.

The chapters gathered in *Under Representation* embody successive attempts to come to terms with the evolving conditions in which any struggle for democratic transformation and justice took place. Throughout, I assume that the critical theorization of the aesthetic, as the realm in which the notion of the subject of freedom was thought alongside the subordination of unfree subjects, is indispensable to understanding the formations of politics and race that shaped the modern epoch among whose ruins we continue to work. I seek to supplement the analysis of race that has been advanced so powerfully of late but that, surprisingly, has almost entirely left the terrain of aesthetic theory aside. This is especially surprising given the importance of artworks of every kind to both the imaginative survival of the racialized and the critical resistance to racism. *Under Representation* as a whole argues that to ignore the aesthetic as a crucial domain within which the modern idea of the human was forged is to overlook its continuing force in the formation of the racial and political structures of the present. It is that formation that I name throughout the racial regime of representation, tracking its genealogy from Enlightenment thinkers like Kant and Schiller to late modernist critics like Adorno and Benjamin.

This book emerges out of my longstanding engagement with postcolonial theory and seeks to challenge the no less peculiar occlusion of race from the major works of that field. That postcolonial engagement has been inflected by an ongoing dialogue with critical race theory and in particular with black studies, which over the last few decades have entirely transformed the thinking of race as a historical and philosophical category. My own entry point into the analysis of race and colonialism as an Irish undergraduate in England studying Irish nationalism was through Frantz Fanon. His analysis of language and colonialism in *Black Skin, White Masks* was to me a startling revelation of the colonial nature of British rule in Ireland, opening the way to an analytical framework that was then, in the late 1970s, virtually never considered. Fanon's work has remained an indispensable touchstone for me. Throughout *Under Representation* he opens a passageway between predominantly US analyses of race and the neglected question of raciality in postcolonial studies and between these fields and that of aesthetic theory. Hence what might otherwise seem a peculiarity of this book: its frequent juxtaposition of Fanon's insights with readings of European critical thinkers. Fanon's fundamental interrogation of the cultural imposition of racial colonialism that goes by the name of assimilation already implied the outlines of a critique of the racial structures of the aesthetic.

Though this is a theoretical work that intervenes primarily in the traditions of aesthetic thought, the conditions out of which I have written were always collective and dialogical. Given the many years over which it has been in the making, it would be impossible for me to acknowledge every individual from whose conversation or writing I have learned or whose criticisms I have absorbed in revising my thinking. But over those years, the common work of a number of groups and collectives has proven indispensable to my own and this book could not have been written without their sustaining commitment to dialogue as the essential medium of thought. I still think of the Group for the Critical Study of Colonialism, which met in Berkeley from about 1984 to 1991, as an inspirational example of the creative work that can be done with minimal material resources and an abundance of determination. Later, the University of California Multicampus Research Group on the Subaltern and the Popular, organized by Swati Chattopadhyay and Bhaskar Sarkar at UC Santa Barbara from 2005 to 2014, was indispensable to thinking through the question of subalternity and furnished an intellectual community that never failed to prove that laughter and enjoyment are the companions of dialectic. These were truly symposia in the original sense of the term. Most recently, the informal gatherings of the Anti-Colonial Machine have offered since 2010 the kind of insurgent spaces that generously and generatively allow one to risk venturing unfinished thought in the confidence that it will be returned augmented and enhanced. To the members of all these collectives, I am grateful for the opportunities to think together and to learn the gift of an intellectual collaboration that can never be recuperated or institutionalized.

No less formative of my thinking have been the numerous organizations of students who have maintained and pressed the demand for justice on every campus at which I have worked over the last three decades, from the student organizers of the antiapartheid divestment campaign at Berkeley in the 1980s to the Student Coalition Against Labor Exploitation at the University of Southern California in 2007 and Students for Justice in Palestine in the present. Student activism is often seen as a distraction from intellectual work, but I have continually discovered that the commitment of students to campaigns for justice and democratization is a constant source of new and inventive theorization. Time and again, I have found my own thinking questioned and pushed by students for whom intellectual positions that have become habitual are by no means given and who constantly refuse to accept that there are no alternatives. That is a gift for which I have been and will always remain profoundly thankful.

Some chapters from this book were published in earlier versions in the volumes credited in the notes. My thanks are due to the editors of those journals and books for their own comments as well as for the opportunity to receive feedback that has contributed so much to my rethinking of each chapter. To them, as well as to the two anonymous readers for Fordham University Press, I am grateful for the incentive to clarify or extend the arguments of this book. What faults remain are, of course, my own responsibility.

A number of individuals have, in a practical and a moral sense, been instrumental in bringing this project to fruition. At a time when I despaired of bringing the various chapters that compose the book into any coherent shape, Clare Counihan brought to bear her inimitable editing skills and, with an extraordinary eye for detail and attention to the unfolding of arguments, ensured whatever consistency this book has finally achieved. I cannot thank her adequately. Tom Lay at Fordham University Press has been an admirable editor in a quite different way. I owe him thanks for seeing this project through. I also want to acknowledge the editorial labor that has gone into maintaining at Fordham a list of publications that has kept faith with the work of theoretical reflection at a time when many publishers might have abandoned the endeavor. It is my hope that *Under Representation* will do the Press and its editorial legacy at least some justice.

Finally, this book would never have come together without the benefit of Sarita See's sustained moral and practical encouragement. From her I have received not only a renewed belief in the value of the work and the example of unwavering intellectual and ethical commitment but also the daily gift of living abundantly. For such gifts, no thanks are ever enough.

Under Representation

The modern times that W. E. B. Du Bois once
identified as the century of the color line have now
passed. Racial hierarchy is still with us.

—PAUL GILROY, *Against Race*

The Erasure of Race

The brief moment in which the thought of a postracial West could be
entertained has imploded, leaving a lingering afterglow of its all too premature declaration of a wishful intent. White supremacy is on the march
in the United States with renewed energy and arrogant violence while xe-
nophobic nationalism has penetrated deeply into Europe's political core,
from England to Hungary. US police killings of black and brown people
proceed with numbing regularity and virtually complete legal impunity.
Racist rage and police violence likewise target indigenous peoples across
the white settler colonies, from Canada to Israel to Australia. At Standing
Rock and elsewhere, militarized police confront Native water protectors
who struggle to preserve both lands and lifeways from the increasingly
brutal inroads of capitalist accumulation. Racially driven anti-immigrant
sentiment has been sanctioned by state policies of border control and de-
portation, set in motion by Donald Trump's Departments of Justice and
Homeland Security but also by those of Barack Obama, first black president of the United States. Trump's border wall was preceded by both Israel's apartheid wall and Fortress Europe, around whose edges refugees
from two continents are detained in grim camps or consigned to death by

drowning. For the most part, they are fleeing the chaos of the Western war against the Islamic world, from Afghanistan to Libya, that has been prosecuted without interruption since the first Gulf War. The project of the post–Cold War New World Order that held out the prospect of a universal democratic dispensation spearheaded by armed force has foundered in the morass of unending wars. Humanitarian interventions in the name of rights and democracy have succeeded only in displacing millions and shattering fragile economic and social infrastructures.

All this has taken place in the name of a postracial order. But it becomes increasingly evident that under that order racial divisions once explicitly predicated on biological marks have given way to categories that render disposable populations subject to violence and what Zygmunt Bauman terms "moral eviction."[1] The alibis of the West's racial ordering of the world may have been reconfigured, but the fundamental discriminations that divide those who can claim respect, rights, and personhood from those reduced to mere disposable existence remain in place. Against this reconfiguration of the color line in the twenty-first century—whether we name it neoliberal, postcolonial, or merely global capitalism—liberal conceptions of the human as a universal value prove to have little to offer beyond defensive appeals. Increasingly it becomes apparent that the concept of the human and the terms that congregate around it—freedom, self-determination, rights, property—do not transcend difference and division. Rather, they constitute the very lines of demarcation that separate human subjects from subjected humans.[2]

In the face of these renewed forms of subjugation in the name of the human subject, I offer this book as a contribution to the genealogy of the racial formation of the human in aesthetic culture. My sense of the necessity of such a project has been underscored by the realization that there have been far too few substantive accounts of the central role of the aesthetic in the emergence and dissemination of that universal human subjecthood. In *Under Representation*, I argue that the constitutive relation between the concepts of universality, freedom, and humanity and the racial order of the modern world is grounded in the founding texts of the disciplines that articulated them and that we now term the humanities. In the late Enlightenment, a discourse on aesthetic experience emerged that furnishes a decisive account of the conditions of possibility for universal human subjecthood. This aesthetic theory is not in the first place a philosophy of fine art, though it may draw on artworks for its examples. Against that common conception of the aesthetic, *Under Representation* insists on the distinction between so-called aesthetic works and the actual ends and effects of the philosophical and theoretical work of aesthetics. I argue that since its inception in the late eighteenth century, aesthetic philosophy has functioned as a regulative discourse of the human on which the modern conception of the political and racial order of modernity rests.

Aesthetic philosophy arises out of the necessity to forestall the revolutionary claims of its epoch and to substitute for the immediacy of political demands and practices an aesthetic formation of the disinterested and "liberal" subject. To become such a subject is the precondition for participation in the public sphere. Moreover, the aesthetic envisages that subject as a universal norm, representative of the human in general. Aesthetic reflection does not contemplate its objects for the sake of sheer delight. It judges, and judges of the human: The terms put in play by aesthetics establish the set of discriminations and distributions by which the Savage comes to be distinguished from the civil subject, the partial and particular human from the universal Subject, and the "pathological" or suffering, needing, desiring human from the ethical human Subject. Aesthetics from its inception has been a regulative discourse of the human. Race is not, therefore, to borrow a term from Nahum Chandler, *exorbitant* to the aesthetic. It is not some historically contingent matter that contaminates the transcendental foundations of pure thought; it is essential to the very possibility of positing a "common sense" on which the subjective but universal claims of the aesthetic could be based.[3]

Under Representation demonstrates the constitutive rather than contingent role that race thinking has played in the formulation of aesthetic thought since Kant's *Critique of Judgment*, contaminating the ideal disinterest of that sphere with its very material role in determining the hierarchies of human being. Though several brilliant essays have addressed Kant's *Critique of Pure Reason* in order to tease out its fundamentally racialized structure, remarkably few philosophers have analyzed how race *structures* critique. Much is at stake in this apparent reluctance. As Rei Terada puts it, it is critical "to expand the methodology of the study of race beyond attention to instances that already assume that the reader can recognize what counts as race and racism (and therefore what counts as a reference to it), or attention that limits itself to what a period text thinks race is."[4] Such a reorientation expands the horizon of race critical analysis beyond specific instances of race and racism as objects for thought and beyond the domains of thought that appear self-evidently apposite to discussions of racism into those in which race operates as a discretely structuring assumption. Race is, in other words, not simply the concern of the social and life sciences: It equally permeates those fields that are ostensibly most free of its long historical shadow. The aesthetic has been the prototype of the disciplines that claim to represent "Humanity" as such and not its different groups or classes that are supposedly the objects of anthropology or sociology.

Indeed, as Chandler points out, race, or the problem of the Negro, has all too long been considered exorbitant to the concerns of philosophy and the humanities, as epiphenomenal or of merely anecdotal or historically contingent interest. Certainly, historians of philosophy have assembled Enlightenment thinkers' statements about race, but the resulting collections have rarely succeeded in doing more than indicating a compendium of ignorance and prejudice that can still be dismissed as an effect of the general cultural conventions of the time.[5] Marking the racial bias of Enlightenment thinkers has had all too little impact on the reading of the philosophical texts themselves, since the often egregious, pseudo-empirical observations on race are held apart from the systematic work in which the strictly philosophical universal moral or epistemological claims are made. Robert Bernasconi, for example, observes how historians of philosophy recognize Kant's crucial contribution to modern racial thought but fail to bring his essays on race "into relation with his teleology, his moral philosophy, or his essay on universal history, in spite of the obvious question that they raised: how could his racism coexist with his moral universalism?"[6] Yet even Bernasconi continues to focus on the racial schemas that appear in Kant's quasi-scientific or anthropological works with their empirically based classifications of races rather than investigating the racial foundations of the critical works.[7]

Accordingly, the racial structures of aesthetic theory as such, and of its decisive formulations of the conditions of possibility for thinking the categories of the human and the universal, have remained virtually unexamined.[8] As Simon Gikandi remarks, "from the very beginning the modern idea of art and its judgment was theoretically connected to powerful racial economies. . . . And yet, it is not accidental that the ideas of race and the aesthetic are separated, almost instinctively, in all major discussions of modernity."[9] The investment that Gikandi notes in the "purity" of the aesthetic as a domain of freedom and unconstrained development forecloses the critique of the aesthetic as an intrinsically racial and political discourse. With the possible exception of Gayatri Chakravorty Spivak's *Critique of Postcolonial Reason*, which I discuss at some length in Chapters 2 and 4, we lack any extended treatments of the constitutive rather than contingent role played by racial judgments in the very formation of aesthetic theory and in its ongoing regulative function for other cultural domains.[10] This absence in the field of critical race theory and postcolonial studies is deeply consequential precisely because, as *Under Representation* argues, aesthetic theory has furnished the indispensable terms that regulate the production and reproduction of the idea of the human subject of modernity.

The Aesthetic Division of the Human

That racialization is at once coeval with and constitutive of modernity is no longer in question. As Chandler argues, "the theme or question of race . . . takes us close to the root of that which we consider constitutive of our world, of our modernity, of our common colonial nexus."[11] Chandler's insight extends the long line of black radical scholarship on race and modernity that runs from W. E. B. Du Bois to Eric Williams's history of the Atlantic slave trade to Cedric Robinson's *Black Marxism*, but it also chimes with a range of recent scholarship in other fields, from Aníbal Quijano's theorization of the coloniality of power/knowledge to Patrick Wolfe's comparative work on the racial regimes of settler colonialism in *Traces of History*.[12] Sylvia Wynter conjoins those traditions and ambitiously articulates how the advent of European colonization at the onset of the modern era produced and depended on a fully racialized "self-description" of the human, or "Man." In a series of essays beginning in the 1980s, Wynter argues that the colonization of the Americas and the global expansion of the West impelled the emergence of a new "descriptive statement/prescriptive statement of what it is to be human." This new statement introduced a categorical "human/subhuman distinction," inaugurating a "coloniality of *being*" in addition to that of power/knowledge.[13] This epochal "redescription of the human" displaced the medieval Christian/pagan opposition and instituted a secular conception of Man that at once divided the world between rational humans and irrational subhumans and produced the subject of the newly sovereign European states.[14]

Subsequently, this early modern conception of the human and its division of those endowed with Reason from the irrational Other would be displaced by a second secular variant that emerges at the end of the eighteenth century in the form of the "bio-economic subject" of modernity.[15] Both versions of Man coincide in representing their Other as ontologically lacking and, within the developmental schema of the later model, lagging behind or failing to adapt to modernity.[16] However, as Wynter proposes in an earlier essay, those who belong to "the set of Ontological Others" of Western Man do in fact offer "the alternative modes of being human" by which that unilaterally declared "figure of *man*" might be disenchanted and dethroned.[17] It is their capacity, as Katherine McKittrick parses Wynter,

"to ethically question and undo systems of racial violence and their at-
tendant knowledge systems that produce this racial violence as 'common-
sense' [*sic*]."[18]

Powerful as Wynter's overarching narrative is, and sympathetic as I am
to her arguments, her account of the racial ordering of post-Enlightenment modernity strangely ignores the role of aesthetic theory in constituting the terms of that order. Wynter indicates her interpretive investment
in specific literary works, from *Don Quixote* to *Invisible Man*, and in the
possibilities of literary critical interventions outlined in her 1987 essay
"On Disenchanting Discourse." But her later focus on "the limits of the
purely biocentric order of consciousness that is genre-specific to the Western bourgeoisies's *homo oeconomicus*" risks overemphasizing the biological
dimension of a pseudo-scientific racism that has largely been supplanted,
without diminishing the virulence of racial categories, by the appeal to
culture on which contemporary articulations of difference rest.[19] As she
argues, the nineteenth-century episteme "virtually partitioned off 'the Humanities' as the discourse of the Human Self from 'anthropology' as the
discourse on the particular 'native' Other."[20] But bracketing the formative
role of aesthetic philosophy in constituting the subjects of the humanities
and the objects of anthropology leaves that crucial boundary unanalyzed
and thus still powerfully operative.

Modernity operates not by positing a "purely biocentric order" but
through the differentiation of spheres wherein individuals fragmented by
the division of labor find compensation in the universalizing claims of political and aesthetic subjecthood. Aesthetic theory enunciates the conditions of possibility for this modern political subject of the liberal state that
succeeds the earlier subject of the monarch that Wynter identifies in the
West's first descriptive statement of Man. The aesthetically governed articulation of those distinct spheres through which the modern subject moves
distinguishes the unfree subject of heteronomy from the self-determining
subject of autonomy and the latter from the racialized anthropological object of an undifferentiated culture. Of course, the differentiation of the social sciences from the humanities goes some way toward accounting for the
absence of a developed discourse on race and the aesthetic: If race appears
as the proper object of the former, aesthetic judgment, in its abstraction
from particular conditions and its claim to universality, supposedly transcends racial differences, as Gikandi notes. And yet the aesthetic domain
functions within the order of modernity to regulate those very distinctions. Accordingly, the occlusion of its critique from the most comprehen-
sive critical genealogies of modern racial formations permits, as we will

see further, the persistence of racial subordination even in and through proclamations of its abolition in a postracial moment.[21]

In what follows, I argue that the aesthetic gives rise to what this book terms a racial "regime of representation." This term echoes both Cedric Robinson's "racial regimes," which designate "constructed social systems in which race is proposed as a justification for the relations of power," and Patrick Wolfe's cognate "regimes of race," which compose a shifting and diverse body of "regimes of difference with which colonisers have sought to manage subject populations."[22] Though I seek to maintain their mutual focus on how such regimes articulate relations of power and domination, my aim is to elaborate the ways in which the aesthetic structures those relations, even in the name of universality, through a complex conceptual matrix of representation. Representation here signifies not merely the mimetic depiction of the world or a means of securing political advocacy within democratic or republican institutions. As it is conceived within aesthetic philosophy, representation is an activity that articulates the various spheres of human practice and theory, from the most fundamental acts of perception and reflection to the relation of the subject to the political and the economic, or to the social as a whole. Ultimately, aesthetics naturalizes representation, forging the modern subject's disposition to be represented through an aesthetic pedagogy whose end is the submission of the subject to the State. Above all, representation regulates the distribution of racial identifications along a developmental trajectory: The Savage or Primitive and the Negro or Black remain on the threshold of an unrealized humanity, still subject to affect and to the force of nature, not yet capable of representation, not yet apt for freedom and civility. They stand, in Hortense Spillers's resonant phrasing, as "vestibular to culture," serving "as the route by which dominant modes decided between the human and the 'other.'"[23] The narrative of representation conceptualized in aesthetic theory, from Kant to Theodor Adorno and Walter Benjamin, constantly replays this distinction between the pathological or "affectable" subject that demarcates the threshold of the human and the aesthetic subject in and of representation.[24] It shapes an aesthetic anthropology prior to any philosophy of art.

Thus, while aesthetic theory is usually taken to promote a "liberal" or noncoercive relation to its objects, it is, in fact, structured through and through by a symbolically violent figure of the impassable threshold. This threshold none can pass without a splitting that severs the corporealized human being from the formal subject of aesthetic judgment that is identified with the universal Subject of humanity. Racial figures haunt that threshold, marking the boundary between the subjects of civility and the undeveloped space of savagery and blackness. Frantz Fanon's graphic portrayal of the petrifaction of the colonized speaks not only to the corporealization or somatization of this stasis at the violent material thresholds of the colonized society, to the sense of being "hemmed in," but also to the symbolic place of every colonized subject as a kind of "boundary stone" that bears witness to the founding violence—material and symbolic—of every racial order.[25]

The convergence of two distinct racial figures, the Black and the Savage, as markers of the threshold of emergence of humanity resides in the productive ambiguity of what constitutes unfreedom—subjection to determination—in aesthetic thought. The Black as slave is the extreme instance of a social condition of material or corporeal unfreedom, economically, juridically, physically. But unfreedom in the case of the "pathological" subject in general is defined as a condition of subjection to nature—a state of necessity, as da Silva economically puts it—that is at once internal and external: subjection to nature as outer force meets inward subjection to nature as need, fear, or desire.[26] This natural state of determination, inner and outer, precedes and justifies the social condition of enslavement even as it legitimates the dispossession and obliteration of the indigenous "savage" by the free settler.[27] To be in such a state of heteronomy blocks the path to autonomous and disinterested judgment wherein, as we will see, aesthetic philosophy locates the very condition of possibility of identifying with the representative subject of universality.

Three racial figures circulate through *Under Representation*. The third is that of the Subaltern, a figure that differs from the Black and the Savage in that it is not defined in relation to freedom as such but in direct relation to representation. The Subaltern stands, as I argue in Chapter 4, as the negation of representation. Though it appears as a moment rather than as the collective noun for any group or class, it designates historically those colonized populations that exist in a relation of exteriority to the state and its institutions. These never enter into representation by the state or by the intellectuals whose ethical and discursive formation has shaped them as the exemplary instances of the racial regime of representation. The Subaltern stands as the destruction of representation rather than its threshold and cannot be reconciled to the state by the promise of self-determination: Historically, it has proven as recalcitrant to nationalist modes of decolonization as it has to the colonial state. Subalternity, therefore, offers the possibility of alternative modes of life to those shaped around the matrix of freedom, self-determination, subjecthood, and universality that constitute the terms of representation grounded in the aesthetic.

Under Representation thus offers an account of modern aesthetic thought that is decisively at odds with the notion of the "representative regime" given currency by Jacques Rancière in his recent and influential works on politics and aesthetics.[28] For him, that regime belongs with an earlier practice of representation as mimesis and the subsequent modern "aesthetic regime"—a new "distribution of the sensible" (*partage du sensible*)—allows for the gradual emergence of voices to which a "share" (*part*) had been denied. From the perspective of *Under Representation*, as I argue in Chapter 1, Rancière's widely accepted history of the aesthetic is mistaken and misleading, enacting the reinscription of an "aesthetic regime" that has been politically hegemonic and instrumental in the regulation of racial form since the Enlightenment. Instead, *Under Representation* tracks the intricate relation between the various domains of representation in post-Enlightenment aesthetics. As first outlined in aesthetic philosophy, representation is far from being a mere matter of inclusion in canons or institutions, or of more or less stereotypical depictions, or of demands for demographic equity. It is a fundamentally regulative and operative concept that supplies the form in which racialization takes place and to a large extent accounts for the obstinate persistence of racial judgment even in supposedly postracial times. The powerful work of naturalizing representation performed by aesthetics is an indelible determinant of the modern racial regime.

Rancière's rehabilitation of the aesthetic is not unprecedented. Long after philosophy declared the end of art, and like the faint gleam of an almost sunken sun, the aesthetic continues to exert a perennial fascination. Over the last three decades alone, approaches to the aesthetic have been as diverse as they have been multiple and recurrent. At times they have been suspiciously critical, aiming at "aesthetic ideology" or the "ideology of the aesthetic," though neither term accurately communicates how the aesthetic functions as the very form of political and racial ideology and not merely as one mode of ideology or one domain of human practice shaped by ideology.[29] At other times, the returns to the aesthetic have sought its vindication, asserting a persisting nonideological moment in aesthetic experience or even reclaiming the utopian or emancipatory potential of the aesthetic.[30] The frequency of these "returns to the aesthetic" should hardly seem surprising.[31] The discourse on the aesthetic that emerged in the late Enlightenment, especially in the work of Kant and his interpreter, Friedrich Schiller, consciously assumed a founding role in the reconfiguration of the liberal arts or the humanities as disciplines. These were to be concerned not only with the refinement of taste but with the formation or cultivation of human beings as civil subjects, necessarily defined, as this book will maintain, against the undeveloped racial other. To return to the aesthetic is, then, to return to the founding claims of the cultural disciplines within or against which critical intellectuals continue to operate.

Those disciplines are riven by a set of contradictions that derive from the ambiguities that have informed the aesthetic since its inaugural formulations. The aesthetic grounds a body of disciplinary practices whose institutionalization in the course of the nineteenth century aimed at the formation of subjects for the state. This task, which is not merely assigned to the aesthetic but first envisaged in it, performs its ideological function through its claim to compensate for the fragmentation of humans by the division of labor and social conflicts with an exemplary experience of wholeness and harmonization. Aesthetic experience is endowed with such a capacity precisely by its removal from practical engagement with the world into a realm of disinterested contemplation, meaning that its social effectiveness is a function of its withdrawal from the social. The aesthetic is still commonly believed not just to address the realm of art and its reception and appreciation but to represent, moreover, a domain of creativity and imagination in which we enjoy the freedom denied to us in the actual world of domination or heteronomy. Far from simply being a disciplinary formation, the aesthetic dimension, to borrow Herbert Marcuse's phrase, prefigures a realm of liberation that is (always) yet to arrive and through its own ideal autonomy allows us to enjoy the anticipation of a world emancipated from coercion and arbitrary constraint.[32] Its very emancipation from political or ideological motives ensures its true political effect: the deferral of freedom's actualization in the world. This conception of the aesthetic and of its prefigurative relation to emancipation runs through the tradition of aesthetic philosophy, from Schiller to Marcuse, from Matthew Arnold to Rancière, from the right to the left of the political spectrum.

The persistence of such a conception, often unsuspiciously embraced in spheres quite remote from philosophical contemplation, is apparent in the still-pervasive image of the artist as the epitome of the free being, a distinction that quietly consigns most nonaesthetic social practices to the realm of unfreedom. Since the Romantic epoch, the creative freedom of the artist has always appeared in contradistinction to the heteronomy of subordination to alienated labor or social convention. The product of this freely creating artist, the artwork or "aesthetic work," is all too easily confused with the work of aesthetic philosophy that identified the separate sphere of Art (or "fine art") and declared itself the domain in which the very possibility of a universal human subject could be posited. The confusion of these quite distinct, if intersecting, practices—artworks and the aesthetic philosophy that takes them as its object—enables the misleading conception that aesthetic culture transcends the coercive apparatuses of the state or the unfreedom of the racial regimes that have informed the post-Enlightenment era. The moments of projected freedom or dissidence that both artworks and aesthetic theory do actually manifest emerge as critical effects of the contradictions through which they work. Artworks above all, charged as they are with the burden of subjective and particular articulations of social life, cannot but give voice to the painful grappling of individuals and communities with the coercive constraints that everywhere confront their efforts at undominated living. As such, however, rather than representing a sphere of freedom, they bear the signifying scars of unfree existence. It is in that sense that I read, in Chapters 3 and 4 of this book, novels that render the contradictions that in the racialized colonial sphere foreclose the full development of the subject, the emancipatory end that aesthetic philosophy promises and that has formed the core project of liberal arts pedagogy and its canons of exemplary works. *Season of Migration to the North* and *Wide Sargasso Sea* powerfully exemplify the critical antagonism of artworks to the false promise of aesthetic liberation.

Crises of Representation

Under Representation engages with the continuing and informing effect of late Enlightenment aesthetic theory on the fundamental racial and political formations of modernity down to the present. It was in the early 1990s that I began to frame the outlines of *Under Representation* in an effort to understand the foundations of the racial system of education—or the racial foundations of education—in relation to a more critical concept of representation than was then in circulation. That concept could not be restricted to notions of political or demographic representation. Already it was clear that the institutions were saturated at every level with questions as to who could be represented and who was representative that had only marginally to do with the counting of and accounting for bodies. The initial conception of this book, indeed, arose in a moment that we might now think of as the last crisis of the liberal state even as it was succumbing to neoliberalism. At that moment, the claims of minoritized subjects for redress and access to state institutions, and not least to the educational apparatus, threatened not so much a demographic adjustment as a complete transformation of those institutions. The questions thrown up by that moment, even now that the forms of struggle have been contained and altered by unforeseen exigencies, continue to linger. The "multicultural" project or, in conservative terms, the "culture wars" of the late 1980s and 1990s, was, for many of us who participated, aimed not at mere demographic inclusion but at the radical rethinking of the protocols and ends of those institutions. The right's anxiety about the fate of Western civilization, while it masked the devastating inroads of privatization and monetization that were quietly advancing beneath the noisier cultural struggles, signaled something that was at stake in those struggles beyond the demand for affirmative action as a means to diversify the campuses demographically. A particular regime of inclusion, or assimilation, was being challenged by students and by social movements bent not simply on gaining access to existing institutions but on a radical democratization of learning such that the spatial assumptions encoded in terms like *inclusion* and *access* no longer made sense. A complete dismantling of the enclosure of the means to thought and study was what was ultimately envisaged "as a political and cultural intervention into the white supremacist university."[33] But even such compromise formations as affirmative action and multiculturalism—rubrics that sought to contain the more radical potentials of desegregation within logics of equivalence and parity—already led inevitably to a certain derangement of the university.[34] Subjects for whom the protocols of aesthetic education or the still-colonial disciplines of civility did not appear self-evident were questioning en masse the order of the classroom and the ends of their schooling.

The response of the professoriate was markedly aesthetic, circling around various expressions of distaste or disgust and driven by the sudden realization of being embodied—gendered and raced—in classrooms that had once guaranteed their abstraction and transparency as disinterested representatives of the ethical ends of the institution. Such consternation in face of the simple fact of the limited democratization underway, incomplete and insufficiently theorized as it was, betrayed not a merely contingent but a constitutive racial disposition. Liberal intellectuals, who would have disavowed any "vulgar" racial prejudice, resisted with remarkable tenacity any form of diversification that aimed beyond the incorporation of a greater number of cultures in the student body or curriculum in order to pursue an ongoing interrogation of the forms and ends of education. Above all, faculty rankled at the demand that collective learning should include the questioning of their own embodiment in the classroom. The familiar adjustment of including one or two "representative" minority authors in the literary or general education syllabus, as if to prove their equal access to humanity, was no longer enough. It became clear that a concept of representation that exceeded either its demographic or its mimetic relation to communities or cultures was at stake.

It was also clear that a certain understanding of representation was so normalized, so self-evident, as to form the common sense of the university. And not only its common sense. As I argue, especially in Chapter 4, the narrative of representation produces what we might call an "ego-ideal" for the intellectual, furnishing at once the means for their identification with the Subject of universality and the ethical guarantee of their representative relation to humanity. The investment of the professoriate in the racial regime of the university thus far exceeded—as it still exceeds—the lingering investment of oppositional intellectuals in "the empirical fact of our ongoing production and reproduction of our order."[35] It betokened, rather, the constitutive ground of their formation as—in da Silva's terms— "subjects of transparency"; accordingly, when challenged by those who are consigned to liminality, they were threatened in their very identity. Their crisis of representativity thus appeared no less as an emergency, a state of exception provoked by the movement of the racialized from the margin to the center: "The liberal grammar efficiently translates demands for racial justice back into the logic that renders any mechanism deployed to bring it about—such as affirmative [action] and voting rights—into something *extraordinary*, that is, beyond the usual, regular, and established, in short, exceptional and temporary."[36]

In the reactionary containment of that emergency by the neoliberal institutions that were installed in response to it, the insurgency of racial subjects has been reduced to their partial inclusion "as commodified and domesticated 'difference' that performs the ideological and material labor of buttressing late-capitalist mantras such as 'diversity and excellence' and 'global citizens.'"[37] Such "mantras" restore to institutional logics the common sense by which racial difference is reabsorbed by a regime of representation that proves constantly capable of reabsorbing a diversity of subjects precisely insofar as they are abstracted from the dense particularities by which they are differentiated. The neoliberal or corporate university signals the latest refunctioning of the regime of representation as institutional common sense, reworking the language of inclusion and multiculturalism into the postracial idiom that asserts the color blindness of the institution and the permeability of its threshold on the condition that difference be reduced to minor inflections of equivalence.[38] This has been, indeed, the principal mode by which, as Roderick Ferguson puts it, "dominant institutions attempted to reduce the initiatives of oppositional movements to the terms of hegemony."[39]

The following chapters map in part a long effort to account for that enfolding of representation with common sense and for the crisis that threatened it by tracking back to the foundational texts in which that conjunction was initially theorized. The first chapter of *Under Representation*, "The Aesthetic Regime of Representation," therefore focuses on the work performed by German idealist aesthetic thought in the political context of the bourgeois revolutions of America and France. With an emphasis on Kant's *Critique of Judgment*, it considers the "turn to the aesthetic" as a means of forestalling the immediacy of revolution and installing an implicitly pedagogical and developmental system of representation that defines the human and the political subject alike as universal and disinterested. That system relies on a notion of common sense that is undecidably the foundation and the product of an aesthetic education, a capacity latent in the human that nonetheless requires to be developed by an intervention that separates the civil subject from the Savage that stands at the threshold of humanity. In this respect, the foundations of aesthetic philosophy are at the same time the foundations of a "regime of representation" that differs markedly from that proposed by Rancière and others, offering not a means to inclusion through dissensus but a mode of regulating access to recognition as a fully human and politically capable subject.

The second chapter, "The Pathological Sublime," shows in greater detail how Kant's predication of the aesthetic not on physical sensation (as in the original meaning of the term) but on form and on the subjective yet universal judgment of taste is crucial to the elaboration of a concept of representation that is fundamentally racial and developmental in form. His distinction of his own mode of deduction from that of his precursor Edmund Burke explicitly aligns the latter's physiological approach to the analysis of aesthetic affects with the "pathological," meaning by that term a determinate relation to the world based on sensation, fear or desire, and gratification. These are the characteristics of the pre-ethical subject and also those that for Kant typify the Savage. The pathological is the constitutive antithesis of the ethical human who can participate in civil society and enjoy what Kant denominates the sensus communis or common sense that is the aesthetic ground of universality and that, while latent in all human beings, must still be developed in the Savage. The chapter concludes by examining the place of blackness as the index of the pathological by aligning Burke's reflections on the sublime horror inspired by the sight of a black woman with Frantz Fanon's exploration of the phenomenology of being seen in *Black Skin, White Masks*. While Fanon's famous account of being the object of a racist gaze dramatizes his "lived experience" of being barred from the human, Burke's anecdote throws into relief the anxious abyss into which the encounter with blackness throws the white subject and his representational schemas.

Obviously, by retaining the Kantian concept of the pathological I am not endorsing the sociological pathologization of racialized communities that underwrites their subjection to the technologies and interventions of disciplinary governmentality. I seek, rather, to underscore at every point how a distinction fundamental to the Kantian account of the human and of the capacity for subjecthood consistently institutes the threshold between the racial subordinate and the human subject of judgment. This distinction, of course, continues to underwrite the instrumental pathologization of the racial and colonized Other that is a constant of Western epistemological and civilizational orders. As Fred Moten puts it, "the pathologization of blacks and blackness in the discourse of the human and natural sciences" corresponds to "the corollary emergence of expertise as the defining epistemological register of the modern subject who is in that he knows, regulates, but cannot be black."[40] My own use of the term as it is positioned by Kant in differential counterpart to the formation of the ethical and aesthetic subject aims to elaborate critically the racial regime of representation within which the modern civil subject is produced.

Accordingly, Chapter 3, "Race under Representation," extends the argument as to the constitutive role played by the aesthetic regime of representation in modern racial formation. Working from the aesthetic thought of Kant and Schiller, it elaborates how metonymy and metaphor function in the formation of the stereotype in relation to the concept of representation as the means to assuming universality. On the one hand, racialization works at the "minimal" level of the organizing tropes of representation; on the other, those tropes embody an order of representation that appears as a recurrent civilizational narrative within which the terms of inclusion always function simultaneously as a rationale for excision. The metaphorical place of whiteness, representative of what I term the (universal) "Subject without properties" is—as I show through the work of two black writers, Tayeb Salih and Frantz Fanon—constitutively unavailable or barred to the racialized subject. Inclusion always requires the effective but impossible erasure of race even as it repeatedly constitutes its positions. Sylvia Wynter invokes the "*overrepresentation* of Man" as the fundamental challenge to dismantling the coloniality of the West. I seek here to disengage the notion of "underrepresentation" from its demographic usage in antiracist campaigns that aim only at proportional inclusion of racial and other minorities in existing institutions. Far from transforming those institutions, such a goal merely consolidates their claims to universality while reaffirming the violence by which, in the racial regime of representation, the racial other is barred, always relegated to the exteriority of race *under representation*.

Recent work in postcolonial studies has been preoccupied with the problematic status of the Subaltern as a category that eludes the very possibility of representation. Commencing with a sympathetic critique of Gayatri Chakravorty Spivak's foundational essay "Can the Subaltern Speak?," Chapter 4, "Representation's Coup," pursues a further elaboration of the regime of representation, arguing that the full force of that essay can only be grasped once the ethically representative function of the intellectual as aesthetic subject is comprehended. My reading of Marx's *Eighteenth Brumaire of Louis Bonaparte* then establishes the ways in which the performance of representation stands historically as well as conceptually as the means by which the intellectual has mediated the relation of subjects to the state. The aporia of subalternity lies, therefore, in the Subaltern's constitutive exteriority to representation: Where the Savage or the Negro stands as the threshold of humanity and of the developmental narrative of representation, the Subaltern is radically exterior, unavailable for identification or assimilation, and troubles the ethical self-identification of the intellectual as representative figure of the human. The chapter concludes with a reading of Jean Rhys's novel *Wide Sargasso Sea* as a critical allegory of the failure of identification with the racialized subaltern that lies at the heart of her rewriting of nineteenth-century aesthetic realism. The breakdown of novelistic representation in this modernist work correlates to a postcolonial—or, strictly, postabolitionist—crisis in the overarching regime of representation that frames it.

This question of subalternity and its relation to the modernist crisis of representation throws into relief the fault lines in the regime of representation that continues to regulate racial formation into late modernity. The final chapter of *Under Representation*, "The Aesthetic Taboo," concerns the fate of the aesthetic in the passage from its first major formulations to its modernist reconsideration by two major and symptomatic critical thinkers, Walter Benjamin and Theodor Adorno. It has long been known that Frankfurt School critical theory attempted a methodological synthesis of Freudian psychoanalysis with Marxism. What has not been observed is the extent to which Freud's writings on primitive culture, and on its survival in contemporary civilization, saturate the aesthetic thought of Walter Benjamin and Theodor Adorno. This chapter traces the resonances of Freud's thinking through a complex of topoi in their work: myth, magic, and, in particular, aura, as Benjamin theorizes that concept in terms drawn almost verbatim from Freud's *Totem and Taboo*. Neither thinker, I argue, ever manages to escape the ideal historical schema of aesthetics, which is the serial transition from a state of necessity, to a state of domination, to an ideal state of freedom. Insofar as the state of necessity is that which defines the Savage as pathological subject, this remains not contingently but immanently a racial schema. Adorno and Benjamin remain on the side of the threshold that both Enlightenment and the dialectic establish, that threshold that divides the Savage into the latent or protohuman and the outcast, the being discarded to the realm of mere affectability.

From another perspective, however, magic emerges in Adorno's *Aesthetic Theory* less as the positive practice of the primitive than as the negation of representation. It partakes of that dimension of the artwork that is an ineluctable materiality that resists formalization or the sensuous remnant that withstands rationalization. This "pathological" moment restores to the aesthetic its foundations in pleasure and pain and would then be the moment where the artwork, like the Subaltern, appears as the performance of the violence of the pathological—that is, as the moment in the system whose very insistence demands the destruction of the law and the possible inauguration of another conception of life in common, predicated on the pains and pleasures of the suffering, desiring, necessitous subject. This is the "occult" moment of magic and superstition that so disturbed Fanon in his capacity as post-Enlightenment thinker and political activist and that yet so clearly fascinates and compels him.

In the cusp of that unrepresentable subaltern moment, Fanon's reasonable will to a politics of well-regulated decolonization finds a counterlogic in the "program of complete disorder" that is, in fact, the aleatory throw of decolonizing movements.[41] Under this condition of permanently renewed possibility, the appeal to a postracial humanism proves not merely premature: It represents the lure of the eradication of difference in the name of a globalized humanity whose advent cures the woundedness of a world divided by pathological "identities."[42] But the differential emergence and persistence of diverse forms of living, provisional solutions to the painful negotiation of mortality and vulnerability as well as varying improvisations of pleasure and sensuous enjoyment, are not predicated on identities forged out of the damage they suffer. Difference is not solely the sign of an imposed lack, the "minor term" of an overbearing dialectic. It is the counterclaim of those who "suffer differently in their bodies" and for whom determination, necessity, is the condition of unanticipated possibilities to alternative conceptions of the world and its futures.[43] Even "damaged life," as I argue elsewhere, imagines forms of living that are not merely reactive but rather discover new forms of resistance and enjoyment, of survival and creation.[44]

These differences may have been negatively encoded and subordinated by the masters of representation as indices of racial inferiority, among other terms like *gender* or *queerness* that establish hierarchy on the back of alterity. But only out of differentiation, in its multiple proliferating tracks, is the possibility of just relation forged. This is not to seek the replacement of one "overrepresented" genre of the human with another, or even with multiple possibilities of human being; it is to intend the destruction of the racial regime of representation that has subtended for two centuries the order of colonial capitalism in all its self-evidence and its violence. So profoundly does that regime of representation continue to saturate our modes of thinking, of perception and of feeling, that we do not yet know what possible spaces its rupture might open for us. But whatever those spaces may eventually allow, the return of the aesthetic to the feeling, desiring, even the fearing, pathological subject continues to offer the prospect of a living otherwise in the face of the generalized state of exception with which the neoliberal state has displaced the "unilateral declaration of universality" of the liberal racial order.[45] Out of the ruins of representation we may envisage collectively the possibilities of other worlds altogether. It is to that hope that this book is dedicated.

CHAPTER I

The Aesthetic Regime of Representation

The Antinomy of Aesthetics

From its inception, the aesthetic has been shadowed by the political sphere from which it sought to declare its independence. Against the conflicting interests and partiality that define political practice, aesthetic thought has traditionally proclaimed its foundation in the disinterested judgment of the spectator. Where the object of judgment is natural, it is an object regarded merely as it appears and gives pleasure, not as one to be conquered, possessed, or fought over, however much appropriation, enclosure, and the displacement of indigenous populations may have furnished historically the material conditions for a terra nullius suitable for the aesthetic contemplation of landscape. Where it is an artwork, it is free of ulterior designs on the subject, whether didactic, dogmatic or ideological. It is an object of pure contemplation or, where it does reflect on social concerns, it reflects on them in their unresolved complexity rather than insisting on the justice of a particular point of view. Aesthetic contemplation reconciles subject and world or it entertains the undecided and undecidable. Such was, at least, the idea of the aesthetic that shaped cultural pedagogy as it came to be institutionalized, from Friedrich Schiller's *Aesthetic Education of Man*, through Mathew Arnold's *Culture and Anarchy*, down to the

New Criticism and beyond.[1] The ego-ideal of the disinterested and ethical subject—an ideal whose genealogy in the aesthetic this book traces—continues to exert a powerful influence over the humanities and over the distaste of the professional scholar for engagement in political activism.

At the same time, aesthetics has also always been the terrain of political contestation: The actual capacity of art to influence and form not only moral and political opinions but also fundamental subjective dispositions has long been valued and activated. The instrumental appropriation of art has its origin in precisely the "cultic" or religious function from which aesthetics, properly speaking, sought to emancipate it and the challenge to art's ideal disinterest preceded the era of its "politicization." That politicization has ranged from the nationalist imperative to deploy art in the service of forming popular consciousness to the various and conflicting claims made by radical aesthetics as to art's function in relation to ideology and to popular mobilization. Over and over again, indeed, radical aesthetics has confronted contradictory but equally plausible prescriptions for effecting social change through art. The contradictory stances that confront materialist thinking in this domain are several, ranging from the antithesis between the political claims of formalist defamiliarization and those, equally cogent, of agitprop or of Lukácsian realism, to the more recent debates on the relative efficacy of postmodernism and modernism that have been complicated in turn by questions as to the relation between postmodernity or poststructuralism and postcolonial or "Third World" aesthetic production.[2]

The confrontation of materialist aesthetics with a certain kind of antinomy goes back to Karl Marx's early speculations on Greek art in the "Introduction" to the *Grundrisse*, in which the question is raised as to how an artwork's "eternal charm" can persist across history when art, like every other human product, must be determined historically in the mode and means of its production. The question is inseparable from that as to whether art is ideological per se or is a form of cognition inassimilable to or even revelatory of ideological formations.[3] In this chapter, I make no attempt to resolve such antinomies, since I argue that they are strictly irresolvable within the terms of aesthetic thought. Rather, I seek to show in the first place that the question is not whether the aesthetic can or should be politicized but how the aesthetic "represents" politics in the sense both of furnishing the conditions under which the modern representative sphere can be thought at all and of displacing or deferring political divisions in the name of reconciliation. This is, strictly speaking, a critical project, in that it proceeds by considering the apparent political impasse of radical aesthetics "in relation to the foundation of the knowledge upon which the question is based."[4]

It might be more precise to say that one must attend here at once to the form of the knowledge, insofar as that is determined by theoretical exigencies, and to the material conditions that ground it. In reading Immanuel Kant's *Critique of Judgement* (1790), generally taken to be the founding text of aesthetic philosophy, I explore the overdetermined conditions both for the emergence of the aesthetic sphere itself and for the formal structures that shaped the discourse on the aesthetic from the start. The argument of this chapter is that the discourse on the aesthetic supplied a theoretical resolution to the contradictions of an emerging liberal politics, resolutions that came to inform not only subsequent ideological discourse but also its material institutions. If that formulation has a certain smack of idealist prioritization of the theoretical, that is not necessarily surprising. In its emergence aesthetics was a theoretical intervention, the historical conditions of late eighteenth-century Germany requiring a theoretical solution to the impasses of liberal politics that could not be resolved in practice given both the political fragmentation and the material "underdevelopment" of the region. The young Marx famously observed: "The Germans have *thought* in politics what other nations have *done*. Germany has been their *theoretical conscience*."[5] The observation is no less apposite to German aesthetic philosophy than it is to their political thought. Entailed in both the aesthetic and the political theoretical solutions is the production of a human Subject in the form of an inner disposition toward the ethical that is prefigurative of, because preconditional for, a public sphere and a state that were yet to be. This sense of the aesthetic as furnishing the very condition of possibility for the political is the focus of this chapter; the fundamentally racial organization of those conditions, deeply implicit in if not essential to it from the outset, will be sketched here and elaborated further in those that follow.

Both in view of what I will show to be its narrative mode of production, which derives the formal and universal from the material and singular, and in view of its putative representativeness for man in general, this Subject comes to give the form in which the modern individual is interpellated ideologically. The aesthetic Subject is produced "as if" a unity but in necessary division from the material conditions of the concrete individual: It becomes what I will call in Chapter 3 the "Subject without properties." Further, this "as if," which is the principal ideological moment of the aesthetic domain, is held in place by the rhetorically analogical structure and movement of aesthetic thought itself. In the very process of formalization that its analogical structure produces, aesthetics displaces the historical conditions of its emergence on to a universal claim to deduce the "supersensible substrate" that is the identity of the human.

From this formalization, programmatically forgetful of the conditions that required it, derives the capacity for transhistorical and transnational dissemination that has characterized the discourse of aesthetic culture as an ideological formation. This European usurpation of all other modes of being human that Sylvia Wynter has dubbed "the overrepresentation of Man" underlies the covert raciality of both the aesthetic and the ideal "formal" political and legal subjects that furnish the template for the global juridico-political order of modernity.[6] For that reason, although I outline here some of its historical conditions, I concentrate on the formal analysis of the aesthetic. In the very formality of liberal ideology, for which aesthetics arguably supplies the indispensable model, lies the secret of its formidable efficiency and its capacity for reproduction and transformation. As I shall propose at the end of this chapter, it is also this formality of the aesthetic, determined by its differentiation as a sphere of human practice analogous to but distinct—by its formality—from the political and the economic, that accounts for its apparently irreducible resistance to appropriation for radical political ends. And that division of spheres of human practice, each one of which is conceived of as the transhistorical end of human development, subtends an ideological system that is never more historical than in its will to deny or put an end to history.

Dividing the Subject

Bourgeois hegemony has always sought to legitimate its universal claims by appeal to common sense. The abstraction that this entails has so often been pointed out, by critics of bourgeois political thought as disparate in their political standpoints as Edmund Burke and Karl Marx or Antonio Gramsci, as to need no further analysis here.[7] That abstraction is part and parcel of its own self-evidence, the figure of universal Man being at once the foundation and the object of common sense, with much the same circularity of origination as a Declaration of Independence that must constitute the people in whose name it claims to speak.[8] As we shall see, such a circulatory relationship between common sense conceived as permitting the unity or accord of human judgment and its production through judgment itself is fundamental to aesthetic theory. Ultimately, it articulates together the figure of Man as the universal subject of the political and a humanity divided by and subjected to a distribution of particular positions, racialized, gendered, classed. This aporia of common sense in liberal political theory was already manifest in Thomas Paine's *Rights of Man*, a text coeval with the emergence of aesthetic philosophy in the late eighteenth century. Produced out of his attempt to reconcile the practical contradictions that the abstractions of bourgeois ideology at once dissemble and perpetuate, the aporia that Paine so well exemplifies for us generates, in turn, an incessant discourse that seeks to provide universal human grounds for liberal common sense.

In a passage crucial to his refutation of Edmund Burke's attempt to limit the rights of Man by adducing binding precedents, Paine counters aristocratic or monarchical genealogical claims by the simple strategy of taking them at their word. His deduction of the natural—and universal—rights of man accordingly takes him back through antiquity to "the time when man came from the hand of his Maker. What was he then? Man." Paine's grammatical isolation of the substantive *Man* in this passage rhetorically underpins what will be his next claim, that the origins of man, as recorded in all human traditions, likewise indicate the "unity of man." The unity of man is the guarantee of that absolute equivalence of men in which the conceptual equality of all men is grounded.[9]

At this point, Paine's argumentation, which is aimed at the legitimation of a new republican form of government, begins an unacknowledged slip from principle into historical deduction. For the necessity of governmental organization, always a negative moment for Paine, cannot be deduced rationally from the unity and equality of man, depending as it does on the historical recognition of conflict and difference between humans as social individuals. Whether because he is engaged in the defense and legitimation of the new society or, more probably, because the universalism of his revolutionary republican principles precludes its acknowledgment, Paine is unable, unlike previous political thinkers such as Hobbes, Locke, or Rousseau, to recognize the origins of conflict in the appropriation of property.[10] This lacuna in Paine's deductions is exemplary for understanding the contradictory developments of liberal individualism and political theory. From Paine's repression of the origins of conflict in appropriation results an ungrounded assertion of a split in a hitherto putatively unified human subject, a split that takes place in the division between "the intellectual" rights of the individual, on the one hand, and those rights "which relate to security and protection," on the other.[11] This division between the "natural" and "civil" rights of the individual, a memory of whose material origins is betrayed in Paine's metaphors of "common stock," "capital," and "proprietorship," defines in nuce the fundamental problematic of liberal political theory. For if the security of the individual (that is, of his property) can be guaranteed only by superior force of the collective over each and every individual, what significance, other than merely formal, does the autonomy of the individual in whose name society is legitimated actually have? Alternatively, given that the individual retains the right to dissent, how, without the exercise of a coercive force that would effectively annul that individual freedom, is conflict between the individual and society to be averted? What appears here as a split between the private and the public man, or between what Marx would come to term the "real man" and the abstract man of civil society, originates in a prior division between the human subjected to arbitrary force, the state of necessity that is that of nature, and the universal Subject that is truly representative of humanity and that will find its final expression in the State.[12] As I will argue in what follows, this fundamental splitting of the human between the abstract figure of the Subject of civil society and the human subjected to force or necessity is not only constitutive of liberal political and legal thought in all its contradictions but also determinant for the racial formation of modernity that aesthetic theory grounds and regulates.

The representative institutions that appear as the practical solutions of the liberal democracies to the actuality of the contradiction between universal claims and social differences are thus, at the theoretical level, no solution at all. For in the conflicts of interest assumed in representative bodies there constantly emerge those political differences that belie the universal claims of liberal ideology. One might say, indeed, that representative institutions are the stage on which the return of the repressed of liberal ideology—namely, the multiple forms of inequality that belie formal political equality—is played out in sublimated forms. But, as I shall argue, the insolubility of the contradictions of liberal ideology within either its political institutions or its political theory entails the migration of the discourse on universality and common sense into other spheres that emerge more or less simultaneously in liberal society. The inadequacy of representative institutions within the political sphere is supplemented by an all-the-more universalizing discourse on representation and common sense, that of aesthetics. As the aesthetic comes to represent or take the place of the formerly political sphere of universality, it becomes its function to produce the specific forms of representation that, at every level of human being, are to seem self-evident to common sense. The aesthetic sphere is held to transcend all contingent differences, and, with less paradox than might at first appear, it is in defining this domain as beyond political interest that the formal terms of bourgeois or liberal ideology are constituted.

Analogies of the Aesthetic

At the conclusion of "The Methodology of Taste," the closing section of the first part of *The Critique of Judgement*, Kant evokes as an exemplary moment a cultural situation that resembles what a series of critics, notably Georg Lukács and Mikhail Bakhtin, would conceive to be the moment of epic:

> There was an age and there were nations in which the active impulse towards a social life regulated by laws—what converts a people into a permanent community—grappled with the huge difficulties presented by the trying problem of bringing freedom (and therefore equality also) into union with constraining force (more that of respect and dutiful submission than of fear). And such must have been the age, and such the nation, that first discovered the art of reciprocal communication of ideas between the more cultured and ruder sections of the community, and how to bridge the difference between the amplitude and refinement of the former and the natural simplicity and originality of the latter—in this way hitting upon that mean between higher culture and the modest worth of nature, that forms for taste also, as a sense common to all mankind, that true standard which no rules can supply. Hardly will a later age dispense with those models.[13]

It is a moment of appealing utopianism in a heretofore rigorously theoretical work, one whose appeal can scarcely have been negligible in the disintegrating postfeudal condition of late eighteenth-century Germany. It can be taken as a document for a historic compromise between an intellectually powerful bourgeoisie with a comparatively underdeveloped economic base and a traditionally powerful but embattled aristocracy confronting the specter of revolution. As such, this passage may appear as a blueprint, if not the blueprint, for defining the political function of aesthetic culture. For this idealized representation of cultural harmony marks the turn of a "disinterested" aesthetic into an interest that is not merely moral—for the explicit function of judgment is indeed to mediate from sense and understanding to ethics and reason—but also political. The universal claims of aesthetic culture, especially the postulation of aesthetic judgment as if it were valid for all men—precisely, "a sense common to all mankind"—are most political, even revolutionary, just where they claim to be least so. They represent, in their very denial of interest, a bourgeois interest in forging a sphere of purely formal equality and identity for all mankind, irrespective of cultural or economic distinctions.

Nonetheless, although Kant's *Critique of Judgement* was published in the year following the French Revolution with its Declaration of the Rights of Man and the Citizen, in the entire text he makes only one direct reference to the political events of his time, and then to the American rather than to the French Revolution. This note comes at a critical juncture for the articulation of the two "wings" of the *Critique*'s structure—on aesthetic and teleological judgment respectively—and, to use a very Kantian analogy, forms a bridge or passage between the two halves. The note runs as follows:

> We may, on the other hand, make use of an analogy to the above mentioned immediate physical ends to throw light on a certain union, which, however, is to be found more often in idea than in fact. Thus in the case of a complete transformation, recently undertaken, of a great people into a state, the word *organisation* has frequently, and with much propriety, been used for the constitution of the legal authorities and even of the entire body politic. For in a whole of this kind certainly no member should be a mere means, but should also be an end, and, seeing that he contributes to the possibility of the entire body, should have his position and function in turn defined by the idea of the whole. (*CJ*, II, 23)

The typological features of the state here presented—its organic nature, the reciprocal relation between individual and totality, its reference to an organizing idea—will of course become essential to a certain generally "Romantic" and nationalist tradition of political theory. Kant, however, does not present the organic analogy of the state with any such conceptual finality but rather in the spirit of the free play of the philosophical faculty within the field of analogies. The analogy between the state and a natural organism is presented here as explicitly an idea of reason that regulates rather than determines the constitution of the state and the relationship of the individual to the whole.[14]

At the same time, the note serves to clarify the limits of another common analogy of which it is the inverse ("on the other hand," *umgekehrt*)—namely, the analogy between the natural organism and the work of art. The paragraph is pivotal for the "Critique of Teleological Judgement," which unlike the first part of the Critique concerns how we make judgments that actually subsume phenomena under determinate concepts of the Understanding. It concerns the very possibility of thinking of organisms as intrinsically physical ends. Here the analogy between work of art and natural organism finds its limit. Although "natural beauty may be termed the analogue of art" (since then we refer the natural object only to a subjective principle of judgment regarding the artwork and make no assertion about its own nature as an object), seeking to explain intrinsic physical ends by reversing the analogy, such that art would be the analogue of nature, leads us to contradiction: "For what is here present to our minds is an artist—a rational being—working from without. But nature, on the contrary, organises itself, and does so in each species of its organised products" (*CJ*, II, 23, §65). The limitation of analogical thinking discovered here, and the discovery that "the organisation of nature has nothing analogous to any causality known to us," leads, however, not to the absolute limit of analogical thinking itself but rather to its "complete transformation" (*gänzliche Umbildung*) in the sense that it becomes the ground of a regulative conception of the reflective judgment, "for guiding our investigation of objects of this kind by remote analogy with our own causality according to ends generally, and as a basis of reflection upon their supreme source" (*CJ*, II, 24). That is, the analogy enables us to appreciate in nature an appearance of causality that conforms to those with which we are familiar without, however, making the mistake of taking such kinds of causality to be demonstratively at work in natural things themselves.

This transitional function of analogical thinking, in its very limitation, is fundamental to the organization of the Third Critique itself. It is a text saturated with analogies, from the most fundamental to the apparently incidental.[15] Hence the importance of the structural function of an apparently marginal note on analogy. It is not merely that, by reversing (*umkehren*) the direction of the analogy to read "human creation is like natural organism" instead of "natural organism is like human creation," Kant saves a domain for analogical jurisdiction at exactly the point where analogical thinking is ruled out but, more importantly, that this note forms a bridge back to a point in the first part of the *Critique*, "Of Aesthetic Judgement," which is analogous to the point being made in §65. For at only one other point in the *Critique* is the state treated by analogy with an organism: that is, in §59 where Kant formulates the manner in which the beautiful may be held to be a symbol of the moral. This is a crucial moment for the afterlife of the *Critique*, offering as it does the means by which a supposedly disinterested aesthetic philosophy could become in the hands of its interpreters a blueprint for its pedagogical institutionalization.[16]

Here again a transition takes place by way of an analogy, in this case from the sensible intuition to the ethical judgment, the transition across the threshold that divides a mere concept of the understanding from one of reason:

Schemata contain direct, symbols indirect, presentations of the concept. Schemata effect this presentation demonstratively, symbols by the aid of an analogy (for which recourse is had even to empirical intuitions), in which analogy judgement performs a double function: first in applying the mere rule of its reflection upon that intuition to quite another object, of which the former is but a symbol. In this way a monarchical state is represented as a living body when it is governed by constitutional laws, but as a mere machine (like a handmill) when it is governed by an individual absolute will. But in both cases the representation is merely *symbolic*. (*CJ*, I, 222–24, §59)

As in the case of the analogy with physical ends in §65, it is exactly where analogy meets its limits in one respect that the transition is effected into a higher domain. The intuitional or the concrete, sensible content of the analogy fades out here at the service of a purely formal reflection upon the common, ideal elements that made the comparison possible in the first place. Accordingly, the idea of a totality in which the individual members are at once ends in themselves and means to an end allows the analogy between two so entirely different entities as a state and an organism to be made, though only insofar as we do not forget that we have to do here with regulative concepts of the subjective judgment and not with constitutive concepts that would determine the object for the understanding. That is, the state is not actually like an organism, but the principles that govern the relations among its constituent parts can be thought of in the same way as the relations among the parts of an organism. Analogy thus performs here the function of moving from the particularity of "empirical intuitions" to the formal abstraction through which identity can be predicated that we will see metaphor performing in racial judgments in Chapter 3. Analogy is, in other words, the form in which common sense is produced, furnishing the bridge between the evidence of the senses and the self-evidence of the abstraction.

In the same way the beautiful comes to symbolize the moral. The judgment of the beautiful must always refer at first to an object that is presented in a sensible intuition. As will become apparent in later chapters, this insistent materiality of the object fatally precludes the final formalization on which the aesthetic depends. For now, however, Kant insists that the pure aesthetic judgment, as opposed to the logical or teleological judgment that is subordinated to the understanding, is in no way directed toward the knowledge of that object. It is engaged in a purely formal reflection on the object as a possible object of intuition, and therefore on the object solely as it is presented to the subject: "What is formal in the representation of a thing, i.e., the agreement of its manifold with a unity (i.e., irrespective of what it is to be) does not, of itself, afford us any cognition whatsoever of objective finality. For since abstraction is made from this unity as *end* (what the thing is to be) nothing is left but the subjective finality of the representations in the mind of the subject intuiting" (*CJ*, I, 70, §15).[17] The subjective formal finality of the aesthetic judgment (that is, the finality with which the object is represented for the subject without reference to any concept of its actual or objective ends) alone allows for the possibility of beauty becoming symbolic of the ideas of reason. For while the moral ideas of reason, such as freedom or the good, are not susceptible of sensible intuition, the "as if" of aesthetic judgment, which represents the object only as a possible object of cognition by the understanding, allows the transition (*Übergang*) through the "double function" of analogy from the determinate, logical judgment of the object to the pure form of the judgment that can become symbolic of the ideas of reason. The rhetorical form of analogy that guides the move from the singular intuition to the formal reflection on its possibility replicates a corresponding movement in the individual from sense to reason, a movement that will turn out to be constitutive of the human Subject itself. The overarching faculty that governs or regulates this transition from material particularity to formal universality is representation, *Vorstellung*.

The Ascent of Common Sense

This movement, from sense to Sense, as it were, grounds the transformation of each individual into the identical form of the human Subject whose possibility is given by the idea of a "common sense." For the subject of judgment, in both the formal possibility of its determinability and in its grounding of the free play of the faculties, necessarily presupposes the existence of a common sense (*CJ*, I, 83, §20). Presupposes, since Kant cannot establish whether this common sense is indeed "a constitutive principle of the possibility of experience" or is "formed for us as a regulative principle by a still higher principle of reason, that for higher ends first seeks to beget in us a common sense" (*CJ*, I, 85, §22).[18] Nonetheless, the reasons for this presupposition are clear enough in the conditions Kant establishes for the possibility of an aesthetic judgment at all. Since the judgment is to be the mediating concept between reason and understanding, the apparent necessity, universality, and objective form of the judgment can be derived from neither of these domains. Yet the judgment, "this is beautiful," seems to take the form of an objective predication (as Kant puts it, it is made by analogy with predication) and at the same time implies a necessary assent by all other human subjects: "The assertion is not that everyone *will* fall in with our judgment, but rather that everyone *ought* to agree with it" (*CJ*, I, 84, §22).[19] How can this be possible for a subjective judgment of a singular intuition, which the aesthetic judgment must be in order not to be merely a logical judgment?

Kant's solution to this problem is articulated somewhat later, in the "Deduction of Pure Aesthetic Judgements":

> However, by the name *sensus communis* is to be understood the idea of a *public* sense, i.e., a critical faculty which in its reflective act takes account (*a priori*) of the mode of representation of every one else, in order, *as it were*, to weigh its judgement with the collective reason of mankind, and thereby avoid the illusion arising from subjective and personal conditions which could readily be taken for objective, an illusion that would exert a prejudicial influence upon its judgement. This is accomplished by weighing the judgement, not so much with the actual, as rather with the merely possible, judgements of others, and by putting ourselves in the position of every one else, as the result of a mere abstraction from the limitations which contingently affect our own estimate. This, in turn, is effected by so far as possible letting go of the element of matter, i.e., sensation, in our general state of representative activity, and confining attention to the formal peculiarities of our representation or general state of representative activity. (*CJ*, I, 151, §40)

Here, in what amounts to a formalization, or aestheticization, of the "censorial" function of the common or public sense in earlier liberal thinkers like Locke,[20] Kant gives his most lucid single statement of the relationship between the formality of the aesthetic judgment and its universal (or commonsensical) claims. Only by presupposing the same formal conditions to inhere in every human's representative activity can one make a judgment that will claim not only universality of assent but also necessity (an *ought*): So long as the judgment is pure and unaffected by peculiar conditions of interest or sensation, every human necessarily judges in a formally identical manner—that is, as the Subject in general. Accordingly, also, the matter of the judgment becomes a matter, if not of indifference, at least of *Gleichgültigkeit*, equivalence. No matter the matter of the object, everyone's representation (*Vorstellung*) of it is formally identical.

This indifference of the matter of the judgment helps us to understand further the way in which the beautiful comes to symbolize the moral and the process by which, as Kant has it in §59, "taste makes, as it were, the transition from the charm of sense to habitual moral interest possible without too violent a leap" (*CJ*, I, 225). First of all, in the "Solution of the Antinomy of Taste" (§57), Kant reconnects the formal finality of the judgment that founds the presupposition of common sense with both its universal validity and its ground in the "supersensible substrate":

> The judgement of taste does depend upon a concept (of a general
> ground of the subjective finality of nature for the power of judgement),
> but one from which nothing can be cognised in respect of the Object,
> and nothing proved, because it is in itself indeterminable and useless
> for knowledge. Yet by means of this very concept it acquires at the same
> time validity for every one (but with each individual, no doubt, as a
> singular judgement accompanying his intuition): because its determin-
> ing ground lies, perhaps, in the concept of what may be regarded as the
> supersensible substrate of humanity. (*CJ*, I, 208)

The very formality, that is, of the aesthetic judgment allows one to glimpse the possibility of the "unity of man" in his "supersensible substrate": In the formal unity of aesthetic judgments is symbolized the ethical unity of mankind to which the reason will give determinate laws. That same formality equally ensures that while an aesthetic judgment must be intuitive and singular in order not to be merely subordinated to the understanding, it does not succumb to the status of a "mere" sensible intuition, of a purely private judgment on the "agreeable." Each particular aesthetic judgment, through its act of reflective representation, represents and enacts the moment of universal humanity, the Subject, in every individual who judges. In this way, as Rebecca Comay puts it, "political judgment is an extension of the aesthetic judgment that simultaneously finds and founds the cosmopolitan collective as the *sensus communis* of the enlarged community: judgment performatively invents what it discovers."[21]

A narrative of ascent is likewise built discretely into the deduction of pure aesthetic judgments, initially as an ascent from the sensible to the supersensible. A series of analogical gradients, analogous to the transition within analogy itself, generalizes this upward transition into every field that comes under jurisdiction of the aesthetic judgment and causes the scheme of each to replicate that of the others within the general developmental system of universal history. Thus, the supersession of the matter of the intuition by reflection upon its form (and thence on the form of the reflection), which Kant sees as the very condition of a universally valid judgment, is matched by the "emancipation" of the subject from the charm of sensation on the way to habitual moral reflection. Furthermore, since these transitions within the individual involve the transformation of private sensation into a "public sense," the way is opened to an analogous development of human societies in general from a state of dependence upon the charm of sensation to one in which "universal communication" is of prime value. In this process, the aesthetic judgment, as generally formative of taste, is at once an agent and a symptom:

> Further, a regard to universal communicability is a thing which every one expects and requires from every one else, just as if it were an original compact dictated by humanity itself. As thus, no doubt, at first only charms, e.g., colours for painting oneself (roucou among the Caribs, and cinnabar among the Iroquois), or flowers, sea-shells, beautifully coloured feathers, then in the course of time, also beautiful forms (as in canoes, wearing-apparel, etc.) which convey no gratification, i.e., delight of enjoyment, become of moment in a society and attract considerable interest. Eventually, when civilization has reached its height it makes this work of communication almost the main business of refined inclination, and the entire value of sensations is placed in the degree to which they permit of universal communication. (*CJ*, I, 155–56, §41)

Thus, the liberal public sphere appears as the apex of universal history, its emergence germinally prepared for by an "original compact" (*einem ursprünglichen Vertrage*) converted here into significantly aesthetic form.

Because it is a presented as a universal history, and as the condition of possibility for a "public sense," the apparently incidental examples of the Iroquois and the Carib, not yet capable of "letting go of the element of matter" and therefore not fully participant in the civilized "business" of communication, turn out to be very precisely positioned along an axis of development that gives the form to racial judgments. Their appearance as incidental or contingent examples (*Beispiele*) is crucial and they are haphazardly substituted for one another throughout the text. Elsewhere, the "Iroquois sachem" is distinguished by his preference for the eating houses of Paris to its fine architecture, a judgment that is counterpoised to the moral and political judgments of the unmarked European subjects (*CJ*, I, 43, §2). Standing only on the threshold of the development of common sense, these beings do not enter fully into the historicity of the aesthetic (the aesthetic is always historical in form); the specificity of their tastes or practices, of their forms of art or pleasure, is as much a matter of indifference as their actual existence is, from the perspective of the universal, of doubtful necessity.[22] The Savage is a racial figure located still within the domain of nature that is the realm of necessity and, subjected as he is to the "charm" of sensual gratification, is subjected equally to heteronomy of fear, desire, and force that confine what Kant in the Second Critique defines as the "pathological" subject: the one subordinated to feeling and necessity. Its opposite, the ethical, civilized subject, representative of the human as such, is instantiated in the white European who occupies the apex of development. As J. Kameron Carter puts it in a compelling account of Kant's empirical writings on race, whiteness "is a present reality, and yet it is also still moving toward and awaiting its perfection. The teleological end, which is the consummation of all things within the economic, political, and aesthetic—in short, within the structural—reality called 'whiteness,' is on the one hand made present and available now in white people and in white 'culture.' And on the other hand, it is through these white people and culture that the full reality of whiteness will globally expand to 'eschatologically' encompass all things and so bring the world to perfection."[23]

The distribution of racial positions and the conditions of possibility of political order predicated on human universality thus turn out both to be fundamentally regulated by the aesthetic that supplies their conditions of possibility. This intimate linking of the racial and the political through the discourse on the aesthetic is what I will discuss more extensively in later chapters as the racial regime of representation.[24]

Analogies for Politics

Kant's work is saturated with politics even, and perhaps especially, where it is ostensibly not at all political.[25] If it is true, as Odo Marquard persuasively argues, that in a situation where the social conditions prescribed by a liberal moral philosophy of history cannot be realized in practice, the aesthetic takes over, it is not the case that a utopian issue is merely tacked on, out of intellectual exhaustion, to an otherwise inherently completed aesthetic philosophy. The "as if" of the aesthetic is too intrinsically enracinated in its structure for that final "as if" not to ramify retroactively throughout the whole.[26] Since the analogical structure of the "as if" is the formal structure of the act of judgment itself, it is inseparable from that ethical "wishful thinking," the deferral of ends, which its very logic produces.[27]

In consequence of the failure of bourgeois revolutions to produce the conditions of "universal communicability" that would be the effective realization of common sense, liberal politics was historically obliged to turn to representative institutions.[28] In liberal political theory, the state-form, the ensemble of such institutions, represents or stands for the disinterested space of common sense, which should in principle require no such mediation. The recourse to force in turn represents the limit of the state's disinterest and is the symptom of the return of an economic repressed, legitimated as the defense of a universal and fundamental right to private property. The insistence of this contradiction between the ethical claims of the state, based, as my preliminary reading of Paine's example indicates, on the attempt to regulate the uneven division of property and on an ultimately violent preservation of private property is what requires the supplementation of aesthetic culture. Against that monopoly on violence, confronted as it was in a revolutionary era by the counterviolence of the "men without property," the aesthetic offers, in Schiller's apt terms, a purely formal "that which is common to all" to be enjoyed in the liberal or *freie* relation of contemplation rather than by its appropriation.[29] Indeed, what the aesthetic assures, the unity of man that is grounded in common sense, merely formalizes the quasi-historical deduction that legitimates the liberal state in the first place. It remains to be shown that the division of the human subject that "allegorical" political man, the citizen, is supposed to overcome recurs in the field of the aesthetic as an ineradicable effect of its analogical relation to the political sphere it displaces.[30]

It was in Germany, where the conditions for a representative politics had not yet emerged, that aesthetics first came to represent a forestalled politics. The universal ethical claim that originated in extrapolitical spheres in the course of the Enlightenment proving politically unrealizable, the ethical "ought" had to be supplemented by the "as if" of the aesthetic: Given the foreclosure of the social realization of the ethical demands of liberal common sense in the sphere of immediate political revolution, one must live *as if* the ethical state were a reality. As Schiller put it, "In the realm of Aesthetic Semblance, we find that ideal of equality fulfilled which the Enthusiast would fain see realized in substance."[31] Quietly, the claims of the aesthetic come less to prepare for than to displace permanently the realization of the political desires of the "Enthusiast." To whatever extent this specific historical condition may be thought to have determined both the internal structure of the aesthetic sphere and its differential relation to the political, that structure and that relation proved to have a considerable capacity for translation exactly as the achieved domination of the local bourgeoisie in other nations came to require the aesthetic supplement of cultural and pedagogical institutions as a displacement of, rather than a detour for, the political. Marx suggested that Germany produced the theoretical where France and Britain produced political and industrial revolutions. The aesthetic dimension of that theory would become rapidly adaptable, on account of its very formalism and in unanticipated accord with the political impasse that was its condition, to states where what was required ideologically was the deferral of political and economic freedoms that had obliged the turn to aesthetics in the first place. In the process of translation, the terms of aesthetic culture established by writers like Kant and Schiller continue to work as a template, allowing one to formalize in general terms the continuing relationship of the aesthetic to the political through the longer history of liberal cultural formations.

The multiple ramifications that stem from these historical conditions for the emergence of the aesthetic, shaping the hegemonic institutions of liberal culture even when and where that culture has achieved dominance, can be succinctly formulated in a German rendering of the aphorism "Aesthetics represents politics": "*Die Ästhetik vertritt die Politik.*" For it is not simply that, in some form of negativity with regard to social and political developments, the aesthetic sphere articulates utopian desires that have no other means of expression or realization. Marcuse and others are certainly correct in this, but only to a limited extent.[32] The limitation of this view is that, in emphasizing the deputational or advocatory function of representation, *Vertretung*, it underestimates the powerful institutional function that was assumed by an aesthetic culture that, in substituting for (*vertreten*) politics, simultaneously blocks the way (*den Weg vertritt*) to it.[33] They underestimate the enormously important hegemonic role played by the institutional dissemination of just such an aesthetic of representation through humanist education and the equally important role of that aesthetic in legitimating, naturalizing, and exemplifying the universal claims made by that humanism. The structure of deferral that informs Kant's figure of Man recurs ubiquitously in the perpetual "as if" of a humanist education that, on the one hand, seeks to defuse political activism by assimilation to the "civil" forms of the institution and, on the other, defers the actualization of freedom in any form of economic democratization into the ideal sphere of free aesthetic judgment.[34] For this reason, one might reasonably conclude that the engrained racism and political conservatism of the very institutions that claim to represent the essential liberalism of Western values, the universities, are not merely contingent consequences of their historically lagging behind changing social values but rather constitutive effects of their formation. As we shall see in later chapters, the liberal narrative of gradual inclusion by the extension of rights, the narrative of representation that informs both pedagogical and political institutions, is the form that regulates the modes by which the discordant subject is barred from access.

If aesthetics sublimates, in turn, economic and political discontent, it is not without being affected in its own structure by that which it debars. In the transference that takes place, the analogy with the other spheres carries over, as indeed it must where the ground of possibility of the analogy itself is not interrogated critically. I examine elsewhere how the analogies between the concept of representation in the political and aesthetic spheres determine the form that the politics of the aesthetic takes.[35] But the claim to the universal validity of the aesthetic judgment is equally inextricable from material developments in the broadest sense. The gradual emergence of the autonomous work of art—about whose precise distinction from artisanal products Kant remains uncertain (§§43–44, 51)—is inseparable from the advent of newly developing modes of production, observable by German thinkers at least in other lands if not so clearly yet at home. It is equally inseparable, both in its conditions of consumption and its theoretical description, from a gradual process of "civilization" that the German middle and upper classes were undergoing. Kant's concern with the liberation of the aesthetic judgment from the conditions of mere sensation is part of, at once reflective of and programmatic for, a continuing process of education and refinement aimed at disciplining the senses and subjecting them to the goals of longer-term rationalization.[36]

For all the claims that it is produced as a unity out of a unified consciousness, the autonomous work is accordingly divided in itself, retaining, as it were, the symptoms of the repressions to which it owes its identity. In the first place, it is split in relation to the objects from which it is to be emancipated. It is defined originally against commodity production, against the division of labor and the fragmentation it entails of a human nature whose "totality," as Schiller famously proclaims, "a higher Art" would have to restore.[37] Paradoxically the sign of its dependence upon a market rather than a system of patronage, this differentiation of the autonomous work from the functional artifact will nonetheless become the ground of the former's apparently negative, utopian function. The ethical claim that underpins this function is equally the supposed consequence of the autonomous artwork's simultaneous emancipation from and substitution for art's former religious or cultic function. What both these forms of emancipation demand, however, is that the subject of the work be both universal and unified: If the artwork is to oppose both the division of labor and religious interests, it can validly do so only in the name of a universal and undivided mankind.

Yet this very demand leads intrinsically to an internal splitting of the individual by a logic that is best articulated in the sphere of the autonomous artwork's emancipation from nature and sensation. For reasons that are clear enough from the foregoing analysis of the Third Critique, the aesthetic work is predicated on its separation as form from nature as matter. This would seem to imply, in turn, the unity of a judging subject posed over against the unity of nature. But a problematic moment in Kant's analysis of the "dynamically sublime" would seem to indicate that this is not, and cannot logically be, the case. The dynamically sublime finds its object in "Nature considered in an aesthetic judgement as might that has no dominion over us" (*CJ*, I, 109, §28). However, if nature's might has no dominion over us, it can have dominion only over itself, and over the nature that inheres in us as animal beings, with the result that the concept of nature as the unity of phenomena set over against the unified human subject perforce disintegrates. The very origin of the sublime affect in such cases lies in the fact that we can be, and often actually are, subject to nature's dominion. It is the condition of mortality entailed on humans as sensible organisms (i.e., as nature). That the ethical interest of the sublime is to be derived from the intimation it gives of a "supersensible substrate" elevated above nature within and without man is well known and is, indeed, Kant's next point: "This saves humanity in our own person from humiliation, even though as mortal men we have to submit to an external violence" (*CJ*, I, 111, §28). In a peculiar way, Kant's analysis of the sublime nicely repeats Paine's division between the individual subjected to the coercive force of others and the individual as member of civil or political society: Both are divided between their particular mortal vulnerability and their identity as representative subjects of humanity abstracted from material conditions. As we will see in the following chapters, this division between what Kant calls the "pathological" subject, subordinated to nature and sensation, and the universal Subject "saves" humanity at the cost of installing a regime of racial judgment or discrimination.

It seems unnecessary to rehearse here the already frequently analyzed ethical and ideological functions of the sublime.[38] What must be stressed is the manner in which the ethic invoked here requires the dissolution or suppression (*Untergang*) of the empirical person in the name of humanity. In a not so extensive detour, the social meaning of this ethic would be articulated, by Schiller and Goethe among others, as the necessary consequence of a continuing division of labor, according to which the narrowed and specialized individual was sacrificed to the necessary general progress of humanity.[39] An aesthetic harmonization of the subject might restore a sense of wholeness to the individual but only at the cost of once again erasing the individual as a concrete particular through identification with the universal. If the autonomous aesthetic sphere gains its legitimacy through

a compensatory pedagogical function, long the rationale of humanist education in face of the principally technical/professional institutions within
which it shelters, it is not without bearing the marks of this suppression
of the very individuals whom it so often claims to represent. The formal
identity of the subjects that aesthetic education seeks to shape is in fact
their "indifference." For what this *Subject* finally represents is the ideological figure of the individual summoned and annulled in the same moment.
The "individual" that capitalism supposedly unleashes from the traditional
ties and identity models is so unleashed in the purely interchangeable form
of abstract labor. It is in this form, that of the unemployment line as the
ground of universal identity, that the *vertretbares Subjekt* of aesthetic culture is actualized in all its representativeness and exchangeability.[40]

To play back the "double function" of the analogical structure of the
aesthetic in this inverse sense indicates the grounds for the antinomial
structure of radical aesthetics. The very positing of the aesthetic as a separate sphere reproduces that division of the human subject into the material domain of the economic and political practice per se and the abstract
domain of formal subjectivity that is that of the human. More important,
however, it obscures the categorical status of the aesthetic as what we might
term, after Marx, a "rational abstraction." Against Marx's own mystifica-
tion regarding the apparently eternal value and affective charge of a historically dated mode of art, we can now pose the historicity of the aesthetic
as a very specific conceptual system. The aesthetic emerges in time with
the "autonomous" art that is its necessary object, but then both that autonomous object and the mode of its reception as undetermined judgment
are imagined to be transhistorical phenomena.[41] Like production, labor, or
exchange, the aesthetic, in occluding the historical process by which the
differentiation of a specific aspect or modality of human feeling emerges,
becomes ideological in its naturalization or universalization. It is similarly
an abstraction whose critical analysis directs one toward the destruction of
its conditions of possibility. Accordingly, while the only conceivable radical art may be that produced under the conditions of a general strike that
would, in Walter Benjamin's terms, seek the deconstitution of the political
system as a whole, the only coherent materialist aesthetics is one devoted
to the critical analysis of the history and function of the category itself.[42]

The Regime of Representation

Aesthetics is a historical discourse that occludes the historicity of its own
emergence by simultaneously insisting on the pure formality of its judg-

ments and disavowing the specifically political function it performs in its claim to disinterest or indifference. As in the famous case of the "Purloined Letter," then, its function is hidden precisely where it is most visible, in the "common sense" that constitutes the very possibility of the political. By the same token, this discourse that furnishes the instance of universal, representative Man—the Subject—proves to regulate the distribution of difference, the division of the human according to degrees of emancipation from sensation and necessity, along a developmental trajectory. This trajectory is not historical in a strict, chronological sense; more effectively than that, it is a formal history of development—an aesthetic history. Within this aesthetic history, the political subject of civil society and the racialized human that is not-yet-subject fold apart at the threshold that divides them. As we have seen, the latter does not (yet) enter into the space of representation that constitutes the former as the subject of the public sphere. Not capable of "letting go the element of matter" and therefore still pathologically subject to mere stimuli, whether charms or terrors, the Savage is not yet the possible subject of representation, incapable of moving from the *Darstellung* (presentation) of a mere sensation to the *Vorstellung* (re-presentation) that reflects on its formal properties "as if" from the standpoint of humanity in general. It does not, constitutively cannot, attain to that vantage of the Subject without annulling itself as matter is (almost) annulled in representation.[43] The following chapters will pursue further the ramifications of this categorical predicament.

This aesthetic history evidently operates both at the level of an ideal phenomenology—the movement from sensuous presentation to reflective representation—and at that of a universal or developmental history—the barred trajectory from the Savage to the subject of civil society. Both levels are governed by the idea of the Subject as the representative instance of the human. This linking through parallel trajectories of the formalization of distinct levels of perception and reflection and of their organization through and around a category of the Subject grounded in and produced by the aesthetic is what I referred to above as the narrative regime of representation. Narrative because—as I hope to show in full in subsequent chapters—representation is not a mere matter of depiction or mimesis but is this movement of formalization through which the Subject emerges or by which the pathological is barred. There is always a temporality to representation, as there is to its principal figures, metaphor and analogy, a temporality that is the double time of the material or sensuous particular and the form or abstraction that supervenes upon it. I term this a regime, because representation has the function of regulating and distributing the access of human individuals or groups to the place of the Subject. The regime of representation articulated in and through the aesthetic divides the human into the moment of the pathological and that of the representative and representable subjects. In doing so, it distributes racial positions along a temporal and a spatial axis: The temporal axis is that of development, from the Savage to the Subject, that coincides with the narrative of representation; the spatial axis is that of the interiority of civil society and the exteriority of those constitutively barred from it.

This aesthetic regime of representation is thus a very different conception than that which Jacques Rancière terms the "representative regime" (*régime représentatif*) of aesthetics. For Rancière, this regime "identifies the substance of art . . . in the couple *poiesis/mimesis*," in the sense that art—the arts in general—is defined and judged as forms of making and that "it is the notion of representation or *mimesis* that organizes these ways of doing, making, seeing and judging."[44] This "Aristotelian" representative regime is distinguished from the "ethical regime of images," more or less Platonic in its emphasis on the truth and the ends of the images art presents (20–21), and from the "aesthetic regime" to which we shall return. It clearly offers a very different conception of representation than the one I have been elaborating in this chapter. Although the three "regimes of identification" are not intended to designate a strictly historical sequence of modes of art, the representative regime is explicitly identified with a Classical Age within which the norms are established for "a well-founded domain of imitation" (21). This framework regulates "partitions between the representable and the unrepresentable; the distinction between genres according to what is represented; principles for adapting forms of expression to genres and thus to the subject matter represented; the distribution of resemblances according to principles of verisimilitude, appropriateness of correspondence; criteria for distinguishing between and comparing the arts; etc." (22). What Rancière's representative regime regulates, in other words, is limited to the forms and the propriety of representation as depiction or mimesis.

His "aesthetic regime," by direct contrast, "is the regime that strictly identifies art in the singular and frees it from any specific rule, from any hierarchy of the arts, subject matter, and genres" (23). This regime is, accordingly, "initially the breakdown of the system of representation, that is to say of a system where the dignity of the subject matter dictated the dignity of genres of representation" (32). Two consequences flow from this opposition between these two regimes: First, as Rancière elsewhere puts it, "There is nothing that is 'unrepresentable' in the aesthetic regime of art."[45] Second, and as a consequence of that dismantling of the Classical proprieties of representation, it suffers a "constitutive contradiction" that "makes art into an *autonomous form of life* and thereby sets down, at one and the same time, the autonomy of art and its identification with a moment in life's process of self formation" (26). This regime, for which Schiller's *Aesthetic Education* "constitutes an unsurpassable reference point" (27), thus enables a recurrent "identification of art with the life of the community," from the German Romantic program to the Futurist or Constructivist "end of art" in the forms of communal life (25–27). The relation of aesthetics and politics for Rancière thus takes place at "the level of the sensible delimitation of what is common to the community, the forms of its visibility and its organization" (18).

Rancière's aesthetic regime, in displacing the representative regime's legislation of the proper and in lodging the autonomy of art not in specific forms of making but in "the autonomy of a form of sensible experience," accordingly produces a "metapolitics." As we have already seen, and as Rancière affirms, "it is as a function of its purity that the materiality of art could stand as the anticipated materiality of another configuration of community."[46] The idealization of the common in both Kant's common sense and in Schiller's notion of aesthetic apprehension—that "pure instance of suspension, a moment when form is experienced for itself" (24)—implies, in Rancière's own terms, that there is "no conflict between the purity of art and its politicization."[47] This is precisely because the mode of the political proper to the aesthetic is not "the support art forms give to the cause of political emancipation" but, rather, "a politics that opposes its own forms to those that construct the dissensual inventions of political subjects." Accordingly, the aesthetic, as experience and as mode of education, is a mode of metapolitics that passes "from the appearances of democracy and forms of state to the infra-scene of subterranean movements and the concrete energies that found them." Marxism may have long furnished such a metapolitics in emphasizing the relations of production underlying those appearances, but "the revolution of the producers is itself only thinkable on the basis of a revolution that had already happened in the very idea of revolution, in the idea of a revolution in the sensible forms of existence opposed to the revolution in the forms of the State."[48]

This metapolitical moment of the aesthetic regime functions in and through what Rancière calls "dissensus." Politics is in the first instance not the theory of the state or of the means to gain power over it but the emergence into visibility of those whom the original distribution (*partage*) of being and not being part of the community has consigned to invisibility. That distribution or partition establishes the forms of common sense or self-evidence that determine "a distribution of what is visible and what not, what can be heard and what cannot."[49] Dissensus interrupts the consensus established by that initial or constitutive "distribution of the sensible." If, then, the politics of aesthetics is a matter of "the sensible delimitation of what is common to the community," the aesthetic regime can be seen as performing a dissensual redistribution of the sensible. Emancipating art from the representative regime and its delimitation of what it is proper and improper to represent, the aesthetic regime makes space for the successive irruption into the visibility and audibility of those who had previously had no part, whether in realist novels or photography (32–33). Passing beyond the Kantian analysis of common sense, Schiller's aesthetic education becomes an instance of such a moment of dissensus: "Aesthetic common sense is, for him, a dissensual common sense. He is not content to bring together distant classes. He puts in question the distribution of the sensible that founds their distance."[50] Thus, we might say, Rancière saves Schiller from what has been seen, at least since Lukács, as the profoundly ideological work performed by the *Aesthetic Education*. That work, after all, institutes what we have seen and will see further in Chapter 3 to be a quite specific set of "distributions of the sensible" under the aegis of representation and the state, distributions that put in place both a deferral of the political and a developmental narrative that designates the place of the Savage under the iron law of the state of necessity.

Here we see the theoretical limitations of Rancière's division of the representative and aesthetic regimes, a division that rests on a somewhat impoverished conception of representation confined to the field of mimesis or depiction. Focused as it is on the modes and objects of aesthetic representation, Rancière's "representative regime" could at best allow us a description of what gets excluded from the aesthetic canon and, as if by extension, from the realm of a political culture of representation. Its tendency is to promote inclusion within the exclusionary forms of the aesthetic regime. But it cannot furnish the terms for a complete analysis, or a complete destruction, of the regime of representation inaugurated in Kant's Third Critique and disseminated by Schiller. What I have termed here the regime of representation is, on the contrary, not merely inseparable from but actually constitutive of both the moment and the mode of the aesthetic regime. Aesthetic theory is fundamentally a theory of representation, distributed through every level of reflection on the human to the point that it eventually has come to seem the self-evident mode of our relation to the world.[51] Furthermore, the regime of representation is a narrative regime. It regulates the process and the rhythm by which subjects enter into representation in the dissensual form of visibility or audibility and in a highly differential relation to the archetypal or canonical form of Man that Schiller identifies with the State itself.[52] As Rancière asserts, the partition of the sensible is nomothetic, "the dividing up of the world (*de monde*) and of people (*du monde*), the *nemeïn* upon which the *nomoi* of the community are founded."[53] So too, we have seen, is the aesthetic: It divides the pathological subject from the ethical, capable of engaging—communicating—in the sphere of public or common sense. It regulates both the deferral of the political right to participation until aesthetic education has raised the subject to representation and the permanent racial exception of the subject defined categorically as pathological, the Savage. The successive and always dissensual entry of certain subjects into that public sphere ends up confirming rather than displacing or destroying that regime of representation and its carefully calibrated distribution of "being part." The entry of the one into representation always reconstitutes the line that divides the remainder from those incorporated in "the *nomos* of the community."

Insofar as the political is defined as the manifestation of dissensus, as the irruption of the "part that has no part" into the public sphere, but does not engage with the regime of representation that determines that sphere and regulates what can appear as sensible within it, it can never unfold beyond its successive and repeated manifestations. Dissensus is a repeated because already incorporated effect of the demand for representation, a moment contained by the regime rather than a shattering of its nomos. It remains, in other terms, a *Darstellung* that cannot enter into *Vorstellung*. In order for the political defined, in the somewhat different terms of this book, as a disruption of that regime of representation that actualizes as a movement rather than just a moment, the larger task of that regime's destruction must be envisaged. That entails not the desire to be represented, the assumption into *Vorstellung*, but the willingness to dwell at the threshold where common sense defaults into what at first will seem to make no sense. In this chapter, I have emphasized the ways in which the aesthetic regime of representation consigns the racialized subject to the space of an exception on which the structure of any possible politics rests. In the following chapter, I will begin to pursue the logic of Kant's distinction between the pathological and the aesthetic subject to the point where the ineradicable difference of the racialized body returns as the abyss in which that regime of representation founders on the brink of the dissolution of its categories of sense and non-sense.

CHAPTER 2

The Pathological Sublime:
Pleasure and Pain in the Racial Regime

Aesthetic Culture

In the past few decades postcolonial theory has been preoccupied by two categories that underpin the operations of colonial discourse: that of the subject and that of history. Indeed, as Ranajit Guha's magisterial essay "The Prose of Counter-Insurgency" suggests, the categories are so intimately intertwined as to be virtually inextricable.[1] And, rightly or wrongly, for better or worse, we tend to trace these categories to the late eighteenth century, regarding them as the products of an Enlightenment in which they find their determinant forms for modernity. Although European colonialism, in its violent conquest of the Americas and of parts of Asia and Africa, evidently originates in earlier centuries, the late eighteenth century stands as a kind of conceptual threshold for postcolonial theory, marking both the emergence of categories that assert their own universal validity and the formation of political states in which they are to be instantiated. As J. Kameron Carter succinctly puts it of the emblematic figure of Enlightenment, "the Kantian outlook is only the discursive maturing of the racial colonialism inaugurated in the mid-to-late fifteenth century."[2] Paradoxically, since clearly both the subject and history have traceable prehistories, their emergence is seen, even in this moment, as revolutionary, as establishing a new order of things by rupture with a past that nonetheless already contained the very forms now declared for the first time to be self-evident. As Marx notes of political economy—that other "new" discourse of the bourgeoisie—a discourse that claims universal validity cannot help but descry retroactively in human history the categories that are its own invention and part of its own prehistory.[3] It is not, however, from political economy that I will seek to derive here the categories of the subject and of history but from the aesthetic: not from the laboring body but from the body that registers pleasure and pain.

In characterizing the aesthetic as a discourse on the sensible body, I am evidently recurring to a notion of the aesthetic that predated its main current usage to denominate reflection on taste, on beauty, or on the philosophy of art. The trajectory by which the aesthetic shifts from a concern with pleasure and pain or disgust to reflection on the properties and characteristics of art is inseparable from the shift in its focus from material objects and their impact on the body as an organ of feeling to questions of form and the judging subject. This formalization of reflection on the beautiful, as I discuss in the preceding chapter, entails various decisive shifts in the discourse on the aesthetic and in its social function. The shift, from the properties of the object that affect the subject to the subject that judges, places the claim for the universal validity of judgments of taste in the disposition of the subject in general rather than in specific characteristics of the object. For this to take place, the judgment must be of the formal rather than the material properties of the object, since the latter may affect only the idiosyncratic gratifications and desires of the individual. The second shift, that discounts the corporeal differences of individual subjects and predicates the capacity for aesthetic judgment on the properties of the Subject in general, endows the aesthetic with the function of determining the very possibility of a universal subject. The discrimination of taste ceases to be a matter for polite consensus among the learned and wealthy elites and becomes, at least in potential, a field open to all subjects.[4] Accordingly, the aesthetic mediates the cultural formation of subjects who accede to universality only through the cultivation of taste. Taste, or the capacity for disinterested contemplative pleasure, becomes, as we have seen, an index of human development and a means of discriminating a savage subordination to immediate pleasure and the coercive force of objects from the reflective mediations that characterize civilization. At the same time, formalization of the aesthetic object enables the already emergent autonomous work of art to be considered as an end in itself and aesthetics becomes the philosophy of fine art.

The trajectory of this discourse thus gradually distinguishes a domain of "aesthetic culture" (I avoid the term "high" culture because the distinction of high and low still takes place within the domain of aesthetic judgment). Differentiated from useful artifacts (the products at first of "arts and crafts" and later of industry whose form is subordinated to their practical purpose), the domain of aesthetic culture—autonomous art—will in turn be differentiated from culture understood as the lifeways of whole groups or societies. That early anthropologists like E. B. Tylor could popularize the idea of "primitive culture" by the mid-nineteenth century signals the discriminatory regime that was secreted in the original distinction of aesthetic culture from culture-in-general. The emergence of a distinct field of aesthetic culture, made possible by the emancipation of autonomous art from political or religious ends and, crucially, from the demand to furnish gratification, differentiates the civilized or developed society from the primitive or underdeveloped one, as a taste for autonomous art distinguishes the cultivated from the uncultivated individual. The civilized society, with the complex differentiation of spheres that distinguish modernity, *has* culture. The uncivilized, who fail to differentiate the spheres of religion, art, labor, and so forth, *are* culture. They lack the capacity to separate out the subject as autonomous agent either from the external forces of nature or from nature in the human that subordinates the individual to the coercive force of its needs and desires. Rather than free, deliberative subjects, the uncivilized are the vessels and objects of a nature and a culture that are themselves barely distinguishable.[5]

It is this—in its full range of meanings—*discriminating* function of aesthetic culture that makes rethinking the aesthetic from the place of the sensible body, as a locus of differentiation rather than identity, critical to postcolonial theory. Beyond recognizing the genealogy of aesthetic discourse and its constitutive function in both subject formation and racial or colonial judgment, postcolonial theory must undertake the more complicated but no less necessary self-critique that its own theoretical terms have come to demand. In its critique of decolonizing nationalism, postcolonial theory has generally tended to displace the former's emphasis on the colonial body as the object of epistemological and physical violence, configured by racialization and objectification as the not-yet-emancipated human subject. For Frantz Fanon, the impact of colonial oppression could be read on the very body of the native and in his bodily comportment: the violence of racism registered in the corporeal encounter between white and black, colonizer and native.[6] Unlike black studies, which has carried Fanon's insight beyond the body into the matter of the flesh, postcolonial theory has preferred to focus on the psychic traces of colonialism, whether in the form of hybridity, mimicry, or melancholia.[7] Neither the body of the colonized nor the physical violence inflicted by colonialism have been its principal objects, and this displacement of the body has entailed post-colonial theory's peculiar and related neglect of the dynamics of racism in the colonial sphere.

There are sound reasons for this shift in postcolonial theory's commitment to the critique of those anticolonial nationalisms whose Manichean analysis of the colonial structure and restricted and patriarchal conception of "traditional" identities for the nation-people contributed to the failure of most postcolonial states. Postcolonial theory valuably seeks to offer an account of subjecthood freed of the notions of transcendental universality and representativeness that undergird both Western aesthetics and ethics and their counterpart, nationalist versions of the representative popular subject. However, if postcolonial theory turns to alternative accounts of culture for another conceptualization of human subjecthood and agency, it slips all too easily into an anthropological model of culture for which the person is the expression rather than the subject of cultural formations.[8] The dilemma is clearest in the predicament of the theory of subalternity, where the desire to account for subaltern agency founders between the two tendencies. Since the Subaltern is by definition the formation that eludes assimilation to Western forms, it cannot be conceived, even by analogy, as acting "like a subject" or by way of representative subjects. Yet to conceive the Subaltern as a group formation acting without subjecthood forecloses the possibility of thinking its autonomy or agency in any form, leaving it rather to appear as a kind of automatism operating on the impulse of exterior forces—subjected, that is, to necessity or, in Kantian terms, nature. This is, indeed, the dilemma framed both by Ranajit Guha in "The Prose of Counter-Insurgency" and by Gayatri Chakravorty Spivak in "Deconstructing Historiography."[9] The dilemma, however, is one already determined by the framework of a discourse on the aesthetic in which the discrimination between two domains of culture is first established. Hence, in order to reground postcolonial theory in an analysis of racial regimes, the need to take postcolonial theory back to the founding moments of that discourse of culture before returning to this question of the subaltern in Chapter 4.

For now, I propose to turn to a telling moment in the formation of aesthetic discourse where the grounds for the elimination of the body and for the formalization of the subject are most clear: Kant's dismissal in the *Critique of Judgement* (1790) of what he terms the "physiological" logic of

Edmund Burke's earlier *Philosophical Enquiry into the Origin of Our Ideas of the Sublime and Beautiful* (1757). The distance that separates Edmund Burke from Immanuel Kant, theoretically and politically, furnishes resources for thinking the recalcitrance of the colonial body to the normative force of the subject and its history.[10] Via Fanon's racial phenomenology in *Black Skins, White Masks* (1952), I read that peculiar moment in Burke's essay where the sudden appearance of a black body fissures a text that promised to locate the universality of aesthetic response in the universality of the sensible body itself. Through Fanon, I elaborate the ways in which the black body appears to present an abyss for white attempts to establish the universality of certain cultural norms and responses. That abyss will appear, however, not as the domain of merely excluded matter but as immanent to the system that produces it in seeking to erase difference and materiality themselves.

The Narrative of Development

Let me start, then, with some assertions whose logic I work out more fully in other chapters.[11] The first assertion is that, for all its apparent separation out from other domains and its consequent antagonism to political or ideological claims, the domain of the Kantian aesthetic constitutes and regulates the very "condition of possibility" of the political as a category of modernity. It does so, as I argue in the previous chapter, by furnishing an account of the subject that grounds its formal universality in an a priori common sense. The second assertion is that, although that common sense has the appearance of a disposition universally present in all humans, it is nonetheless only realized as the product of a developmental history that we have come to call cultivation or the civilizing process. That case I will elaborate further in the following chapters. The first of these assertions is in accord with, but somewhat stronger than, for example, Terry Eagleton's argument for the secretly political significance of the supposedly apolitical claims of culture or Hannah Arendt's powerful demonstration of the "interrelation and mutual dependence" of the spheres of culture and politics.[12] The *Critique of Judgement* is concerned with such interrelations but also seeks to give an account of the very conditions of possibility of the political in its demonstration of the transcendental grounds for a "public" or common sense in the disposition of the judging subject.

As I argue in the first chapter, Kant achieves this in the Third Critique by locating the properties that are strictly aesthetic—beauty and sublimity—not in the object itself but in the "disposition" (*Bestimmung*) of the reflecting and judging subject. Unlike the teleological judgment, which is interested in what a thing is for—its actual conformity with a given end—and unlike a moral or ethical judgment—which is interested in whether a thing is good—a pure aesthetic judgment is entirely disinterested and independent of either moral ends or mere sensual gratification. It is through aesthetic judgment, or Taste, that the empirical individual becomes the autonomous Subject in a universal sense, a movement that is achieved by the judgment's reflection on the formal properties of the object's mode of representation. In the case of the beautiful, the pleasure that attends the aesthetic judgment derives from the formal accord of the understanding and the imagination (which for Kant is merely the faculty by which sense presentations are borne to us as representations): that is, the pleasure is not in the realization of what a thing is, its concept, but in its "formal finality," its possibility as a thing with ends. In the case of the sublime, the pleasure derives from the capacity of the reason to apprehend forces or magnitudes in nature that exceed the representative capacity of the imagination. The sublime overwhelms the senses and the imagination but is nonetheless a manifestation of the supersensible in the mortal human.

As with the beautiful, then, the sublime has reference to the state of the judging subject, not to any quality inherent in its object:

> Therefore, just as the aesthetic judgement in its estimate of the beautiful refers the imagination in its free play to the *understanding*, to bring out its agreement with the *concepts* of the latter in general (apart from their determination): so in its estimate of a thing as sublime it refers that faculty to *reason* to bring out its subjective accord with *ideas* of reason (indeterminately indicated), i.e., to induce a temper of mind conformable to that which the influence of definite (practical) ideas would produce upon feeling, and in common accord with it.
>
> This makes it evident that true sublimity must be sought only in the mind of the judging Subject, and not in the Object of nature that occasions this attitude by the estimate formed of it. Who would apply the term "sublime" even to shapeless mountain masses towering one above the other in wild disorder, with their pyramids of ice, or to the dark tempestuous ocean, or such like things? But in the contemplation of them, without any regard to their form, the mind abandons itself to the imagination and to a reason placed, though quite apart from any definite end, in conjunction therewith, and merely broadening its view, and it feels itself elevated in its own estimate of itself on finding all the might of imagination still unequal to its ideas.[13]

And what is common or universal to the human as subject cannot be derived merely from experience but must have transcendental grounds. Further, the universal "ought"—the "objective necessity of the coincidence of the feeling of all with the particular feeling of each" (*CJ*, I, 84, §22)—by evident analogy with the *Critique of Practical Reason*, is categorical rather than actually realized or enforced, which thus appears to save it from the shadow of its coerciveness. These considerations will furnish the principal basis for Kant's critique of Burke.[14]

Kant ostensibly defers the lingering problem that common sense must be at once a constitutive element of any judgment and a product of the exercise of judgment until after the analysis of the beautiful and the sublime and after grounding common sense in the subject's formal reflection on its mode of representation. In the following section, however, he resolves the apparent aporia of common sense in a manner that is surely momentous for subsequent Western thought about the place of culture in the formation of the subject. Kant assumes the latency of that "common sense" while making its actualization subject to a "narrative of development." In doing so, he makes a certain form of historicity intrinsic to the history of the subject: The two categories become inseparable. In the first place, the narrative of subject formation that folds into a larger history of human civilization furnishes a kind of master narrative for a racialized understanding of human development itself. In the second, that narrative of civilization is universalized in accord with what are posed as the collective ends of humanity itself. Finally, in grounding it in the sphere of aesthetic judgments that are political in their effect, he incorporates equally a set of cultural judgments that determine the level of development of any given human community, its capacity for autonomy and representation. As the ground of sociality, this "common sense" only emerges in society and appears rudimentary at best in the "primitive" or "savage" states of Kant's exemplary Caribs and Iroquois (*CJ*, I, 155–56, §41). We recognize in this schematic narrative, as I suggested in the previous chapter, the history of human development that poses the emergence of civil society and the public sphere—"universal communicability"—as both its privileged end and as the actualization of a capacity always latent in the human at whatever stage of development. What I want to insist on here, in an extension of my claims in the previous chapter, is that the constitutive limit of the aesthetic, by the same token, is a cultural difference specified in racial terms and comprehended within this developmental narrative as a state of "underdevelopment."

The Savage—Carib or Iroquois—stands at the threshold of a development that culminates in civil society but remains subject to the "charm of sense," as Kant earlier calls it. This heteronomy of the senses over the judgment must be overcome for the full history of the subject to unfold. The Savage represents at once the instance of subjection and the latent potentiality of the aesthetic. Accordingly, we should not understand the "native" to be "foreclosed" from this Kantian history, as Gayatri Chakravorty Spivak suggests, but rather to be its limit point, at once outside the temporality of civilization and the "informing" moment of its emergence: The Savage is the "vestibule" of civility, to borrow again Hortense Spillers's apposite term.[15] What effectively makes this a racializing judgment rather than, as might be argued, a merely contingent historical or comparative anthropological example is its structural necessity to Kant's account of the development of the civilized subject. The Savage is required as a permanent instance of the "not-subject," the object of heteronomy both in the form of external natural forces and in that of the immediate gratification of his own desires. To deploy Denise Ferreira da Silva's terms, the Savage is opposed to "the subject of transparency, for whom universal reason is an internal guide," as a "subject of affectability," subordinated as an object both to reason and to nature as a force that it has yet to master.[16] The Savage thus marks a threshold in the historical development of humanity and stands as a permanent figure of the inner division of the human between the pathological and the (at least potentially) autonomous subject.

The anthropological assumption that the Savage is subordinated to the senses thus corresponds to the theoretical subordination to immediacy of sensation from which Kant's own aesthetic philosophy, and, in particular, his analytic of the sublime, struggles to emancipate itself. It is well known that what Kant calls his "transcendental exposition of aesthetic judgments" (*CJ*, I, 130, §29) marks a decisive turn away from the eighteenth-century preoccupation with the phenomena of pleasure and pain that formerly constituted the object of aesthetic philosophy. In seeking to ground the judgments of taste in a priori faculties of the human mind, Kant seeks to emancipate the aesthetic from its dangerous subordination to physical gratifications or affects, giving pre-eminence to formal modes of judgment rather than to the exquisite cultivation of sensation. Even such civilized refinements retain for him the marks of heteronomy, of the force of need and desire that continues to exert its sway through the body over the mind. This consideration explains the peculiar supplement to his "General Remark upon the Exposition of Aesthetic Reflective Judgements," inserted at the end of §29 and marked off from the rest of the text by a horizontal bar or boundary. Kant is at pains here to emphasize the distance that separates his analysis from the "physiological" exposition most eminently exemplified in Burke's *Philosophical Enquiry into the Origin of Our Ideas of the Sublime and Beautiful.*

Kant's objections to the "physiological" exposition of aesthetic judgments are twofold. First, Burke's analysis of the "origins" of the sublime and the beautiful remains attached to sensation and therefore to the "gratification" of the senses from which Kant has been at pains to separate the disinterested and autonomous reflecting subject. Second—and this is yet more telling for Kant—this attribution of delight to the "charm of the senses," which he had associated with the condition of the Savage, prevents the "universal accord" that is the standard of taste from being achieved by anything but a coercive exaction of agreement:

> But if we attribute the delight in the object wholly and entirely to the gratification which it affords through charm or emotion, then we must not exact from *any one else* agreement with the aesthetic judgement passed by *us*. For in such matters each person rightly consults his own personal feeling alone. But in that case there is an end of all censorship of taste—unless the example afforded by others as a result of a contingent coincidence of their judgements is to be held over us as *commanding* our assent. But this principle we would presumably resent, and appeal to our natural right of submitting a judgement to our own sense, where it rests upon the immediate feeling of personal well-being, instead of submitting it to that of others. (*CJ*, I, 132, §29)

For Kant, the physiological aesthetic in its very principle undermines the possibility of a universally valid subjective accord, leaving judgment either subordinate to the despotic "command" of an arbitrary standard of taste or dissolved in the potential anarchy of assertions of individual idiosyncrasy.

Kant here, if discretely, acknowledges the political stakes of the aesthetic: The ideal republic that consists of autonomous subjects, whose possibility is given by the common sense instantiated in the reflective formal subject of judgment, is threatened by the immediacy of judgments predicated on sensations of gratification or pain. Burke's analysis of the sublime and the beautiful, being thus predicated on sensation, undermines for Kant the ethical substrate of the judgment, its categorical form, that is crucial to the social function of taste. The "psychological observations" that "supply a wealth of material for the favourite investigations of empirical anthropology" (*CJ*, I, 131, §29) turn out not to be so easily relegated to the status of mere data but actually pose a dangerous immediacy of sensation in place of the delight that for Kant is "*immediately* connected to a representation" (*CJ*, I, 132, §29): Burke's empirical laws "only yield a knowledge of how we do judge, but they do not give us a command as to how we ought to judge, and what is more, such a command as is *unconditioned*" (*CJ*, I, 132, §29). The crucial term here is that of immediacy: Kant's aesthetic judgment must appear to take a delight *as if* it were immediately in the object itself, whereas it is actually, mediately, a delight in the disposition of the subject in relation to the representation of the object. He accordingly judges Burke's aesthetic to be predicated all too empirically on the immediate sensation provoked by the object itself. The description of Burke's aesthetic as "physiological" thus slips into its critique as pathological. It is literally pathological, being derived from what the subject undergoes or submits to (*pathein*). At the same time, the figurative connotations of sickness or pathology are readily available, suggesting that Burke's aesthetic is one that is disordered or contaminated by its subjection to heteronomy, to forces that make the subject determined or conditioned rather than self-determining or autonomous.

The distinction between Kant's and Burke's aesthetics could not be clearer in the passages that Kant actually cites. In the first passage, the sublime is said by Burke to be "grounded on the impulse towards self-preservation and on *fear*," while the other, on the beautiful, reduces it to "the relaxing, slackening, and enervating of the fibres of the body, and consequently a softening, a dissolving, a languor, and a fainting, dying, and melting away for pleasure" (*CJ*, I, 130–31, §29). In both cases, Burke's aesthetic experience approaches the dissolution rather than the affirmation of the subject, a dissolution that takes place by way of the intimacy of the subject and "mere" sensation. In the case of the sublime, the distance from the phenomenon that allows Burke's subject to survive the forces that threaten his "self-preservation," and that permit "a sort of tranquility tinged with terror," is entirely contingent. It is the lucky accident of his location that allows the subject to be an observer of the storm rather than its victim and leaves him gasping all at once with relief and fear, shock and awe. For Kant, on the contrary, the sublime is the effect of a quite different understanding of the subject's superiority to danger and is the product of its very opposition to the despotism of the senses, being precisely "what pleases by reason of its opposition to the interest of sense" (*CJ*, I, 118, §29). The sublime is the pleasure taken by the subject in the recognition of its superiority as subject to the forces of nature, in its own triumph over mortality and limitation. This is equally true of the mathematical and the dynamical sublime:

> In the immeasurableness of nature and the incompetence of our faculty
> for adopting a standard proportionate to the aesthetic estimation of
> the magnitude of its *realm*, we found our own limitation. But with this

we found in our rational faculty another non-sensuous standard, one
which has that infinity itself under it as unit, and in comparison with
which everything in nature is small, and so found in our minds a pre-
eminence over nature even in its immeasurability. Now in just the same
way the irresistibility of the might of nature forces upon us the recognition of our physical helplessness as beings of nature, but at the same
time reveals a faculty of estimating ourselves as independent of nature,
and discovers a pre-eminence above nature that is the foundation of a
self-preservation of quite another kind from that which may be assailed
and brought into danger by external nature. This saves humanity in our
own person from humiliation, even though as mortal men we have to
submit to external violence. (*CJ*, I, 111, §28)

Nothing could be further from Burke's derivation of the sublime from the
sensation of an overwhelming power that, though actually it threatens the
life of the subject, does not destroy him. Kant's sublime is precisely one
in which "the interest of sense" is overcome by the mind's pre-eminence,
freeing the subject into an autonomy predicated on its identity with all
other humans as rational subjects: "Humanity is saved in our person."[17]

We will return in a moment to Burke's physiology of the sublime. But
first, what is implicit in Kant's aesthetic is once again profoundly political, though here in its refusal of the despotism of sensation rather than
in his grounding of "common sense" in the universal subject. Although,
with self-preserving circumspection, he does not spell this out, the Kantian subject is both one that refuses the fear on which despotism is predicated, cleaving instead to the quasi-republican equivalence of moral and
autonomous subjects, and one that grounds its political claim to autonomy
discretely in a quite Protestant relation to the Godhead. That is, while
fear of God is acknowledged to be a proper and customary relation to the
divine power, it is by no means a source of the sublime. On the contrary,
the sublime relation to the divine is one of the reflective judgment that opposes superstitious awe:

> In religion, as a rule, prostration, adoration with bowed head, coupled
> with a contrite, timorous posture and voice, seems to be the only
> becoming demeanour in presence of the Godhead, and accordingly
> most nations have assumed and still observe it. Yet this cast of mind is
> far from being intrinsically and necessarily involved in the idea of the
> *sublimity* of religion and of its object. The man that is actually in a state
> of fear, finding in himself good reason to be so, because he is conscious
> of offending with his evil disposition against a might directed by a will

at once irresistible and just, is far from being in the frame of mind for admiring divine greatness, for which a temper of calm reflection and a quite free judgement are required. Only when he becomes conscious of having a disposition that is upright and acceptable to God, do those operations of might serve to stir within him the idea of the sublimity of this Being, so far as he recognizes the existence in himself of a sublimity of disposition consonant with His will, and is thus raised above the dread of such operations of nature, in which he no longer sees God pouring forth the vials of the wrath. (*CJ*, I, 113–14, §28)

Though Kant refrains from doing so, the traditional analogy between divine and monarchical power suggests that we should extend this "sublime" relation to God to secular authority and to read in it a republican commitment to nondomination or an enlightened refusal of submission to autocratic power entirely in keeping with his other writings, such as "What Is Enlightenment?" and *The Conflict of the Faculties*.[18] Kant's critique of Burke here implicitly manifests the political stakes of the Third Critique, posing an aesthetic and political claim for the autonomy and universality of the judgment against the heteronomy and arbitrariness that characterizes the despotic.

In contradistinction to Kant's "republican" aesthetics, with its disinterest toward the realm of the senses, Burke's essay presents the experience of the sublime and the beautiful as intimately linked to a dissolution of the subject in the face of powerful sensation. As Kant's paraphrase indicates, the feeling of beauty is closely linked to the effects of love, the subject "being softened, relaxed, enervated, dissolved, melted away by pleasure."[19] Furthermore, the effective cause of this pleasure lies in the qualities of the object itself and in the sensations they arouse in the subject rather than in the independent disposition of the subject himself. Burke is at pains to spell out the properties of the object that induce love or the feeling of beauty— properties like smallness, smoothness, sweetness, and variation—that are specific to the object rather than to any relation into which it enters, such that he explicitly excludes "proportion" and "fitness" as sources of beauty insofar as these have to do with comparative judgments rather than immediate sensations.

If beauty, then, has to do with properties in the object that induce a relaxation of the subject, the sublime, on the contrary, induces a tension that is indeed predicated on fear and the instinct of self-preservation. Again, however, the motive force of the sublime lies not in the subject's independence from the object but in his subordination to it. Several times, Burke emphasizes that in the experience of the sublime, sensation overwhelms the reason, hurrying it in a way that defies the act of reflection that for Kant is crucial to the judgment: "The passion caused by the great and the sublime in *nature*, when those causes operate most powerfully, is Astonishment; and astonishment is that state of the soul, in which all its motions are suspended, with some degree of horror. In this case the mind is so entirely filled with its object, that it cannot entertain any other, nor by consequence reason on that object which employs it. Hence arises the great power of the sublime, that far from being produced by them, it anticipates our reasonings, and hurries us on by an irresistible force" (*OSB*, 95–96). Later, of Milton's portrait of Satan, Burke writes that: "The mind is hurried out of itself, by a croud of great and confused images; which affect because they are crouded and confused. For separate them, and you lose much of the greatness, and join them, and you infallibly lose the clearness" (*OSB*, 106). This displacement of the reason by poetic language is similarly induced by actual crowds and the violence of mobs: "The shouting of multitudes has a similar effect; and by the sole strength of the sound, so amazes and confounds the mind, the best established tempers can scarcely forbear being born down, and joining in the common cry, and common resolution of the croud" (*OSB*, 151). Ultimately, for Burke, the sublime is the effect of a power that comes close to overwhelming the subject, "bearing it down," "hurrying it out of itself," "hurrying us on." Indeed, he remarks, apart from terror itself, "I know of nothing sublime which is not some modification of power" (*OSB*, 110). As Burke admits in the second edition of the essay, the archetypal figure of power is the Godhead and fear is a proper response to that power, fear that overpowers the reflective judgment:

> Some reflection, some comparing is necessary to satisfy us of his wisdom, his justice, and his goodness; to be struck with his power, it is only necessary that we should open our eyes. But whilst we contemplate so vast an object, under the arm, as it were, of almighty power, and invested upon every side with omnipresence, we shrink into the minuteness of our own nature, and are, in a manner, annihilated before him. And though a consideration of his other attributes may relieve in some measure our apprehensions; yet no conviction of the justice with which it is exercised, nor the mercy with which it is tempered, can wholly remove the terror that naturally arises from a force which nothing can withstand. (*OSB*, 119–20)

Far from deprecating this fear, Burke, unlike Kant, regards it as a "salutary" and necessary element of "true religion."

The secular correlative of divine power is, as for Kant, the power of monarchy or of despotism, and its effect, like that of both natural and divine power, is to "take away the free use of [the] faculties" (*OSB*, 116–17). Srinivas Aravamudan has finely demonstrated how Burke's invocation of despotism draws on and relates to the notion of oriental despotism, in relation both to religious and to secular power.[20] What I am interested in here is another aspect of Burke's analysis of terror, which is his extraordinary and fascinated intimacy with it. His derivation of the effects of both the sublime and the beautiful enters in minute detail into the modifications of the musculature of the body, from the straining of the eye in the face of darkness or obscurity, to the enervation or swooning away of the bodily sinews in relation to the loved object, to the labor of the ear in attending to repeated or intermittent sounds. The essay registers, in a way that Kant's critique never could, the thrill that attends the relation of the subject to objects that in one or another way threaten its autonomy, dissolving or overwhelming it in the passions of love and terror. Burke's is, as Kant seems to have descried, strictly speaking, a pathological and not merely a physiological account of aesthetic pleasure. His subject undergoes or suffers the sensations that cause the terrors of the sublime or the pleasures provoked by beauty, a willing subjection to the heteronomy of sensations that would, for Kant, slip over into the other sense of a pathology, that of a subject distempered by its passions—or, in da Silva's terms, a subject of affectability.

Burke, indeed, insists that the universal claims of taste, as his introduction "On Taste" makes clear, are derived from the physical rather than the formally subjective universality of the human. The human is an object that suffers its passions as much as it is a subject that reflects upon its objects. Accordingly, the senses are the foundation of any universal claims that can be made about human relations to the world: "All the natural powers in man, which I know, that are conversant about external objects, are the Senses; the Imagination; and the Judgement. We do and we must suppose, that as the conformation of their organs are nearly, or altogether the same in all men, so the manner of perceiving external objects is in all men the same, or with little difference" (*OSB*, 7). Accordingly, the objects of the aesthetic, human pleasures and pains, are universally felt in the same way.[21] By the same token, the imagination is also universal:

Now the imagination is the most extensive province of pleasure and pain, as it is the region of our fears and our hopes, and of all our passions that are connected to them; and whatever is calculated to affect

the imagination with these commanding ideas, by force of any original
natural impression, must have the same power pretty equally over all
men. For since the imagination is only the representative of the senses,
it can only be pleased or displeased with the images from the same
principle on which the sense is pleased or displeased with the realities; and consequently there must be just as close an agreement in the
imagination as in the senses of men. (*OSB*, 17)

The universality of Taste, as a complex of the senses, the imagination,
and of reasoning thereon, is predicated upon this commonality of human
sensation: "For as the senses are the great originals of all our ideas, and
consequently of all our pleasures, if they are not uncertain and arbitrary,
the whole ground-work of Taste is common to all, and therefore there is
sufficient foundation for a conclusive reasoning on these matters" (*OSB*,
31).[22] Far from regarding taste as the prerogative of the rational subject
and as a yardstick that divides the cultivated subject of civilization from its
savage or barbarian other, Burke's argument on the sensational foundation
of taste seems almost radical in its inclusiveness, bringing the oriental despot into community with the shoemaker: "On the subject of their dislike
there is a difference between all these people, arising from the different
kinds and degrees of their knowledge; but there is something in common
to the painter, the shoemaker, the anatomist, and the Turkish emperor, in
the pleasure arising from a natural object, so far as each perceives it justly
imitated; the satisfaction in seeing an agreeable figure; the sympathy pro-
ceeding from a striking and affecting incident. So far as Taste is natural, it
is nearly common to all" (*OSB*, 24).[23] For such an analysis, differences in
knowledge and in station are less important than the common element of
pleasure in the object of judgment.

Such a "naturalist" account of taste is far from the Kantian one.[24] Not
only is Kant's subject of judgment expressly indifferent to the gratification or pain of the senses, focusing solely on the formal aspects of the
representation, that subject emerges, moreover, only in consequence of a
process of cultivation. This is particularly true in relation to the sublime.
For despite the fact that Kant derives the capacity for taste from a "common or public sense" latent in all men, aesthetic judgment in the fullest
sense, and a capacity to appreciate sublimity in particular, is predicated on
the development in the individual of a certain level of cultivation. Unlike
the appreciation of the beautiful, in the case of the sublime "a far higher
degree of culture, not merely of the aesthetic judgement, but also of the
faculties of cognition which lie at its basis, seems to be requisite to enable

us to lay down a judgement upon this high distinction of natural objects" (*CJ*, I, 115, §29). This "degree of culture" is based on a varied and extended acquaintance with aesthetic objects and has specifically to do with the development of the mental capacity for ideas:

> The proper mental mood for a feeling of the sublime postulates the mind's susceptibility for ideas, since it is precisely in the failure of nature to attain to these—and consequently under the presupposition of this susceptibility and of the straining of the imagination to use nature as a schema for ideas—that there is something forbidding to sensibility, but which, for all that, has an attraction for us, arising from the fact of its being a dominion which reason exercises over sensibility with a view to extending it to the requirements of its own realm (the practical) and letting it look out beyond itself into the infinite, which for it is an abyss. In fact, without the development of moral ideas, that which, thanks to preparatory culture, we call sublime, merely strikes the untutored man [*dem rohen Menschen*] as terrifying. (*CJ*, I, 115, §29)

For Kant, the unmediated confrontation with the sublime leaves the savage or the peasant overwhelmed by the abysmal terror of the phenomenon that exceeds the imagination. As Spivak comments: "The raw man has not yet achieved or does not possess a subject whose *Anlage* [blueprint] or programming includes the structure of feeling for the moral. He is not yet the subject divided and perspectivized among the three critiques. In other words, he is not yet or simply not the subject as such, the hero of the *Critiques*, the only example of the concept of a natural yet rational being. This gap between the subject as such and the not-yet-subject can be bridged under propitious circumstances by culture."[25]

In a certain sense, it is precisely the requirement of mediation, the mediation of culture and of the ethical formation of the disposition of the subject, that enables the subject to partake of the public sense that the aesthetic both forms and instantiates. The pedagogical aims of the aesthetic that Schiller will draw out into a program of education, transforming the "raw man" into the citizen, are already deeply, if less evidently, inscribed in Kant's Third Critique.[26] Within such a pedagogy, the developmental history that separates the Savage from the modern subject is spelled out more fully than it is in Kant's exposition, and the terms of the racializing judgment of culture are established in ways that are decisive for what in Chapter 3 I will characterize as a liberal discourse of colonialism. And yet, as Spivak remarks, it is only under "propitious circumstances" that the bridge can be made by culture between the "raw man," object of heteronomy, and the autonomous subject that is defined against that state. The differential example of the Savage is a requirement of the thinking of autonomy itself and cannot therefore be cultivated out of the system: It is the threshold instance on which the narrative of development at once founds itself and founders.[27]

For Burke, in contradiction to Kant, the effects of the sublime are intimately bound up with the actual physical experience of the mind's incapacity to separate itself from the "interest of sense." The surety of self-preservation is not by any means the given of those endowed with cultural capital, like Kant's exemplary scientist de Saussure among the Savoyard peasants, but seems everywhere predicated on the exertions of human bodily labor. Even the work of theorizing the origins of taste becomes such a labor, one that "exercises" the mind and strengthens it for future labors: "Whatever progress may be made towards the discovery of truth in this matter, I do not repent the pains I have taken in it. . . . Whatever turns the soul inward on itself, tends to concenter its forces, and to fit it for greater and stronger flights of science" (*OSB*, viii–ix).

Yet it is not my point here to suggest that the conservative Burke paradoxically offers on the basis of a common experience of labor a more democratic foundation for aesthetic thought than the proto-republican Kant. On the contrary, as is well known, the thrill that the younger Burke is able to entertain in the effects of the crowd, the transport that carries all along with it, became, in the face of the French Revolution and the seizure of Marie-Antoinette, the basis of a reactionary critique of the immediacy of revolutionary violence.[28] That critique, in turn, feeds into the suspicion that informs British cultural discourse in its founding thinkers from Samuel Taylor Coleridge to Matthew Arnold as to the disturbing effects of radical politics and what is understood as the unmediated violence of "terror." Indeed, the discourse on culture that founds the humanities as we practice them could be understood precisely as an attempt to contain the potential for violence—and even the heady pleasure in violence—that is the specter of radical democracy. Culture, which defines the work of humanities pedagogy since the Enlightenment, stems from the critique of revolutionary violence as immediate violence that it seeks to counter by forming the reflective subject on whom the possibility of representative democratic institutions is founded.[29] It forgets the unspectacular violence of that formation.

Even as the convergence of a Kantian aesthetic with a Burkean reaction against revolution informs that cultural tradition, a counterdiscourse that retains the traces of Burke's aesthetic sensationalism persists. It is, after all, the radical William Godwin who, in the wake of Burke's *Reflections on the Revolution in France*, derives the very grounds of human equality from the identity of the senses of pleasure and pain:

> Justice has relation to beings endowed with perception, and capable
> of pleasure and pain. Now it immediately results from the nature of
> such beings, independently of any arbitrary constitution, that pleasure
> is agreeable and pain odious, pleasure to be desired and pain to be
> disapproved. It is therefore just and reasonable that such beings should
> contribute, so far as it lies in their power, to the pleasure and benefit of
> each other. Among pleasures, some are more exquisite, more unalloyed
> and less precarious than others. It is just that these should be preferred.
>
> From these simple principles we may deduce the moral equality of
> mankind.[30]

Godwin's radical account of the grounds for human equality short-circuits the discourse of culture with an appeal to an aesthetic foundation for political justice that is located immediately in corporeal sensations. It could, I think, be argued that such a refusal of the separation of the subject from sensation is articulated throughout a radical countercanonical discourse that insists, in defiance of the canons of "high culture," on working through the terrain of corporeal pains and pleasures in ways that vividly apprehend the workings of and resistance to what Foucault will come to term "biopower" in the emergence of industrial capitalism.[31] It is, in other words, in the pained flesh of the dominated and not in the autonomous subject of the political or aesthetic spheres that we first locate, following both Fanon and Spillers, the stirrings of resistance to the states of subjection over which the universal holds sway and against which it takes its form.

The Abyss of Blackness

Although Foucault notoriously ignored the colonial sphere in his explorations of the genealogy of modern forms of power, there is probably no space in which the conjunction of power and violence more consistently and continuously affected the bodies of humans declared not or not yet to be subjects.[32] The distance that separates a "physiological" from a "transcendental exposition of the aesthetic" may also serve to draw our critical reflections back to the intimate linking of violence and terror in the colonial project, an issue that postcolonial theory has notably veered away from addressing. Luke Gibbons has persuasively argued that Burke's intimacy with the corporeal sensations of violence and despotism, as well as his apprehension of the "sublime" impact of mass politics in "carrying away" the subject, derives from his experience in colonial Ireland.[33] Frantz Fanon, to whom the contemporary analysis of colonial discourse owes much of its impetus, was similarly familiar with the impact of colonial violence on the colonized body and with the denial of subjectivity or access to universality to the racialized. The scope of his work critiques the historical unfolding and colonial consequences of a discourse on the human and the body that was only emerging in the late eighteenth century.

In both *Black Skin, White Masks* (1952) and *The Wretched of the Earth* (1961), it is on the visceral, corporeal impact of colonialism and racism, as against the colonized intellectual's appeal to the universal values of Western culture and subjecthood, that Fanon places the weight of his analysis. Whether it is the black man's experience of racism as being transformed into "an object in the midst of other objects"—a sensation that causes him to encounter "difficulties in the development of his bodily schema"—or whether it is the peculiarly "alert" and tensed "tonicity of muscles" of the colonized—a tension that stems from the simultaneously "inhibitory and stimulating" apparatus of colonial power—it is for Fanon always the body that first registers the effects of a racialized culture.[34] It is the sensation of painful terror that calls forth the colonized's violent resistance to a prior colonial violence. For the colonized, the developmental schema that underwrites the civilizational discourse of the colonizer and bars the colonized from recognition as a subject is apprehended as the vertiginous collapse of the subject back into the body, a collapse in which the violence of the colonial state appears unmediated by the cultural apparatuses that undertake the formation of the white subject in the West.[35] Precisely insofar as our own subjectivities as intellectuals are formed within those apparatuses, we risk, even in a postcolonial critique of the subject, occluding the corporeal terror and violence that still constitutes the realm of colonial power.

For Fanon, it is in and on the racialized body that that violence—the violence of a negation that makes the raced body the very limit and other of the civilized—is registered. It is registered in the judgment that denies subjecthood to the racial other. "Look, a negro! (*Tiens, un nègre!*)": In that famous moment of *Black Skin, White Masks*, under the white child's gaze— a gaze of recognition that denominates the difference it observes—Fanon finds himself fixed, "in the sense in which a chemical solution is fixed by a dye," and "bursts apart" in the experience of nonbeing (*BSWM*, 109).

Nonetheless, to be denied being as a subject is not to be outside the racial regime, "For not only must the black man be black; he must be black in relation to the white man," suspended between fixity and explosion (*BSWM*, 110). If, for Spivak, Kant's "*rohe Mensch*," "untutored Man," is the "not-yet-subject," for Fanon, "the black is not a man" (*BSWM*, 10). For all that, the black man is not yet "foreclosed" from the developmental structure but rather caught at its threshold in the lethal mirror stage of racialization that he calls a "dual narcissism" (*BSWM*, 12). In this specular domain, racialization itself prevents the white subject, let alone the black, from actually occupying the position of universality on which the racial judgment itself is predicated: "The black man wants to be white. The white man slaves to reach a human level" (*BSWM*, 11). As Fanon elsewhere puts it, the European declaration of its cultural "normativity" is never more than "unilateral."[36] The continuing presence in the white's vision of the black as an object denied full subjecthood thus constitutively prevents the white subject from realizing his representative universality: He has always already objectified another subject as mere body or matter in order to constitute the narrative of his own development, a narrative that, as Kant obliquely suggests, could not be anchored without that objectification. The predication of universality on the development of taste and common sense thus stumbles on the threshold instance of the racial figures, Savage or Black, that its unfolding requires.

To read back into Burke from the perspective of Fanon is equally to throw open the racial blind spot of the corporeal schema of sensation on which his claims for the universality of taste are predicated. As we have seen, for Burke the aesthetic experiences of the sublime and the beautiful are registered in the first place on the affectable body. Already, however, there is a fundamental asymmetry between the two spheres of taste, one of which regards self-preservation, the other love and sociability. The sublime is an affect that derives its force from its antisociality: It is apprehended in the face of the wilderness or the stormy ocean, or in the face of a political or religious power that crushes the reciprocity on which any sociality is based. At the same time, it is the domain that calls forth labor, a mental labor that is the analogue of the physical labor by which the natural world is subdued and that counteracts the "disorders" that result from overmuch "relaxation" or inaction: "The best remedy for all these evils is exercise or *labour*; and labour is a surmounting of *difficulties*, an exertion of the contracting power of the muscles; and as such, resembles pain, which consists in tension, or contraction, in everything but degree. Labour is not only requisite to preserve the coarser organs in a state fit for their functions, but it is equally necessary to these finer organs, on which, and by which, the imagination, and perhaps the whole mental powers act" (*OSB*, 254–55).

In the economy of Burke's aesthetic, then, the sublime relates to the domain of production as the beautiful, the realm of love and sociality, does to that of reproduction. The sublime calls forth the physical and mental exertions that extend men's domination over the natural and social worlds; the beautiful inhabits those domains that have already been reduced. In a certain sense, the sublime strengthens or forges the subject that it threatens to destroy, "preparing it for further flights," while the beautiful relaxes it. But there is a further, more discrete, asymmetry between the two domains. Where the objects of the sublime actually appear to produce their effects upon the subject, calling forth the countermotion of a certain aesthetic labor, the objects that constitute domesticated nature appear as no more than the supports of the qualities that induce the sensation of the beautiful. Nowhere is this clearer than in the paradigmatic case of love, where the beloved woman who elicits the passion of the male subject nowhere in fact appears: She is only the effect of her effects. Those effects are the remarkably powerful ones that Kant later paraphrases from Burke: "The head reclines something on one side; the eyelids are more closed than usual, and the eyes roll gently with an inclination to the object, the mouth is a little opened, and the breath drawn slowly, with now and then a low sigh: the whole body is composed, and the hands fall idly to the sides. All this is accompanied with an inward sense of melting and languor" (*OSB*, 287).

In a peculiar sense, beauty—which "acts by relaxing the solids of the whole system" (*OSB*, 287)—works as powerfully to threaten the autonomy and integrity of the subject as do any of the objects of the sublime. It induces a "fading" of the subject, a powerful effect of dissolution. And the feminine, which never appears as the subject of taste but only as its support, occupies the peculiar, nonsymmetrical position of being at once outside the system of taste and the exciting object of both the beautiful and the sublime. Situated at the boundary of nature and culture, so to speak, the feminine takes on the ambiguous quality of nature "herself," at once overwhelming power and nurturing servant. In this respect, indeed, woman occupies the same threshold as the Savage or "raw man," belonging both within the trajectory of culture and at the same time standing outside it as its counterinstance. Unable to recognize this parity, and caught perhaps in the dilemma of wishing neither to transform the woman into mere object nor to have her appear as having dominion over man, Burke allows her to fade into an uncanny metonymic absence that haunts the text.

At only one point, however, does woman appear and appear as an object with the effect of the sublime. That moment is when the already asymmetrically gendered subject is also racialized: The black woman arrives as a kind of abyss in the text where the sublime and the beautiful collapse into one another. The passage comes in the course of the chapter entitled "Darkness Terrible in Its Own Nature," which endeavors to show "that blackness and darkness are in some degree painful by their natural operation, independent of any associations whatsoever" (*OSB*, 275). Burke cites the case of a thirteen-year-old boy who was born blind but had recovered his sight after a cataract operation. We are informed "that the first time the boy saw a black object, it gave him great uneasiness; and that some time after, upon accidentally seeing a negro woman, he was struck with great horror at the sight. The horror, in this case, can scarcely be supposed to arise from any association" (*OSB*, 276). What is striking in this passage is only in part that blackness is held naturally, immediately, to provoke uneasiness: Here as in Fanon, the putatively untutored gaze of a child betrays the fact that the apparently unmediated recoil from blackness is already structured retrospectively by what it will have recognized.[37] Every gaze is already snagged in the regime of representation within which it finds its meaning: not "Look, what's that?" but "Look, a negro!" Moreover, the blackness of a woman provokes, far more intensely, "great horror." The feminine, the support of the beautiful that relaxes and dissolves the subject, comes into conjunction with the dark mark of the racialized body, thus bringing about the collapse of the carefully maintained distinction between the domains of self-preservation and of reproduction, of the sublime and the beautiful, of subject and object, of the barred "Savage" and the civilized "social."[38] In short, the black woman's appearance initiates a foundering of the borders between death and life.

Clearly, and for the only time in the essay, Burke assimilates the sublime effects of blackness on the sensations to those of love, only to stage the subject as reacting to that affect with recoil rather than pleasure: "Black bodies, reflecting none, or but a few rays, with regard to sight, are but so many vacant spaces dispersed among the objects we view. When the eye lights on one of these vacuities, after having been kept in some degree of tension by the play of the adjacent colours upon it, it suddenly falls into a relaxation; out of which it as suddenly recovers by a convulsive spring" (*OSB*, 281). Burke poses the shock caused by the "black body" as an abysmal threat to the subject, operating as a "vacuity" that causes a sudden fall. In the play of the contradictory effects of attraction and repulsion, an ambivalence attends the thrill of the sublime here as throughout Burke's essay. Not for nothing, surely, do the three chapters on darkness and blackness (§§xvi–xviii) abut the chapter entitled "The Physical Cause of Love" (§xix).[39]

In this moment, the boundary marks of both the gendered and the raced objects that at once structure and threaten the white male subject converge in a moment of crisis: As Spillers puts it, "The crisis of collapse passes over the black and is 'answered' in the white, whose imaginary is insulted and assaulted by this racially different bodily manifestation."[40] Fanon takes his own experience as such a phobogenic object to critically extend the Lacanian mirror stage into the terrain of racial subjecthood. The pathological phobia that constitutes racism derives for Fanon from the "destructuration" of the white body image that the black body effects: "At the extreme, I should say that the Negro, because of his body, impedes the closing of the postural schema of the white man—at the point, naturally, at which the black man makes his entry into the phenomenal world of the white man" (*BSWM*, 160). The very body of the black man functions as a kind of abyss that shatters the closed circuit of the white familial mirror stage.

It is important to note at this juncture that the black body that here appears as an abyss to the white subject is, unlike in Burke, a black *male* body. For Burke, for reasons outlined above, it is structurally inevitable that the body be female, drawing together as it does a persistent anxiety in the text about the covert sublimity of the feminine with the anxiety provoked by blackness. For Fanon, the focus on the black male body is surely equally overdetermined. The passage is staged autobiographically, and the analysis of the anecdote evidently draws on a very male-oriented body of psychoanalytic work. But beyond these contingencies, we can hypothesize within the terms of the larger argument of this essay more systematic reasons for the negation of the black female in Fanon's corpus. In the terms of the mirror stage, Fanon stands in the anecdote in the place of the image of the father. But rather than representing, as the white father would, the Name-of-the-father, the anchor of the Symbolic or the Law, he represents a terrifying abyss. He is not recognized as a subject who could represent the Subject; his existence is negated. Fanon's means to escape from that predicament is, throughout *Black Skin, White Masks*, to desire what, according to the Lacanian logic of heterosexually asymmetrical desire, the white man desires: the white woman. Pursuing that logic, it is the desire of the white woman that Fanon desires. This places him in the unenviable situation of desiring to become the male subject by way of a desiring of the other's desire, which places him back into the feminized position of the nonsubject. He occupies in this relation the structural position, therefore, of the woman of color who is the object of the white male's desire.

The ineluctability of this contradictory outcome of his apparently simple
desire to be recognized as subject may account for Fanon's often-remarked
misogyny, especially toward women of color, and his simultaneous recognition and denial of the homosociality and the homosexual desires that
circulate through the scene of race and colonialism.[41]

Though he skirts the question of his own desire, Fanon elaborates the
terms of the abyssal negation of black subjecthood in an extended and
complex footnote:

> It would indeed be interesting, on the basis of Lacan's theory of the
> *mirror period* [*sic*], to investigate the extent to which the *imago* of his
> fellow built up in the young white at the usual age would undergo an
> imaginary aggression with the appearance of the Negro. When one has
> grasped the mechanism described by Lacan, one can have no further
> doubt that the real Other for the white man is and will continue to be
> the black man. And conversely. Only for the white man the Other is
> perceived on the level of the body image, absolutely as the not-self—
> that is, the unidentifiable, the unassimilable. For the black man, as we
> have shown, historical and economic realities come into the picture.
> (*BSWM*, 161n)

The asymmetry is marked here: What for the white man takes place at the
level of the ontological, as an ahistorical and immediate abyss, appears for
him as such precisely because of the historical barring of the black from
subjecthood and historicity. For the black man, on the contrary, the historical and the economic conditions of racialization become the means to
an analysis of that exclusion and of the negation of subjectivity.[42] In the
developmental schema of the West, for which the destiny of the racialized
subject is to "become white," as Fanon puts it, that black subject will always
remain the "subject-yet-to-be": an object interpellated by historical judgment but never able to be fully in that history as its subject.[43]

Reading Fanon's analysis in relation to the discourse on the aesthetic
thus suggests that the body—which is for Kant a material to be transcended in the course of universalizing reflection and cultivation and is
for Burke the very foundation of aesthetic universality—is rather the locus of an ineradicable and constitutive difference. As Fanon puts it, in a
riposte to Sartre, "the Negro suffers in his body quite differently from
the white man" (*BSWM*, 138). Because it is constitutively inassimilable to
the unilaterally declared norms of universality, the black body necessarily
evokes violence and objectification.[44] What cannot simply be transcended
must be destroyed, obliterated, in the sublime violence of colonialism. But,

being constitutive of and not merely contingent or external to the very regime that produces the subject as such, it cannot in fact be annihilated and remains an ineradicable if abyssal peril. Hence the persistent rage of the colonizer and the racist.[45] Burke, whose Irish experience would have taught him the disproportionate violence of colonialism toward what resists it, comes closer than Kant to recognizing this fact in his vivid apprehension of the violence of power. Nonetheless, his recognition necessarily falters when the universal eye of the white subject encounters the black body that embodies the difference that denies it universality. The black body becomes the abyss into which the claims of universality, founded as they are on its difference, inevitably founder. Burke's anonymous black woman, about whose name and history aesthetic philosophy has remained consistently and symptomatically incurious, stands in all her abyssal abstraction as the dark counter-figure of universality itself. Invoked merely to confirm the logic of the sublime, she becomes the singular threshold at which the subject confronts the possibility of its dissolution.

Insofar as both the transcendental and the physiological accounts of the aesthetic, and the political subject that they differently underwrite, remain inscribed within what we might call a precocious as well as a unilateral universalization of a singular conception of the human, the discourse of the aesthetic will remain a more or less discretely racialized, as well as a political, discourse on the subject and on culture. In the following chapter, I will argue that the regime of representation that regulates that conception of the human constitutes, in its rhetorical structure as in its topology, an abyss that consigns the racialized subject to the place of nonrepresentability. Where aesthetic theory governs the possibility and the structure of representation itself, the figures of race—the Savage and the Black—stand as the absolute instances of the pathological, arrested at the threshold and barred from access to civility and humanity.

CHAPTER 3

Race under Representation

This racism that aspires to be rational, individual, genotypically
and phenotypically determined, becomes transformed
into cultural racism. The object of racism is no longer
the individual man but a certain form of existing.

—FRANTZ FANON, "Racism and Culture"

Far from having to ask whether culture is or is not a function of
race, we are discovering that race—or what is generally meant
by the term—is one function among others of culture.

—CLAUDE LÉVI-STRAUSS, "Race and Culture"

Racial Formations

The experience and the analysis of racism or race relations have been and
continue to be cast principally in spatial terms. The concept of race has,
throughout its history, been articulated in terms of the geographical distribution of peoples or, as the discreteness of geographical location gradually dissolves, as if there were a spectrum of races in contiguity with one
another. Likewise, in the politics of racism it is the confrontation of races
in opposition to one another and the literally and figuratively spatial disposition of inequitable power relations between them that is most striking.
Frantz Fanon's influential analysis of the colonial sphere as "a world divided into compartments" can hardly be gainsaid any more than one could
dismiss his corresponding insistence that "this approach to the colonial
world, its ordering and its geographical layout will allow us to mark out the
lines on which a decolonized society will be reorganized."[1] Unquestion-
ably, neither the history nor the theory of racism can be thought without
reference to spatial categories, whether we attend to the global geographies
of imperial expansion and international capital or to the more intimate geographies of the inner city, ghettoization, or the displacement of peoples.
The human experiences recorded in these terms are the material substrate

69

of other, equally spatial terms in which the antiracist cultural politics of the last decades have been expressed: Euro- or ethnocentrism, marginalization, exclusion, the Global South, not to mention those categories, Orientalism and the West, whose invocation has become all the more pertinent as Islam once again becomes the object of demonization in the context of the global war on terror. Race manifests, as always, in a spatial division of the world charged with differential powers.

It is not my intention here to critique those categories, without which neither the analysis of nor the political struggle against racism could have been articulated, but rather to argue that these spatial terms must be supplemented by an analysis of the temporal axis that is equally constitutive of racist discourse. Critiques of development and modernization theories have long drawn attention to the manner in which racist and ethnocentric discourses in economic and political spheres deploy a normative temporality of human development that is applied at once to the individual, to individual nations or cultures, and to the human race in general.[2] But beyond such critiques, the discourse on culture that emerges in the "modern era" of the West is itself structured at every level by this normative developmental schema: As I argue, the racism of culture is not a question of certain contingent racist observations by its major theoreticians or of the still incomplete dissemination of its goods but an ineradicable effect of its fundamental structures. These structures, indeed, regulate the forms, casual and institutional, that racism has taken in the post-Enlightenment era, and they account for the generally racist disposition of the "West," understood not as a bounded geographical domain but as a global complex of economic, political, and cultural institutions that represent, in a universalizing temporal schema, the locus of the modern in any society.

The so-called postracial moment represents the extension rather than the negation or even the fulfillment of this schema. It is, in the discourse on race that always subtends the political and the economic, the equivalent of the "end of history," a declaration that no alternative to the present regime can be considered anything other than a state of inadequacy to the cultural norm that is the predetermined end for humanity. Like the end of history, the postracial maintains the differential structures of race in place precisely by relegating them to spaces of excision or "exception" to a humanity redefined as indifferent to difference.[3] Their declaration is no less premature than that of the domain of aesthetic freedom. Within these structures— political, economic, or aesthetic—the discourse of culture is not merely descriptive but crucially productive, in that it directs the fundamentally racial formation of the modern subject both in the geographical west and wherever the West has imposed its institutions. The postracial moment, indeed, is no more than a reinscription of the West in dominance, another moment in the long historical trajectory that Sylvia Wynter has described as relegating every alternative to the condition of lack: "All other modes of being human would instead have to be seen not as the alternative modes of being human that they are 'out there,' but adaptively, as the lack of the West's ontologically absolute self-description."[4] This "overrepresentation" of a singular and partial "mode of being human" is counterpointed by what I call here the relegation of its racialized residue to a state of being *under* representation: constitutively barred by the regime of representation that dictates the racial formation of the human subject.

Michael Omi and Howard Winant have proposed that racial formations operate on both micro- and macrolevels of society to produce a regime that links the cultural domain of representation to social structure. "From a racial formation perspective," they argue, "race is a matter of both social structure and cultural representation. . . . Racial projects connect what race *means* in a particular discursive practice and the ways in which both social structures and everyday experiences are racially *organized*, based upon that meaning."[5] Part of the intention of this chapter is to continue to elaborate a question raised in Chapter 1—namely, how the meshing of racial formations can take place between various levels and spheres of social practice, as, for example, between political and cultural spheres or between the individual and the national level. In doing so, I will be redeploying the concept of "formation," folding the sociocultural sense in which Omi and Winant intend it into the equally important sense that it has traditionally had in aesthetic pedagogy, of self-formation or *Bildung*. Culture will have here not its generalized sense of the totality of life-forms of a particular society or group but quite strictly the sense of aesthetic culture.[6] I contend that the terms developed for aesthetic culture in the late eighteenth century, as constituting the definition of human identity universally, continue to regulate racial formations through the various sites of contemporary practice.[7] Crucial to this function of aesthetic culture is its formulation and development of a narrative of representation, by which I mean not only the representative narratives of canonical culture but also the narrative form taken by the concept of representation itself. As we shall see further, within this narrative the same processes of formalization occur at every level, allowing a series of transferred identifications to take place from individual to nation, and from the nation to the idea of a universal humanity. By the same token, the fissures and contradictions that trouble this narrative are replicated equally at every level or in every site that it informs. In this way, the self-evidence of fundamentally narrative forms works to naturalize the racial regime of representation.

What I will attempt here, then, is to sketch a tropology of racism as it is embedded in the "disposition of the subject" produced and maintained by Western culture. Though I will use the term *culture* throughout to imply, first of all, "aesthetic culture," it will become clear that the idea of aesthetic culture governs not only what is loosely referred to as "high culture" but also, if less evidently, most other subsequent usages of the term. As we have seen, the theoretical construction of a domain of aesthetic judgment in late eighteenth- and early nineteenth-century cultural theory provides the constitutive forms of the "public sphere" itself. Grounding the idea of a common or public sense, the subject of aesthetic judgment supplies the very possibility of a disinterested domain of culture and prescribes the development of that domain through history as the ethical end of humanity itself.

My argument here builds on, and to some degree necessarily reprises, my reading of Kant's *Critique of Judgement* in Chapter 1, where the ordering of "our general state of representative activity" implies a narrative organization of the senses that moves from sensation to form and proposes that the existence of both a public sense and public sphere are contingent upon a "Subject without properties," the judgment of which is purely formal. I further extend the claim presented in Chapter 2 that this narrative of the senses within the individual human subject finds a correspondent form in the development of the human race, in that the capacity for formalizing aesthetic judgment is the mark of civilization; further, the developmental narrative of this gradual organization of the senses is required by the developmental history of the race of which, at every stage of that development, it is the index.

While the groundwork of an aesthetic regulation of racial judgment can be deciphered throughout Kant's work, it is useful to turn to one of his earliest interpreters, Friedrich Schiller, whose schematization and dissemination of Kant's Third Critique decisively contributed to its generalization and institutionalization in the following century. While some have held that Schiller's *On the Aesthetic Education of Man* (1795) performs a reduction of Kant's complexity for pedagogical purposes, it seems more accurate to say that Schiller in fact draws out the necessarily pedagogical infrastructure of the *Critique of Judgement*.[8] By the same token, Schiller draws most clearly out of Kant's aesthetic theory the intertwining of its pedagogically developmental ends with its corresponding racial formation.

Schiller's schematization of Kant can be summarized in the following preliminary propositions:

1. the ordering of "our general state of representative activity" is such as to imply a narrative organization of the senses that moves from sensation to form;
2. this narrative of the senses within the individual human subject finds a correspondent form in the development of the human race;
3. this narrative can be expressed as or, alternatively, depends upon a movement from contiguity to identity, or from metonymy to metaphor.

These formally correspondent narratives, which I will elaborate in the following sections, shape in their conjunction the conditions for the emergence of the public sphere as a racial formation.

On the Aesthetic Development of the Race

As the simultaneously literal and metaphoric usages of both the terms *common sense* and *taste* might suggest, what these concepts describe is the very movement they require from the immediate particularity of sensation to the formal generality of the social. For "sense" to become "common," its conditions must be formalized as a disposition of the Subject in each of us; for "taste" to emerge as a social phenomenon, the cultivation of the senses must proceed from the pleasure derived from the existence of the object that is characteristic of literal "taste" to the contemplative relation to the object that is principally conceived of as a capacity of sight. This narrative of the organization of the senses toward an increasing distance from the object and an increasing formalization of its mode of representation was parallel for Kant to the movement from the merely agreeable, which is private and entirely singular, to the beautiful, which is to be universally communicable. In the discourse of aesthetic culture, which itself emerges in the increasing abstraction of aesthetics itself from the science of pain and pleasure to the discourse on fine art, this narrative organization of the senses in a crucially developmental hierarchy is fundamental. Indeed, in the most minimal moment of perception, such a development is already present within any judgment as the move from *Darstellung* (presentation), in which the senses are merely passive recipients, to *Vorstellung* (representation), in which the object is constituted as a possible object for the reflective or the logical judgment. A process of formalization, the initial abstraction of a form from a manifold of sensations as an object assimilable to other such objects, is inseparable from any completed act of perception.

Schiller puts it with characteristic clarity:

> It is nature herself which raises man from reality to semblance, by furnishing him with two senses which lead him to knowledge of the real world though semblance alone. In the case of the eye and the ear, she herself has driven importunate matter back from the organs of sense, and the object, with which in the case of our more animal senses we have direct contact, is set at a distance from us. What we actually see with the eye is something different from the sensation we receive; for the mind leaps out across light to objects. The object of touch is a force to which we are subjected; the object of eye and ear a form that we engender. As long as man is still a savage he enjoys by means of these tactile senses alone, and at this stage the senses of semblance are merely the servants of these. Either he does not rise to the level of seeing at all, or he is at all events not satisfied with it. Once he does begin to enjoy through the eye, and seeing acquires for him a value of its own, he is already aesthetically free and the play-drive has started to develop.[9]

Schiller makes explicit here the development of the senses that grounds and symbolizes the developmental history of the race and reaffirms the status of the Savage as the being subordinate to external force. In a version of the thesis that "ontogeny recapitulates phylogeny," the movement, as Kant put it, from "the charm of sense to habitual moral interest" that taste makes possible is at once an affair of the individual and of the human "race" exactly inasmuch as it represents a movement from heteronomy to freedom.[10] The same development that produces in each individual a capacity for subjectively universal judgments of taste produces in human societies the civilized form of the public sphere in which the autonomy of the subject is at once exercised and regulated. In a passage I have already cited, Kant thus describes the movement from a primitive interest in the "charms of sense" to "universal communicability":

> Further, a regard to universal communicability is a thing which every one expects and requires from every one else, just as if it were part of an original compact dictated by humanity itself. And thus, no doubt, at first only charms, e.g. colours for painting oneself (roucou among the Caribs and cinnabar among the Iroquois), or flowers, sea-shells, beautifully coloured feathers, then, in the course of time, also beautiful forms (as in canoes, wearing-apparel, &c.) which convey no gratification, i.e. delight of enjoyment, become of moment in society and attract a con-

siderable interest. Eventually, when civilization has reached its height it makes this work of communication almost the main business of refined inclination, and the entire value of sensations is placed in the degree to which they permit of universal communication. (*CJ*, I, 155–56, §41)

As I argue in the foregoing chapters, the narrative of sensual development is here destined to culminate in the emergence of the public sphere and depends clearly on an ever-increasing degree of formalization. Despite its articulation through the ascription to particular races of "essential" characteristics, racism is structured primarily by the cultural regulation of a public sphere and of the subject formation that is its condition of existence. Though this proposition finds some empirical corroboration in the constant appeal of white racism to ethical categories—not least in recent years the invocation of "civility" that seeks to place unruly minorities beyond the pale of acceptable public discourse—its fullest justification is to be found rather in the logic of racist thought and culture, the fuller analysis of which follows.[11] Suffice it to say, it is not the claim of an ethical disposition as a racial characteristic as such but the establishment as the end of humanity of a peculiar and historically specific social form, the public sphere as defined in aesthetic theory, that defines the logical and historicist structure of racist discourses. For this reason, it is possible for an interchangeably ethical, political, and aesthetic judgment as to the inferiority of the "savage races" to saturate post-Enlightenment discourses on race from liberals such as John Stuart Mill and Matthew Arnold to extreme conservatives such as Arthur de Gobineau, Gustav Klemm, Josiah Clark Nott, or James Hunt.[12] The inadequacy of the native to self-government is empirically demonstrated by "his" lack of aesthetic productions or by "his" subordination to immediate sensual gratification, "his" laziness or inconsistency. These frequently cited empirical observations, which appear as ascriptions of an essential inadequacy, are organized by the judgment that in the Savage the capacity for autonomy is either as yet underdeveloped or is lacking and requires to be developed or supplemented by external force.

Though both arguments continue even now to be presented, it is the developmental model rather than that of irredeemable lack that tends eventually to dominate. Sound historical grounds for this gradual transition can be traced. As Colette Guillaumin argues, the discourse on race (as on other categories of heterogeneity) undergoes a crucial shift in the late eighteenth century from a system of arbitrary marks to the ascription of natural signs. We can, as Fanon does, attribute such a shift to the necessity to legitimate, within the context of appeals to universal humanity, the intensified and systematic domination of subordinated peoples. In this case, any discourse on difference must cease to be contingent and casual and establish instead a regular regime of discriminations that at once preserves and legitimates domination. Initially, there may be no absolute correlation between racist and imperialist discourses, since fear of contamination and environmental derivations of racial variation can offer strong arguments for not encouraging interracial encounters or even the colonization of alien climes. Gradually, however, through the intersection of liberal humanism with the necessities of imperial polity, the developmental discourse on race comes to dominate, precisely because it allows for the assimilation of a fraction of the colonized population to the imperial culture in order that they may function as administrators and professionals.[13] The racial regime for which that liberal humanism served as an alibi remains its underlying structure.

To this last point we will return. It is important here, however, to note that Guillaumin's formulation allows us to grasp how racist discourse maintains its capacity to replicate and circulate in several spheres. In describing the transition from allegorical marks, which retain the arbitrariness of their social constitution, to symbolic "natural signs," which represent externally the inner, organic constitution of the object, she indicates the regulatory force of the regime of representation across the social field. Even where a representation is at first a representation of difference, it conforms formally to the general demand for any representation to maintain the structure of identity within which the part can stand for the whole. Across differences, identity is formally preserved; across cultures, human nature is essentially the same and can therefore be developed along identical lines.[14]

As Guillaumin points out, to the "natural mark" (color, gender, facial appearance) that inscribes the dominated corresponds the absence of marks attributed to the dominator: "It inscribes the system of domination on the body of the individual, assigning to the individual his/her place as a dominated person: but it does not assign any place to the dominator. Membership in the dominant group, on the contrary, is legally marked by a convenient lack of interdiction, by unlimited possibilities."[15] This "unmarked" position occupied by the dominant individual belongs to what I would call Kant's "Subject without properties." This Subject with "unlimited possibilities" is precisely the undetermined subject, what Schiller terms the Person, the individual abstracted from the Condition that determines his particularities, whose infinite potential is a function of a purely formal identity with humanity in general.[16] Its universality is attained by virtue of a literal indifference: This Subject becomes representative in consequence of being able to take anyone's place, of occupying any place, in a state of pure exchangeability. Universal where all others are particular, partial, this Subject is the perfect, disinterested judge formed for and by the public sphere.

This Subject without properties is the philosophical figure for what becomes, with increasing literalness through the nineteenth century, the global ubiquity of the white European. His domination is virtually self-legitimating since the capacity to be everywhere present becomes a historical manifestation of the white man's gradual approximation to the universality he everywhere represents.[17] It is still not uncommon to hear it remarked that the human race, as opposed, implicitly, to such particularized and localized categories as Kant's Tahitians or Lapps, for example, is singular among creatures in its capacity to occupy any habitat. The latter begin to "become human" precisely on the occasion of their displacement.[18] But by the same token, emigration from the former colonies is a source of especial ideological and racial scandal not least because it upsets this asymmetrical division of humanity between the local (native) and the universal. Anti-immigrant racism thus notoriously expresses itself through the argument that immigrant adherence to their cultural or religious norms indicates their incapacity to enter the modern Western public sphere: They remain entrapped by their inveterate incapacity to adapt. What governs this distribution, as until quite recently it governed the disciplinary anthropological notion of its object, the ethnic, is the regulative idea of (aesthetic) Culture against which the multiplicity of local cultures is defined. Like Kant's sublime subject Saussure, the anthropologist and the colonial administrator occupy the place of disinterested spectator as representatives of Culture, with the critical consequence that every racial judgment is simultaneously an aesthetic, an ethical, and a political one.[19]

To reformulate the foregoing remarks, it is not in itself the antagonistic recognition of difference that constitutes the discourse of racism but the subordination of difference to the demand for identity. This identity principle governs racism in both its exclusive and its assimilative modes, the former narrowing the domain of identity, the other apparently expanding it but, as we shall see, only at the cost of a dissimulated but logically necessary barring of the nonidentical. As the very expression "assimilation" might suggest, racism elevates a principle of likening above that of differentiation such that its rhetorical structure is that of metaphorization.

Paul Ricoeur observes that the tension between likeness and difference constitutes the metaphoric process: "The insight into likeness is the perception of the conflict between the previous incompatibility and the new compatibility. 'Remoteness' is preserved within 'proximity.' To see *the like*

is to see the same in spite of, and through, the different. This tension between sameness and difference characterizes the logical structure of likeness."[20] Such a description accounts quite adequately for the pleasurable
shock of novel metaphors. What it is unable to do, however, is to grasp the
finally normative function of metaphor that makes it so central a figure for
both an organic poetics and post-Romantic literary pedagogy. The point
can be made most succinctly by remarking that Ricoeur's description would
allow no distinction between metaphor and those poetic figures that a pre-
Romantic poetics terms conceit or wit. Unlike metaphor, which Étienne
Bonnot de Condillac more succinctly and classically describes as "thinking
of the properties in which things agree," wit and conceit derive their effects from the salience of difference.[21] Accordingly, both Ricoeur's definition and Paul de Man's even more radical reading, which sees metaphor as
rhetorically subversive of the identity principle of philosophy by virtue of
its catachrestic foundations, require supplementation. Both arguments fail
to observe that metaphor is not merely the oscillation between sameness
and difference but the process of subordinating difference to identity. This
subordination gives to metaphor a narrative structure that makes metaphor
ultimately compatible with philosophical projects in general and with aesthetic projects in particular.

   Ricoeur virtually acknowledges this narrative aspect of metaphor in another essay when he remarks on the conjunction in Aristotle's *Poetics* of
metaphor and plot. Metaphor functions structurally and mimetically at a
minimal stylistic level as does plot at the largest organizational level. Both
are directed toward uncovering concealed identities, to moments of anag-
norisis.[22] Finally, even the most jarring of metaphors, if it is to be accepted
as tasteful, must allow the recognition of an identity that was already there.
It is recreative, not transformative. The question with regard to metaphor
becomes, not *what* it signifies but *how* it signifies within the larger matrix of
cultural elements. What this shows is the function of metaphoric processes,
as minimal narratives of identity, within the larger plot of self-formation:
both are directed toward the gradual overcoming of difference by identity. Nonetheless, as Ricoeur's own argument implies, it is not merely that
a happy analogy exists between metaphor and the plot of self-formation.
More pertinently, metaphor operates at the most fundamental levels of
feeling to produce effects of identification or "assimilation" in the subject:
"If the process [of metaphor] can be called, as I have called it, predicative
assimilation, it is true that *we* are assimilated, that is, made similar, to what
is seen as similar. This self-assimilation is a part of the commitment proper
to the 'illocutionary' force of the metaphor as speech act. We feel *like* what

we see *like*."[23] This being the case, we can locate in metaphor a minimal element of the processes of cultural formation that is replicated at larger and larger levels of identity and identification. Culture can, so to speak, be understood as a learning to be like what we should like to like. That is, as assimilation. Not unlike a felicitous performative, a felicitous metaphor produces a new state in and for the subject, its gradual assimilation to identity and universality.

Like the notions of "taste" and "common sense," "assimilation" is at once a metaphor and structured like a metaphor. But unlike taste and common sense, which embody the narrative of a movement from immediate sensation to universality, the very logic of assimilation betrays an inverse movement equally intrinsic to the process of metaphorization in general but accentuated by its status as a material practice. The constitution of any metaphor involves bringing together two elements into identity in such a manner that their differences are suppressed. Just so, the process of assimilation, whether in bringing two distinct but equivalent elements into identity or in absorbing a lower into a higher element as by metastasis, requires that which defines the difference between the elements to remain over as a residue. Hence, although it is possible to conceive formally of an equable process of assimilation in which the original elements are entirely equivalent, the product of assimilation will always necessarily be in a hierarchical relation to the residual, whether this be defined as the primitive, the local, or the merely contingent.[24] The process of identification, therefore, whether instanced in metaphorization, assimilation, or subject formation, produces difference and simultaneously gives that difference a determinate sense that is to be resistant to sense. Differences that have no meaning and no law come to signify negatively under the law of identity that produces them. Racial discriminations, accordingly, "make sense" and achieve their self-evidence only in relation to the law of identity that governs equally assimilation and exclusion.

A contradictory logic thus structures equally the abstract, identical Subject and the public sphere that it subtends. Since the production of difference as negative identity is inherent to that logic, the Subject that results may be conceived as obsessionally anxious, since its very formation produces what might undo that formation. It would be proper in this, if not in all instances, to speak of the insistence, rather than the return, of the repressed, since the repressed is here produced in every moment of the Subject's formation. What is true for the Subject is, on account of the logic of doubling analyzed above, true on other levels for the public sphere and for aesthetic culture. In the following section, I examine the consequences of the insistence of the repressed in terms of the resistance it poses to the assimilative drive and developmental claims of a universalizing culture. Since the emphasis here is on the logic of individual self-formation, and since I have been stressing till now how cultural formation works rather than how it breaks down, it is worth remarking that it is racism itself, as a social phenomenon, that brings to light the contradictory nature of the powerful and remarkably effective institutional logic of culture.

Racial Tropes

It is a frequent characteristic of racism that where the apparently neutral ascriptions of difference depend on relations of contiguity and therefore on metonymic indices (for example, skin color for race—black, yellow, white), the racist epithet that asserts relations of superiority is generally metaphoric: black boy, savage, baboon.[25] The metaphoric structure of the epithet here legitimates a violent assertion of superiority by way of the appeal to developmental categories: Against the achieved identity of the white man, the black appears as being in greater proximity to childhood or animality. Yet at the same time, as we already saw in the case of Burke's boy "blind from birth" in the previous chapter, racism constantly makes appeal to the immediacy of its discriminations, to their self-evidence: "You only have to look at them . . ."

The argument of the foregoing section establishes, however, that the appeal to visual immediacy is always illusory. It is not that there is never any difference to be seen but that the significance of the difference registered depends already on the transfer from metonymy to metaphor or on the acculturation of the subject that sees. These processes transform recognizing an indeterminate difference into a determinant positing of lack of identity in the object. Indeed, the very emergence of the subject that sees, or, more properly, the Subject that judges, is already predicated on a prior development of the senses that is ethically structured. The racist vision sees an underdeveloped human animal whose underdevelopment becomes the index of the judging subject's own superior stage of development.

The visual structure of racism can, accordingly, better be compared with what psychoanalysis supposes to take place in the castration complex than, as some argue, with the processes of fetishism.[26] While fetishism is produced out of a disavowal of anatomical difference, the fetishist refusing "to take cognizance of the fact of his having perceived that a woman does not possess a penis," the castration complex emerges in the recognition of difference and its interpretation as a mutilation of identity.[27] The castration complex is the primary agency of the formation of the little boy as at once male and ethical, initiating the internalization of the father in the form of the superego. In a phrase highly significant for the meaning of identity formation, Freud remarks that this process constitutes "the victory of the race over the individual" (*ADS*, 341). However, the castration complex achieves this victory only at the cost of producing an ineradicable anxiety in the subject as to the possibility of itself undergoing a mutilation that would undo that identity. In an associated move, Freud sees the woman, by virtue of her mutilated identity, as incapable of ethical development: The impossibility of a castration complex prevents the internalization of the father as superego and the identity formation of the woman remains incomplete (*ADS*, 342). Freud's interpretation at this juncture nicely recapitulates the little boy's. Where the little boy reinterprets the girl's or woman's "lack of a penis" at first as the sign of an underdeveloped organ and then as a mutilation, Freud reads the "lack of a penis" as the grounds of an underdeveloped ethical sense only then to confront female sexuality as something gapped and interrupted.

That Freud's interpretation should thus appear to recapitulate that of the little boy whom it seeks to analyze is not surprising once we reflect that the boy's judgment is in any case not as immediate as the phrase "first catches sight of" implies but is predicated on a prior development of the organs and of the ethical sense of which the castration complex is only the final stage. Freud is quite clear that the castration complex depends on what he had long before identified as "The Phases of Development of the Sexual Organization."[28] It depends on the movement of the organization of sexual pleasure away from the "polymorphous perversity" of infancy toward the "phallic stage." Once again, the narrative of development moves from a moment of contiguity and substitution to one organized around a single term that—like a metaphor—comes to effect the distribution of phenomena into identity and difference. (For this reason, regression to the point prior to the castration complex in psychosis produces the effects of verbal nonsense and fantasies of physical disintegration.) The development of the organs, like that of the senses in Schiller, is already directed toward an ethical end. Accordingly, the apparent visual immediacy of the little boy's judgment is, in fact, prepared for by an ethical formation of however rudimentary a kind. Freud's revision of his understanding of the process between "The Dissolution of the Oedipus Complex" (1924) and "Some Psychical Consequences of the Anatomical Distinction between the Sexes" (1925) makes this clearer. Where in the first essay, it is the "first sight" of the female genitals that induces the castration complex, in the second essay, the first sight may be attended by disavowal and "irresolution." And it is only "later, when some threat of castration has obtained a hold upon him, that the observation becomes important to him" (*ADS*, 336). The visual index, in other words, only has meaning in relation to a moral development governed by the overvaluation of a specific organ or sense that then appears as a possible object of punishment for transgression.[29] In turn, it is the sense given to the visual as a mark of identity and of difference reinterpreted as the mutilation of identity that structures the Subject in its very identity as always subject to the ineradicable threat of a difference upon which it depends. The identity of the subject is not only structured against difference; its own possibility depends on producing the possibility of precisely the internal difference that threatens it.

In the field of racism, as of sexuality, the appeal to visual immediacy in any judgment of difference may be seen as a disavowal of the contradictory logic of the subject's identity formation.[30] The anxiety of the racist is that what is constantly represented as an immediately visible, self-evident difference in the object is in fact internal to the subject. The racist shares with the obsessional neurotic the anxiety of being found out. Whiteness is never white enough. While it is doubtless the case that the psychic structure of racism depends in large degree on projection, the critical point is that it is the insistence of a difference internal to the constitution of identity that underlies the cultural logic of racism, rather than either the return or the projection of repressed material.[31] Instances of racism where the visual index of difference is by any measure minimal—if not absent—throw the cultural logic of racism into relief with peculiar force. In such instances of white-on-white racism, the fantasmatic projection of differences appears as a wishful resolution of a disturbance in the visual field. In what has become a celebrated passage, Charles Kingsley wrote to his wife of the impoverished Irish in 1860: "But I am haunted by the human chimpanzees I saw along that hundred miles of horrible country. I don't believe they are our fault. I believe there are not only many more of them than of old, but that they are happier, better, more comfortably fed and lodged under our rule than they ever were. But to see white chimpanzees is dreadful; if they were black, one would not feel it so much, but their skins, except where tanned by exposure, are as white as ours." Such perceptions disturb the law of verisimilitude, which governs the metaphorical system of racism. For this law, the identity between ape and black is self-evident, and it is scandalized by the possibility of a conjunction between whiteness, as the outward sign of human identity, and the simian, which, as a metaphor, becomes a metaphor of nonidentity in the very structure of the human. The same scandal to the order of identity is registered in Thomas Carlyle's phrase for the Irish, "the white negroes," an impossible, catachrestic conjunction that persists as an anomaly in English racist discourse: "if only they were black . . ."[32]

The point here is not to underestimate the importance of external marks of difference to racist practices but rather to emphasize how the apparent visual anomaly of white-on-white racism is the index of a prior constitution of the racist Subject-who-judges by which alone the appeal to visual immediacy of discrimination is legitimated. Whiteness is the metaphor for the metaphorical production of the Subject as one divested of properties rather than the natural sign of difference to which the attributes of civilization and culture are in turn attached. Where whiteness is suddenly, forcibly conjoined with the metaphors of difference, the order of development is radically disrupted. And insofar as the metaphoric logic of culture works always through the production of a residual order of difference, what Kingsley or Carlyle discover in the form of an anomaly constantly troubles the discursive and institutional practices of assimilation.[33]

Black Bildung

Different colonial regimes have had quite various policies with regard to the assimilation or the segregation of dominated populations. It is often remarked, for example, that French colonialism differs from British in that French policy tended to emphasize the process of acculturation while British policy tended to institute virtual apartheid systems, especially in its African domains. Though such distinctions may be accurate with regard to the regulatory tendencies of each imperial state, any imperial apparatus, once the initial period of conquest and domination by force is over, requires a greater or lesser number of native administrators and professionals to mediate its hegemony. Even if, as in many British colonies, this caste is relatively small numerically, its political function is crucial both for the colonial administration and for the development of national resistance movements.[34]

Many writers have noted and analyzed the regularity with which nationalist movements are formed among the most assimilated elements of the colonized population.[35] One constant and critical factor in this process is the confrontation with racism precisely as a contradiction in the logic of assimilation itself. Unlike the "subaltern" population, whose oppression and resistance alike remain, by definition, outside the domain of state institutions for which the subalterns have no subjective existence at all, the colonial intellectual confronts racism as a limit to the line of development that cultural assimilation appears to propose to him as a subject. Racism exposes the residual elements required by the logic of assimilation in constituting the colonial subject as a divided self, one part constituted by acculturation as "modern," the other identified by racist judgment as permanently lodged in a primitive moment incapable of development. Nationalism offers to suture this division by relocating the institutions of the modern state on the very terrain that the colonizer regards as primitive. It restores continuity to the interrupted narrative of representation by reterritorializing it within the newly conceived nation. Nationalism, in other words, accepts the verisimilitude of the imperial cultural narrative, merely redefining its terrain, just as its "westernized intellectuals," as Wynter puts it, "continue to articulate, in however radically oppositional a manner, the rules of the social order and its sanctioned theories."[36]

In an essay on the Sudanese writer Tayeb Salih's novel *Season of Migration to the North*, Samir Seikaly expresses the predicament of colonialism's "divided man" succinctly: "For whatever else it may be on the economic plane, colonialism, for every man, or society, who feel its full force, is essentially and permanently deformative, serving to bisect native society. . . . Of the two antithetical halves, the first, because of imperialism itself, is no longer traditional, while the other, because of its longing for a primordial identity, can never become fully modern. This is the origin of the divided man."[37] But in grasping the extent to which one of the cultural and psychological consequences of the assimilative drive of colonialism is the production of divided subjects, we need equally to perceive the extent to which that process can contribute to a transformation of the colonizing as of the colonized culture. The force of novels such as *Season of Migration*, which indeed dramatizes the predicament of the divided subject of colonialism across two generations, lies less in their representation of the damage inflicted than in the radical critique of Western cultural forms that they draw from that damage. What comes into question in Salih's novel is that order of verisimilitude that I have termed the racial regime of representation.

Both the narrator of *Season of Migration* and its other principal character, Mustafa Sa'eed, are British-educated Sudanese, the latter of the generation immediately following the consolidation of British rule in the late nineteenth century, the former of the period of independence. The narrator, returning to his village after a long absence in England, is devoted at every level to the concept of identity. His return seems to be a resumption of identity, "continuous and integral," making him "happy . . . like a child that sees its face in the mirror for the first time." To the villagers' questions as to the nature of the Europeans, he replies repeatedly that "with minor differences" they are "just like us."[38] But virtually from the moment of his arrival, the narrator is confronted by the alien presence of the stranger Mustafa Sa'eed, who is an insistent reminder of their mutual alienation: By the end of the novel, in yet another turn on the mirror stage, the child's narcissistic contentment will be displaced by the narrator's mistaking his face in a mirror for the portrait of Mustafa Sa'eed (*SMN*, 135).

The novel becomes a forensic quest as the narrator seeks obsessively to establish Sa'eed's identity, to reconstruct his past in the Sudan and in England. But the novel refuses to deliver the generic denouement of the classic detective story. Sa'eed's narrative, rendered in fragments of flashback, is a narrative of multiple dislocations, literal and figural, and insistently raises the question of identity rather than resolving it. As the narrator, in the final scenes of the novel, enters the dead or disappeared Sa'eed's library, he finds not a single portrait or identity paper but a proliferation of portraits of Mustafa Sa'eed in various guises and poses together with a blank book that was to have contained his autobiography (*SMN*, 138–39, 150). Rather than a narrative of self-formation or of identification, we are confronted with a proliferation of types unable to cohere into a single form. Just as Mustafa Sa'eed in England manipulates stereotypes of the African man as a means to seducing English women, Salih parodies each of the genres with which the novel seems momentarily to align: detective fiction, racial romance, tragedy, even farce.[39] Above all, however, it is the novel of self-formation that fractures, as even this most successful of colonial intellectuals fails to integrate with the English culture that summons and even idolizes him.[40]

Sa'eed's trajectory, from the streets of Khartoum to the lecture rooms and salons of England, has all the elements of a narrative of self-making. Most significantly, it involves a reorganization of his desire such that at the social level it is directed toward English culture (the narrator eventually finds only English works in the deceased man's library) just as at the sexual level it is directed at English women. In the typical *Bildungsroman*, from *Wilhelm Meister* through *A Portrait of the Artist as a Young Man*, erotic and cultural or economic desires are mapped on one another so as to produce coherence in the subject. For Mustafa Sa'eed, on the contrary, both modes of desire become ultimately sites of frustration and of dislocation, for all his apparent success. In both modes, the logic of the racial stereotype becomes inescapable. As Sa'eed manipulates time and again the stereotype of the sexual African man as a means to seduce, he projects as the truth what he admits to be entirely inauthentic, but does so, with a dogged literalness, as a means to penetrate the culture that is finally closed to him precisely because he represents to it the very stereotypes that he thinks he can control and manipulate.

So much becomes apparent at his trial for the murder of his English wife, Jean Morris. Here, the prosecution represents him as a beast, "a werewolf who had been the reason for two girls committing suicide, had wrecked the life of a married woman and killed his own wife," while the defense, more liberally, represents him as "a noble person whose mind was able to absorb Western civilization but it broke his heart" (*SMN*, 32–33). The stereotypes are logically interdependent: on the one hand, the representation of the colonized as bestial or savage generally requires the at least hypothetical possibility of mistaking them for human—hence the werewolf; on the other hand, for the more common, liberal appeal to cultivation and assimilation to seem legitimate, it must also represent the native, prior to the civilizing process, as a passionate savage, endowed with a desire that can be and requires to be "broken." The first version accordingly arouses the anxiety of those like Kingsley at the spectacle of human simulacra; the second holds out the promise of self-formation but only at the expense of detachment from the native's "authentic" being. The claim of culture to harmonize the self at each and every level devolves, in the colonial relation, into the repetitive production of inauthentic images, like the multiple mirrors of Sa'eed's bedroom (cf. *SMN*, 31).

We are forcibly reminded, accordingly, that if English culture negates and dislocates Mustafa Sa'eed, its confrontation with him brings its own laws of verisimilitude face to face with their founding incoherence. The either/or of racism—the native as savage or as object of cultivation—reveals itself as a contradictory both/and. The law of verisimilitude that governs cultural racism depends, we recall, on the normative temporality of the regime of representation: the regulative or ideal passage from subordination in absolute specificity (which, as pre-existing form, is indistinguishable from absolute indifference) to the pure formality of representative man. The functioning of that narrative, which regulates the formal logic of Western institutions, requires the continual production of a constitutive difference. Mustafa Sa'eed will always be perceived as that problematic category the "black Englishman," as the Sudanese *mamur* puts it, not because of his failure to assimilate to English culture but precisely in time with his success (*SMN*, 53). The closer his identification, the more forcefully his difference insists. Perceived by others as a catachrestic anomaly, Mustafa Sa'eed affirms rather that he is a lie, the figure of nonidentity itself. Rejecting the defense lawyer's attempt to represent him as the victim of "a conflict between two worlds," Sa'eed recognizes that the complexity of his situation lies rather in the manner in which the process of assimilation itself transforms him successively, vertiginously, into subject *and* object.[41] In acting as if he were a subject, he runs against his status as the object of racist discourse. Hence the final proliferation of photographs in which he seems to seek to represent himself as subject for the gaze of others. Hence also two phrases that recur through his monologue take on the status of metaphors of radical ambivalence, doubling at this minimal level what the novel narrates at length, the simultaneity of assimilation and dislocation undergone by the colonial subject in racist culture: "My mind was like a sharp knife. The train carried me to Victoria Station and to the world of Jean Morris" (*SMN*, 31). The rhythms of dislocation, from other worlds or from the body and plunged back into the body, punctuate at every level the normative temporality of assimilation at whose end is identification with the Subject. Racism imposes the limit to the assimilative process but not simply as an external force antagonistic to that process. The developmental logic of culture depends upon the continuous reproduction of a stereotypical otherness that is, in every sense, the expelled origin of its identity.

Under Representation

Tayeb Salih's work, formed under the pressure of British colonialism, shows remarkable affinities with the analytical work of Frantz Fanon, reacting primarily to the racist culture of French colonialism. Salih comments, indeed, that he read Fanon after finishing *Season of Migration* and "discovered that [he] was in total agreement with him."[42] The work to which he is almost certainly referring, Fanon's *Black Skin, White Masks*, analyzes the experience of assimilation as a cultural practice with a dense and contradictory history both at the level of colonial institutions and for each particular subject of colonialism. It also stages the realization that while race may be a cultural construct, racism is the structure of culture. From the very opening pages, Fanon is quite clear that the analysis of racism can only proceed in relation to the discourse on man and on "his" development to which culture itself gives the structure:

> What does a man want?
> What does the black man want?
> At the risk of arousing the resentment of my colored brothers, I will say that the black is not a man . . .
> The black man wants to be white. The white man slaves [*s'acharne*] to reach a human level. (*BSWM*, 10–11)[43]

The identity of the black man is to be a difference defined as lag, always suspended in the developmental trajectory of a humanity figured in terms of whiteness. Only in terms of this trajectory can what Fanon's translator names in the title of one chapter "The Fact of Blackness" be understood in the full network of the social relations that constitute that "fact."[44] If, in the course of that chapter, Fanon makes clear that the appeal to *négritude* has, for him, no longer any sense, it is because the larger trajectory of *Black Skin, White Masks* shows in detail that the appeal to essences is of no account where racist social relations constitute the black in a merely negative relation to another defined as the representative human.[45] The enormous task that this work proposes is the transformation of the nonidentity of the black not into an affirmation of an oppositional identity but into the means to a dismantling of the discourse of racism on several axes: that of the formation of the individual subject, that of the metaphoric structure of culture, and that of the social institutions in which the former are sedimented.

This task involves what at the outset Fanon describes as the attempt "to penetrate to a level where the categories of sense and non-sense [*sic*] are not yet invoked" (*BSWM*, 11). It entails a decomposition of the subject akin to what would be required to break with the effects of the "castration complex" and a collapsing of the metaphoric organization of identity and nonidentity that structures the Subject as such. Fanon is constantly aware how closely his analysis must skirt psychosis, yet it is only in the light of this task that we can grasp the process of transfiguration involved in the remark, late in the work, that "the Negro is comparison" (*BSWM*, 211). This remark first presents itself as an analytic description of the neurotic condition of Antillean society: "We have just seen that the feeling of inferiority is an Antillean characteristic. It is not just this or that Antillean who embodies the neurotic formation, but all Antilleans. Antillean society is a neurotic society, a society of 'comparison'" (*BSWM*, 213). These remarks make quite clear that in every case "we are driven from the individual back to the social structure" (*BSWM*, 213). This suspension in perpetual comparison of self and other is not an individual aberration but the very social condition of being black in racist culture. The "demon of comparison" suspends blackness in its relation to whiteness as lack and occludes the fundamentally differential constitution of race. It is a system, to riff on structural linguistics, composed not of positive essences but of differences that signify only in relation to one another.[46] That recognition transforms an analytic description of a malformation of the black subject into a culturally critical concept that opens up the inherently contradictory metaphoric logic of identity. If the "Adlerian comparison" of the individual neurotic consists only of two terms "polarized by the ego" and is expressed as "Ego greater than The Other," the social neurosis of "Antillean comparison" is "surmounted by a third term: Its governing fiction is not personal but social" (*BSWM*, 215) and introduces the crucial moment of a signifying difference along both the vertical and the horizontal axis of race relations. Fanon expresses the relation thus:

$$\frac{\text{White}}{\text{Ego different from The Other}}$$

The formula is of exceptional analytical force. The surmounting term consists of one self-identical word, the metaphor of metaphorical identity: white. As the citation above from Fanon's introduction indicates, the possibility of placing "White" in this position derives from positing the white man as standing closer to the identity of the human that is the telos of history. The white assumes the position of universally representative man within the narrative of representation itself. That is not to say that the white man is (yet) identical with the position of pure, universal identity that is the Subject without properties but rather that he stands as its representative. In the Kantian terms we have been engaging with throughout this book, the white man stands as the moment of *Vorstellung*, the movement from materiality and particularity that constantly approximates to the universal, barring the black man as the moment of *Darstellung*, mere immediate presentation. What the elevation of whiteness thus produces, in relation to the "Adlerian comparison," is the dissolution of the previous axis of ontological superiority (Ego greater than The Other) into a social relation of hierarchically signifying differences. In one of the few commentaries on *Black Skin, White Masks* that has addressed this Adlerian moment rather than Fanon's Hegelian analysis in the following section, Lewis Gordon summarizes the issue succinctly: "The Adlerian move fails because of the superstructural force of the White Man, under whom people of color find equality only among themselves below whiteness."[47] What this implies, finally, is that there can be no therapeutic adjustment of the neurotic individual because—as Fanon is at pains to point out throughout his work—racist society continually reproduces the conditions of the neurosis. For the white man in the racist system is for Fanon no less neurotic than the black, never quite capable of achieving identity with what he is called on to represent, whiteness and universality. For the black man, any attempt at "adjustment," any effort to "fit in" would necessitate what is systemically impossible, a total crossing of the line that demarcates superior from inferior, identity from difference, white from black.

This is, nonetheless, the demand imposed by imperial culture on its colonized subjects, and of which *Black Skin, White Masks* is an extended analysis.[48] Its larger narrative, schematized in the formula above, is that of a process of *Bildung* that falters in the workings of its own logic. Imperial culture—in Fanon's case, French culture—holds out the promise of citizenship to all its subjects but at the cost of the abandonment of "local cultural originality": "Every colonized people—in other words, every people in whose soul an inferiority complex has been created by the death and burial of its local cultural originality—finds itself face to face with the language of the civilizing nation; that is, with the culture of the mother country. The colonized is elevated above his jungle status in proportion to his adoption of the mother country's cultural standards. He becomes whiter as he renounces his blackness, his jungle" (*BSWM*, 18). It is worth stressing again that the phenomena of race and color, however naturalized they appear, are secondary to and produced by the question of culture and to culture seen as a process of development. There is, as we have seen, no unmediated racial perception. The developmental narrative of representation absorbs the geographical narrative, which is that of the move to and return from the metropolis, allowing the trajectory of displacement to be conceived as a cycle of completion, a *Bildungsroman*: "By that I mean that Negroes who return to their original environments convey the impression that they have completed a cycle, that they have added to themselves something that was lacking. They return literally full of themselves" (*BSWM*, 19n). But *Black Skin, White Masks* is a *Bildungsroman* against itself and demonstrates over and again that taking on imperial culture, whose first embodiment is the language, "is evidence of a dislocation, a separation" rather than a fulfilment (25). If greater mastery of the language is the index of a greater approximation to whiteness (38), it is always precisely as approximation that development takes place, producing in the assimilative process of "likening" the one who can never be more than "just like a white man," "*l'homme pareil aux autres*," a "black Englishman." For the colonized, the process of assimilation discovers within the identity that is to be formed the difference on which assimilation's very logic depends. The process of likening produces a residue of difference that insists as the ineradicable blackness of the culturally racialized subject, "the barring of nonwhite subjects from the category of the human as it is performed in the modern west."[49] For this reason, for the colonized, who had never conceived of themselves as black while "at home," the trajectory of *Bildung* must be "inverted": "More especially, they should become aware that the line of self-esteem that they have chosen should be inverted. We have seen that in fact the Antillean who goes to France pictures this journey as the final stage of his personality. Quite literally I can say without any risk of error that the Antillean who goes to France in order to convince himself that he is white will find his real face there" (*BSWM*, 153n). The end of *Bildung* is not identity but the discovery of the culturally constitutive function of racism; it reveals the insistence of a splitting rather than the fulfilment of a developed subject. Racism appears at once as the product and the disabling limit of the cultural formation of that Subject that subtends and gives the possibility of the "public sphere." At that limit, the racialized individual splits between what assimilation subsumes and what it necessarily produces as its residue. That impossible predicament issues perforce in madness or resistance as the subjective correlatives of the process by which the colonizer's attempt to assimilate the native produces the national consciousness that revolts. Fanon's subsequent writings accordingly become increasingly concerned with the necessity of violence as the only means to the overthrow of colonial domination.

I argue throughout these chapters that aesthetic culture itself constitutes the formal principles of racist discourse, that the indices of difference on which racism relies gain their meaning from a distribution of values determined by an aesthetic philosophy that founds the idea of a universal common sense and its space of articulation, the public sphere. This argument implies that there can be no simply cultural solution to the problem of racism and that all the measures taken by liberal cultural institutions in the name of assimilation are, at best, half measures that dissemble a racial system of differences as a set of equivalent, comparable cultures, at worst, misrecognized means to the reproduction of a singular cultural form that will continue to produce racialized residues. The demand for representation within existent institutions will be self-defeating so long as it is not accompanied by the demand for the transformation of those institutions, since every partial instance of representation of difference succumbs to the larger regime of representation that absorbs it.

The debates on cultural education, on multiculturalism, and on affirmative action, helped to highlight the pivotal role played by educational institutions in the interpellation of individuals as subjects for the state. That said, their eventual containment by insidious slogans like "excellence and diversity" or by the assertion of the postracial society only serves to affirm the continuing force of the regime of representation in our moment. Institutional efforts at assimilation of racialized subjects cannot be divorced from their will to annihilate the determinate difference that constitutes race and the splitting of recalcitrant social practices and modes of life that are the content of that difference from unconditional participation in the public sphere. Fanon's work, in highlighting the cultural or "sociogenetic" dimensions of racism, conversely brings out the necessity to conduct the analysis of racist discourse and practices in relation to the form of the state and to representation as its instrument.[50] The persistence of racism is then to be understood, in keeping with the foregoing arguments, as an effect of ideological interpellation that always forms the subject as a moment within a racial regime. Approximation to the position of the Subject, theoretically available to all, regardless of "race or creed," in fact requires the impossible negation of racial or cultural differences. To Fanon's diagram we can add the formula of "race under representation":

$$\frac{\text{Representation}}{\text{Race}}$$

Just as it is impossible for the colonized individual to escape the social neurosis of colonialism by passing over into identity or "whiteness," so it is impossible for the racialized individual to enter the domain of representation except as that Subject that negates difference and therefore the racialized subject itself. Assimilation is self-negation, "renunciation" as Fanon puts it.

One consequence of this argument is that the concept of the "racial state" developed by Omi and Winant stands in need of supplementation by the idea of the state that regulates the formation of citizen-Subjects fit to participate in what is effectively the state culture. The state is not merely a contingent ensemble of institutions but is ultimately determined by the desire to unify the public sphere that it organizes. What the Subject is to individuals, the state represents for civil society: the site of its formal identity. Obscured as the idea of the state generally is by the contradictions that in practice seem to frustrate it, its unifying ends become quite apparent at moments of pressure. Such was one effect of the multicultural educational debates in the United States, where conservatives appealed explicitly to the need to adhere to a common, central culture as a means to preserving loyalty to the state's institutions, thus inadvertently acknowledging the racial formation of the state. At the same time, "ethnic" cultures were relegated increasingly to the recreationary and preaesthetic domain of private cultural consumption. The failure of the multicultural model to realize its aspiration to a kind of racial democracy or equivalence was already prescribed by the aesthetic model of identity that underlay its notion of discrete cultures, each one of which replicated the function of Culture as such. If race is, as Omi and Winant argue, "a *central axis* of social relations," this is because it is continually, and necessarily, constructed and reproduced as the constitutive negation of the identity that the state, the representative moment of "common sense," represents.[51] No more than class or gender, race is no ontological or essential quality but is constructed in differential relation to the normative culture of the state.

These remarks indicate how the elements of that vexed triad—race, gender, class—can be articulated with one another without collapsing them into false identity or allowing one or other to "be subsumed under or reduced to some broader category or conception."[52] Indeed, the analysis of the formation of these categories in relation to the Subject of aesthetic ideology ultimately requires the counterpart of an unrelenting and historical specificity that I have not attempted here. Both moments are indispensable: on the one hand, the formal analysis of the ideological Subject as a racial function whose effectiveness is inseparable from its very formality, as I argued in Chapter 1; on the other, the material histories of the specific transformations that take place through the dialectic between the state and what it perforce negates as a condition of its existence. This implies, of course, that the theoretical model of the ideological Subject to which I have been alluding, Althusser's "Ideology and Ideological State Apparatuses," falls short insofar as it claims a transhistorical existence for ideology and the impossibility of standing outside it.[53] The analysis of racist discourse is instructive in this respect, precisely because one can show the history of its transformation in relation to specific political or economic demands and, more important, because many of its contradictions derive from the destiny of the racialized individual: to stand at once inside and outside, subject and object of the discourse. The interpellative "Hey, you!" of the police cannot be delinked from the "Look, a Negro!" of the border-guards of whiteness in which the unity of the Subject founders.

The insistence of contradiction in racial formations, their inability to totalize the domain of the Subject, is politically as well as historically instructive. It guides both a theoretical agenda and a practical purpose for that agenda. If the public sphere formed by aesthetic culture furnishes a crucial ideological, and racist, regulative site, its critique is guided by what Walter Benjamin designates as the task of the materialist historian—"to brush history against the grain." This entails, in Gramscian terms, the reconstruction of histories of subaltern classes, of those social groups whose practices fall outside the terms of official culture.[54] To do so is, in effect, to decipher the history of the possible and to trace the contours of numerous alternative countercultures to dominant modes of social formation, those for which, as Cedric Robinson puts it, "the possibilities are the stuff of history."[55] So long as that subaltern project remains unfinished, renouncing any new representative hegemony, its counterhistorical work undoes the narrative regimes of domination, splintering them into multiple possible histories. Without such histories, the universal history of cultural development—the narrative regime of representation—is all the more difficult to displace and the imagination of radical politics becomes all the more constrained by rights-based struggles—that is, to the extension of representation and the implicit affirmation of assimilation.

CHAPTER 4

Representation's Coup

It is not enough to accept the position of the
colonized, it is necessary to be loved by them.

—ALBERT MEMMI, *The Colonizer and the Colonized*

The Disjunctive Subaltern

Following Fanon, I argue that the racialized black subject appears in his
analysis in *Black Skin, White Masks* as barred from fully entering into representation. On the temporal axis of the narrative of representation, the
black subject's movement is arrested on the threshold of difference in a
manner akin to that in which the colonized in *Wretched of the Earth* is "a
being hemmed in" and fixed in "immobility."[1] As Fanon makes clear at this
point in *Wretched of the Earth*, physical or spatial immobility cannot finally be divorced analytically from temporal arrest or from the colonized's
eviction from history as process. And yet the two axes remain distinct.
The subaltern native's sensation of spatial compartmentalization and prohibition of movement differs markedly from the geographical and cultural
trajectory of the colonized intellectual. The latter, like the Antillean black
student of *Black Skin, White Masks*, travels actually or virtually to the metropolis only to find his desire frustrated: He finds his real face there. In the
drama of the essay "Concerning Violence," the intellectual returns to the
colony, seeking to become actually representative there—through political parties, through demands for rights—only to find that the subaltern
masses, having begun to move, dissolve the structures of representation

through which he sought to lead them. The Subaltern, as I shall argue in greater detail here, is a category constituted by its externality to representation. To what extent does it overlap with the black subject barred from representation or the Savage that stands as the interior-exterior of a latent humanity's developmental trajectory? How does thinking the Subaltern as a distinct category open up further this regime of representation and the intellectual's suspension in it?

Let me begin with some observations that have emerged for me over many years of following discussions of Gayatri Chakravorty Spivak's seminal essay, "Can the Subaltern Speak?"[2] My observations do not principally concern the notorious difficulty of that essay, though that difficulty does establish the condition for the effects in which I am more interested. As almost anyone who has engaged with this essay may corroborate, above and beyond the intellectual difficulties it raises, it seems to produce with peculiar consistency certain affective effects that are puzzling and exceed the intervention it makes on a theoretical plane, crucial as that has been to shaping the field of postcolonial and subaltern studies. Discussion of the essay seems to lead inevitably to a sense of ethical consternation, in that it gets read over and again as posing to the reader not merely the pragmatic question "What is to be done?" in relation to the Subaltern but the question, "By what right are you assuming any relation to the Subaltern?" In other words, it seems to raise a question that goes directly to the ethical self-regard of the reader. This could be an interesting and absorbing question, but any response to it exceeds the terrain of intellectual debate. The discomfort the essay arouses seems to strike at the moral identity of the reader, at the right to assume an ethical position at all. One telling, if occasional, counterpart to this response is, of course, the response of smugness, the confirmation that one is oneself the Subaltern who cannot be spoken for, a response that seems predicated on an over-hasty leap to identification, yet that ultimately occupies the same ground of moral identity.

A further affect that correlates with this ethical consternation is melancholy: Over and again, the essay seems to arouse not political conviction or critical insight but a sense of dismayed paralysis. It is as if the question "What is to be done?" here transforms into the assertion "There is nothing I can do." The confrontation with an aporia meets with the mourning of a lost possible object or—what may amount to virtually the same thing—of a lost possible subject. Why should the aura of melancholy hover around the reading of an essay that must surely be understood as a political, feminist, and postcolonial intervention against the epistemological violence of the West? Are these not peculiar consequences of a work written in the mode of critique? To be more precise, why would the critique of the category of representation, which is the core of the essay's intervention, lead to either ethics or mourning at all? My somewhat rhetorical questions prompt a turn from the ostensible object of the essay's inquiry—can the Subaltern represent herself, can the Subaltern be represented—to one that addresses the intellectual, by definition the class of its readers. The underlying question of "Can the Subaltern Speak?" is less its titular one than the question, to which the reader responds quite viscerally, "Can the intellectual represent [the subaltern]?" To that question there is a further, and more disabling, turn, which is "Can the intellectual be representative?"

One further remark before returning to this constellation of melancholy, ethics, and representation: In the penumbra of "Can the Subaltern Speak?" and virtually constitutive of the category of the Subaltern in its larger theoretical and historiographical unfolding is the question of violence. Every approach to the Subaltern seems to be haunted by the specter of violence. This violence exceeds the empirical record of peasant insurrections and riots through which subaltern groups explode into the historical archive, as it exceeds the record of state violence directed at those subaltern movements—a violence that has been intrinsic to the very formation of the state itself, law-making rather than merely law-preserving.[3] What haunts the concept is not the violence done by or to the subalterns but rather something intrinsically categorical: the violence of the Subaltern or, indeed, the Subaltern as violence. Why should a category, a concept that presumes a manifold of social groups that are by definition disempowered and marginalized, to the point of their inability even to speak, appear not simply as violent, or in violence, but *as* violence? That is the question that I shall link to the Subaltern as the lost object of representation.

The constellation of questions clustered around the figure of the Subaltern since the 1980s embraces two issues that have troubled Marxism and colonial and postcolonial theory: agencies and social sites that have proven theoretically and politically unincorporable. Since its inception, subaltern historiography has been concerned with agencies and formations that have at times played a role in anticolonial struggle but have been neither organized nor incorporated fully by elite formations, including state-oriented nationalist movements, nor fully subjected to or by the colonial state or its successor, the independent nation-state. By the same token, the Subaltern occupies or designates social sites that remain exterior to those in which Marxist historiography has traced the development of capitalism and anticapitalist struggle, both in economic and political terms. Whatever it may have encoded in Gramsci's initial formulation, in subaltern studies the

Subaltern is not another word for the proletariat or the working class. On the contrary, it implies those elements of the dispossessed and colonized who, in the wake of primitive accumulation, do not undergo proletarianization and cannot be organized or even analyzed along traditional Marxist lines. So much is signaled in Spivak's invocation of Marx's distinction between a class in itself and a class for itself in the *Eighteenth Brumaire*, as it is by her later remark that "Subalternity is the name I borrow for the space out of any serious touch with the logic of capitalism or socialism."[4]

In its exteriority to both the categories of anticolonial nationalism and of Marxism, the Subaltern cannot merely be dismissed as a lumpenproletariat or as the masses whose destiny it is to become a people shaped by nationalist ideology. It stands outside or to the side of such modernizing, developmental logics and in doing so represents not merely an inert mass awaiting incorporation or assimilation but a specific form, or set of forms, of recalcitrance to colonial capitalist development or to the colonial state— a recalcitrance not primordial and prior to colonialism or capitalism but formed in relation to those forces. In anticolonial theory, the Subaltern is problematic in marking the limit of processes of decolonization that are thought within the terms of nationalism. Nationalism, as a modernizing discourse even in its selective invocation of tradition, follows the path of the colonial state and is just as devoted to the elimination of the subaltern groups as was the colonial state. As the unassimilated element (or moment) of the population, the Subaltern's trajectory—while profoundly affected by the violence of colonialism—has not followed the paths of modernization taken by either the nationalist elites or the "people" defined as the citizenry. The Subaltern, occluded by the political and cultural forms of the nation, thus persistently poses the question of the meaning of a decolonizing process that fails to speak to or for those it seeks to represent. That question is not easily theorized within the terms of colonial discourse or postcolonial theory. If, as I will argue, the Subaltern marks the limit of the nation-state's capacity for representation—if, moreover, it marks a limit to representation in every way—the problem of the representation of the Subaltern leads postcolonial theory into a virtual aporia with regard to thinking practical alternatives to nationalist notions of decolonization. Nationalism envisages decolonization as a decontamination of the population from the influences of colonial culture while at the same time maintaining the modern political forms of the nation-state for which a revived set of national traditions forms the citizens. Postcolonial theory has tended to critique such idealizing versions of decolonization and to emphasize in its stead the productive and performative dimensions of hybridity and *mesti-*

zaje. Such critiques can have no purchase on subalternity, posed as it is on the interface between colonial modernity and the nonmodern social formations of the colonized but without the possibility of being drawn into the assimilative processes that give rise to the hybrid in its own instabilities and ambivalences.[5] While subalternity presents a limit to representation that is at the same time a limit to defining, categorizing, or projecting the modes of agency or subjecthood it entails, it provides no obvious foundation for thinking an alternative to decolonization that would not be predicated on a return to some purified precolonial cultural tradition, or on a culture unevenly assimilated to modernity, but on modes of social relation that are forged within subalternity itself. The modern conceptual terms deployed by the elite intellectual can give no substantial account, not at least without constitutive contradictions, of what processes of decolonization might in fact derive from subalternity itself. "Consequently," as Heather Laird puts it in a very thoroughgoing critique of the subaltern tendencies of postcolonial theory, "it is no longer simply difficult to envisage a means by which the subaltern can transcend subalternity, but undesirable."[6]

This aporia of postcolonial thinking on decolonization cannot be resolved merely by trying to revert to the categories of internationalist Marxism or to state-oriented nationalism. In the regimes of contemporary capitalism, the new international and gendered division of labor within a mode of "flexible accumulation" tends to lay hold increasingly on laboring populations that emerge from sites that we could designate subaltern. This age-old practice of colonial capitalism, from slavery and indenture to the mines and fields of every colony, now occurs on a scale and with a degree of systematicity that are both unprecedented and clearly enabled and regulated by the nation-state itself.[7] Such circumstances oblige a rethinking, perhaps in the wake of Fanon's critique of the limits of decolonization in *The Wretched of the Earth*, of the processes of mobilization and politicization in terms radically different from models of proletarianization or national citizenship. To invoke the lessons of historical materialism itself, the mode of production has changed, and capitalism itself has learned to work, so to speak, on and off with subalternity. It is equally obligatory to detach materialist analysis from the developmental narratives within which its modes of economic and political analysis have traditionally been framed: The Subaltern cannot be thought as a "progressive" historical category in the sense of Benjamin's *Theses on the Philosophy of History* but rather as one whose relation to modernization and development is disjunctive.

The disjunctiveness of the Subaltern cuts across both historical and political domains of analysis. Historically, the agency of the Subaltern does not correspond to some moment in the formation of subjects or citizens for the state. It is marked by recalcitrance to such formation, and by definition subaltern practices cannot be translated into the political categories of state-oriented movements, either in their demands or in their forms.[8] In this regard, the logic of the Subaltern as it has emerged in subaltern studies and in postcolonial theory introduces entirely different concerns than those outlined by Gramsci in his seminal account of the subaltern classes in *Notes on Italian History*. For Gramsci, the subaltern classes would themselves become the subjects of history at the moment of their capture of the state. In postcolonial theory, on the contrary, the Subaltern is the permanent and inexpungible remainder of the processes of state formation. Economically as well as politically, this exteriority of subaltern groups to citizenship or, in the terms of Gramsci's analysis of civil society, to the "ethical state," corresponds to the disjunction between subalternity and proletarianization. The cultural and social formations of subaltern groups cannot be aligned with the classic Marxist understanding of the political or economic formation of an industrial or agricultural proletariat, and it may be crucial to acknowledge that the modes of resistance and self-organization of subaltern groups will differ markedly and unpredictably from those demanded by traditional Marxist theory.[9]

This fundamental disjunctiveness of the Subaltern is of greater theoretical significance than the empirical or archival problems that afflict the subaltern historian—that cluster of problems around the availability of records, the reliability of oral sources, the need to translate back from official documents and elite narratives for the traces and effects of subaltern agency. It is even more significant than the problem for the historian that has been most imaginatively worked on by Dipesh Chakrabarty—namely, the predicament of the insuperable incommensurability between the rationalities of the professional historian and the terms that any subaltern group might deploy to account for their own motivations and modes of action. Spivak formulates this problem as "the subaltern's persistent emergence into hegemony [that] must always and by definition remain heterogeneous to the efforts of the disciplinary historian."[10] Such disjunctions affect the very regime of representation that is the overarching framework of modernity in its self-conception—not merely the empirical or methodological problems regarding the adequacy of a historical narrative to its objects. The question of subalternity occupies the very cusp at which an analysis of metropolitan or "Western" formations intersects with that of colonial and postcolonial ones. There it draws together critically a set of logics that are at once historiographical, aesthetic, or cultural, and, in the largest sense of the term, political. Insofar as the production of the Subaltern "at the periphery" is always in a differential relation to the emergence and consolidation of the metropolitan "core," the question of the representation of the Subaltern cannot but open the question of representation as it is articulated "at the center" and in every domain of modernity. It is in the latter realm that I want to pursue the implications of this argument before returning to the question of colonialism and subalternity.

The Triple Session of Representation

The problematic status of subalternity has been approached, most notably in Spivak's sympathetic critique of the subaltern studies project, "Deconstructing Historiography," as a question of the consciousness of the Subaltern. That question can be reposed in a different if related way as: "What is the self-representation of the Subaltern?" or "[How] does the Subaltern represent herself [to herself]?" However, to pose it in this way is to frame the question in a way that cannot be proper to the Subaltern as such, by analogy with the Marxist distinction between "a class for itself" and "a class in itself." To ask what the self-representation of the Subaltern is—if it is—is to ask whether the Subaltern constitutes something like a class for itself, with a "class consciousness." The distinction is between the objective formation of a class as differentiated from other classes (class in itself) and the subjective or reflective moment of class consciousness— one's self-representation as belonging to or being identified with a class and sharing its interests. As Spivak points out, formally speaking the location of the Subaltern cannot be substantial in the way a class has a concrete and objective, if relational, existence. The location of the Subaltern is "irreducibly differential":[11] The Subaltern, as Ranajit Guha defines the term, does not represent any social positivity but appears as the negation of all other classes. In this negatively defined space, the supposed "consciousness" of the Subaltern can stand only as a counterpossibility to the narratives that underwrite the consciousness of the historian as subject—a "negative consciousness" as Spivak puts it.[12] While accepting the assumption that the Subaltern represents (if it represents) the negative limit to Western historiography—"the absolute limit of the place where history is narrativized into logic," an epistemological more than a social category—I want to elaborate further the system of representation within which such problematics continue to be posed.[13]

At this point we must follow Spivak's own path to the locus classicus of the distinction between class formation in and for itself, Marx's description of the French peasantry in the *Eighteenth Brumaire of Louis Bonaparte*. As Marx famously expresses it:

> In so far as millions of families live under economic conditions of exis-
> tence that separate their mode of life, their interests and their culture
> from those of the other classes, and put them in hostile opposition to
> the latter, they form a class. In so far as there is merely a local inter-
> connection among these small-holding peasants, and the identity of their
> interests begets no community, no national bond and no political orga-
> nization among them, they do not form a class. They are consequently
> incapable of enforcing their class interest in their own name, whether
> through a parliament or through a convention. They cannot represent
> themselves, they must be represented. Their representative [*Vertreter*]
> must at the same time appear as their master, as an authority over them,
> as an unlimited governmental power that protects them against the
> other classes and sends them rain and sunshine from above. The political
> influence of the small-holding peasants, therefore, finds its final expres-
> sion [*Ausdruck*] in the executive power subordinating society to itself.[14]

The French peasants form a class, they do not form a class. This apparent contradiction is resolved by the distinction implicit here between the ob-jective similarity of the conditions in which the peasantry as a whole lives and works and the fact that, as smallholders, they are set in competition with one another and are unable to reach beyond those competing self-interests to imagine themselves as a class in solidarity. Differentiated as a class "in itself" from other classes, their class relations among themselves are merely contingent, predicated on the sheer contiguity of their exis-tence, "much as potatoes in a sack form a sack of potatoes," in Marx's vivid simile for metonymic relations. They fail to represent themselves to them-selves as a class for itself. In a much-cited phrase: "They cannot represent themselves, they must be represented" (*Sie können sich nicht vertreten, sie müssen vertreten werden*) (*Brumaire*, 106).[15] Unable to represent themselves, they look outside themselves to the state, or "executive power," in the per-son of Louis Bonaparte—and in doing so enable his seizure of power in a coup d'état. The peasantry, of course, is thus in no sense to be confused with the Subaltern: It is at once the object and the support of the state and lends itself singularly to representation.[16]

The term that Marx here deploys to designate the representation of the peasantry by an alien power, *vertreten*, signals at once that their support for Bonaparte cannot be understood as the "organic" expression (*Ausdruck*) of their class formation. As I mention in Chapter 1, the term *vertreten* means not only to "represent," as in parliamentary representation, but also "to take the place of," "to substitute for," and, in certain colloquial usages, which may well have been available to Marx, "to stand in the way of" (*jemandem den Weg vertreten*). *Vertreten* thus establishes a somewhat unstable semantic field, allowing the concept of representation to play between standing or speaking for others and displacing them from the scene—as the advocate or *Stellvertreter* speaks for the client but also takes her place, effectively silencing her in the public space of the court.

We can elaborate this self-cancelling doubleness of the term *vertreten* by following Spivak's own elaboration of what she calls "the double session of representation."[17] Spivak isolates two terms for representation from Marx's German: *vertreten* (as in the usage just indicated) and *darstellen*. She further asserts that the two terms are "related but irreducibly discontinuous."[18] This claim to their discontinuity turns out to be richly if damagingly consequential. *Vertreten* is the standard German term for political or legal representation, one whose noun form, *Vertreter*, Marx uses interchangeably with the more Latinate *Repräsentant* throughout the *Brumaire*. However, the German term carries powerful associations of substitution or replacement, and it entails an inevitable logic of displacement in a far more active sense. Marx plays with this sense of representation as a mode of illegitimate substitution in referring to Louis Bonaparte as a kind of *remplaçant* or *Ersatzmann* for his uncle Napoleon. (The *remplaçant* was the poor person who would be paid to take the place of a richer conscript under the terms of French military service.) Arrogating to himself the triple representative role of standing for his uncle, representing the state, and representing the peasantry, Louis Bonaparte became merely a poor substitute for all, entirely ersatz in somewhat dated parlance.

As always, Marx's parodic humor carries serious analytic intent: In the logic of replacement that invests the very term *vertreten* lurks the recognition that we can provisionally condense in the quasi-Althusserian formula that "the accession to representation is the displacement of the subject by the Subject." For the most part, however, Marx's use of the term *vertreten* interchangeably with *Repräsentant* signals not the exceptional or contradictory aspects of the term but its already normative, commonsensical force. I will return shortly to this peculiar play between the normative usage of *Vertretung* in legal and political forms of representation and its underlying connotations of an exceptional coup de main, as entailing an act of forceful displacement.

The no less ambiguous term *darstellen*, as Spivak points out, has among its primary colloquial meanings the theatrical sense of representation: It translates the English "to appear as," as in the phrase "Paul Robeson stellt Othello dar" (Paul Robeson appears as Othello). In philosophical usage, the term generally designates something as it "presents itself" or appears to perception in an immediate way. Marx uses the term in precisely this sense in the celebrated chapter of *Capital*, "On the Fetishism of Commodities and the Secret Thereof," a passage that Spivak cites in "Can the Subaltern Speak?":

> *So stellt sich der Lichteindruck eines Dinges auf den Sehnerv nicht als subjektiver Reiz des Sehnervs selbst, sondern als gegenständliche Form eines Dinges außerhalb des Auges dar.*

> Thus the light impression from an object presents itself not as a subjective stimulus to the optic nerve, but as an objective form of a thing outside the eye.[19]

Spivak's own translation of the term as representation blurs the analytical point of Marx's analogy, which is to suggest that what at first appears (or presents itself) to sensation has to be subjected to reflective analysis in order to gain an accurate comprehension of relations whose apparent immediacy or self-evidence is deceptive. But in order to bring out the force of that usage of *Darstellung*, we must introduce a third and crucial German term for representation into the "double session of representation."

Despite his notorious web of theatrical allusions in the *Brumaire*, Marx seems never to use the word *darstellen* in its theatrical sense. There is, however, another term that he uses frequently in the text and that, while it overlaps semantically with *darstellen*, carries a quite different sense. This is the term *vorstellen*. As we have seen in previous chapters, this term means to represent or to imagine, but always with a certain degree of reflexivity or self-consciousness. In order to become a class for itself, for example, the members of a class would have to represent or imagine themselves to belong to it. Spivak overlooks this usage in the *Brumaire* with significant effects on her elaboration of the concept of representation and, in particular, the role of the intellectual in relation to representation. *Vorstellung*, of course, also translates the French *représentation* in the sense of a theatrical performance, and Marx uses it in this sense continually throughout the *Brumaire* in order parodically to foreground the "masquerade" that is Bonaparte's attempt to replace his uncle:

An old crafty *roué*, he conceives the historical life of the nation and
their performances of state [*Staatsaktionen*] as comedy in the most
vulgar sense, as a masquerade where the grand costumes, words and
postures merely serve to mask the pettiest knavery. Thus on his expedi-
tion to Strasbourg, where a trained Swiss vulture plays the part [*vorstellt*] of the Napoleonic eagle. For his irruption into Boulogne he puts
some London lackeys into French uniforms. They represent the army
[*Sie stellen die Armee vor*]. In his Society of December 10, he assembles
ten thousand rascally fellows, who are to play the part [*vorstellen*] of the
people, as Nick Bottom that of the lion. . . . Only when he has eliminated his solemn opponent, when he himself now takes his role seri-
ously and under the Napoleonic mask imagines he is [*vorzustellen meint*]
the real Napoleon, does he become the victim of his own conception
of the world, the serious buffoon who no longer takes world history
for a comedy but his comedy for world history. (*Brumaire*, 63–64; *Der
Achtzehnte*, 161; translation slightly modified)

However satirical Marx's account of Bonaparte's adventurism may be, the
movement in meaning of the word *vorstellen* from representation as performance, role playing, to a moment of earnest self-representation ("he imagines himself the real Napoleon") that is also a self-elevation to a more universal standpoint than the individual can embody, marks a movement from
particular to general, common to universal, that is intrinsic to the logic of
representation that is inscribed in the term itself. Thus, if we can say that
"Ian McKellen plays Hamlet" in the sense of *Darstellung*, we can equally
say that "Hamlet represents the indecision of the intellectual" in the sense
of *Vorstellung*. That is, the performance of Hamlet as a particular individual
unfolds, at the same time but at a higher level, a more general predicament.
Such a usage of *vorstellen* marks the act of representation as a movement
from the mere presentation of a particular sense image (and by analogy, of
any particular impression) to the reflexive moment where it becomes the
object of a concept, *Vorstellung* meaning also a concept or mental image.

As I remark in the preceding chapters, Kant uses the term in the same
sense in the *Critique of Judgement* to characterize the process of moving
in the act of judgment from a sensuous presentation of an object to a reflective representation of it. It is specifically a movement of generalization
and formalization, "effected by so far as possible letting go the element of
matter, i.e. sensation, in our general state of representative activity [*Vorstel-
lungszustande*], and confining our attention to the formal peculiarities of our
representation or general state of representative activity [*seiner Vorstellung,*

oder seines Vorstellungszustandes]."[20] This act of formalizing representation grounds the universal form of aesthetic judgment and is, as Kant is at pains to argue in this section, the very foundation of what he calls "common or public sense."[21] Similarly, in his *Introduction to Aesthetics*, Hegel makes this move from immediacy to the moment of reflexive representation the definitive characteristic of the human being, not as a particular individual but in his identification with the Spirit (*Geist*): "Things in nature are only immediate and single, while man in spirit duplicates himself, in that (i) he is as things in nature are, but (ii) he is just as much for himself; he sees himself, represents himself [*stellt sich vor*] to himself, thinks, and only on the strength of this active placing of himself before himself is he spirit."[22] In its philosophical usage in the traditions of German idealism, *Vorstellung* is accordingly a term inseparable from the possibility of the individual being brought into accord with the universal, of representing a general rather than a merely particular or private interest. As we have seen, it is a term that in itself maps the processes by which the individual becomes representative.

We can thus break down more completely the moments of representation that I first sketched in Chapter 1, in which the particular subject comes into identification with the universal Subject or with the human as a general category, in a logical series that is also a kind of formal narrative:

1. The notion of *vorstellen*, unlike either *darstellen* or *vertreten*, tends always to have reference to a disposition of the subject, even where it appears merely as the presentation of an object, idea, or action. That is, as both the passages quoted above would suggest, *vorstellen* as an activity always contains a moment of self-reflexiveness. As Hegel goes on to suggest, representation is a labor that produces an object for a subject but in doing so also produces the subject for itself: "He has the impulse, in whatever is directly given to him, in what is present to him externally, to produce himself and therein equally to recognize himself."[23] But this subject is produced, is apprehended, not as a particular content but as subjecthood per se, as purely formal in Kant's terms.

2. The capacity to engage in representation in this formalizing sense is crucial to the formation of the subject as such. As I argue elsewhere, it is the project of nineteenth-century aesthetic education, of humanities pedagogy in general, to form the subject in this sense as the means to becoming citizen.[24]

3. This formation of the subject in representation is no less the formation of a subject that is representative—i.e., a subject that can stand

in the place of any and every subject by virtue of its formal identity with them. That the subject should be representative in this sense is the very ground on which Kant establishes the very possibility of common or public sense—in other words, the very possibility of the political at all.

4. By the same logic, if in reverse, the subject that is representative is capable of being represented precisely because to be representative is also to be interchangeable with other subjects, formally identical with them. The subject that envisages itself (*sich vorstellt*) as representative is disposed (*bestimmt*, determined) to be represented.

5. Thus, we could accurately rewrite Marx's formula on the representation of the French peasantry as "sie können sich nicht *vorstellen*; sie müssen vertreten werden." It is, after all, in the absence of this capacity to represent or imagine oneself as subject that the moment of representation as displacement or substitution comes most forcefully into play.

And yet we would be wrong if in doing so we were to suggest that there exists a domain in which self-representation takes place free of the shadow of representation as displacement. For what the logical series that I have just schematically presented implies is that to assume the disposition to representation is also to assume the disposition to be represented by others. This slippage is crucial to the emergence of political representation as the self-evident form of modern liberal societies. It undergirds the peculiar state function of the intellectual and the pedagogical institutions that, whatever their ostensible practical ends or the content of their training, seek finally to produce the citizen, the subject who is disposed to be represented by another. From Kant's claim for the aesthetic foundations of a common or public sense, elaborated in Chapter 1, to the institution of liberal education as the field in which the ethical formation of the individual takes place as the condition of citizenship, this insistence on the need to form the representable subject regulates the very possibility of modern political life. Within that scheme, it is the coup of the intellectual to represent him- or herself as the one who regulates representation, and therefore the formation of subjects, and to represent that regulative role as ethical—that is, as universalizing—rather than political. In this sense, the convergence between the intellectual and the state, as the ultimate representative of universality, is virtually absolute.[25]

The formative function of the intellectual as the one who regulates the processes of representation, *Vorstellung*, suggests a schematic triad of

moments of representation that is virtually narrative in form and that could
be diagrammed as follows:

$$darstellen \rightarrow vorstellen \rightarrow vertreten$$

The first movement is from the mere presentation of an object to representation as such, the act of formalization in which the subject, through
its reflective apprehension of its objects, comes into identity with other
subjects and is formed as at least potentially universal. The intellectual
oversees pedagogically the repetition and normalization of this movement.
Through the second movement—the coup of representation—the subject
that represents itself as universal by virtue of standing in its formality in
the place of all other subjects is in turn succeeded by a further act of representation that takes the place of the subject, effecting its displacement.
The possibility of this second movement, however, is predicated on the
first: Only the formation of the subject as representational in the moment
of *Vorstellung* underwrites and permits its determination as the exchangeable, indifferent subject, subject to substitution—as what we might call
vertretbar, at once exchangeable and representable, exchangeable because
representable.[26]

The movement through this series can equally be recursively naturalized precisely because it resides upon a process of perception given as
natural. We perceive as impressions present themselves to us and then we
re-present them and in doing so become conscious of (apperceive) both
them and ourselves. The hold of this Kantian and Hegelian dialectic of
consciousness on our common sense is hard to break, so natural does it
seem. It grounds the self-evidence of a set of little histories that form the
common sense of a modernity we have yet to transcend and repeat on ever-
larger scales the triad of representation just outlined:

1. The psychic or moral history of the formation of the citizen-
    subject of and for the state: This is, as we have seen, the movement
    from the particular, partial individual to the subject capable of
    representation.
2. The political history of the formation of the state as the general
    representative of the particular interests of society as a whole:
    This is, in Schiller's resonant terms, the emergence of the state as
    representative of the "archetype of man" or, in Matthew Arnold's
    terms, the state as the "best self" of the nation.[27] In either case, as
    the recent and violent preoccupation with state formation and failed
    states indicates, we are far from abandoning this overarching his-

tory for which the emergence of the state is the index of civilization and development, of accession to full humanity.

3. The history of history itself, as that of the emergence of what Marx would call "species being" from species life—that is, the forging of humanity from mere human existence.

Over and again, this set of little histories, undergirded as they are by the dialectical triad that composes the field of "representative activity," comes to affirm the legitimacy of colonial dispositions of power globally, those that establish the West as the representative of humanity in general, as the bearer of civility and the state and therefore of freedom, as against the recalcitrant particularities and antiuniversalism of the colonized: They cannot represent themselves, they must be represented.

By the same token, this set of little histories is entirely congruent with the formal processes of capital itself, and we can repeat them, mutatis mutandis, as a series of ever-more inclusive narrative movements that schematize the saturation of our representative systems with the logic of exchange:

1. In commodity production, the particularities of the use value of an object are subsumed into exchange value as the object is regarded as formally equivalent, as a commodity, to all other commodities: The commodity is no more than the formal representation of value. Difference is subordinated to identity.

2. Within commodity production, the "real labor of men"—the particular work that they perform—is equally transformed into "abstract labor," labor "represented as value." In a real sense, the proletariat is not composed of those who work together but of those who in turn represent themselves as units of value, of abstract labor. The capacity for self-representation and, therefore, for being represented is the very condition of possibility of politicization in Marxist terms even as it is the condition of participation in social democracy.

3. The "fetishism of commodities" itself assumes that social relations among productive human subjects are replaced and represented by imaginary relations among their objects. A fetishism of representation displaces relations among human beings with relations among their representations, of which the commodity would be but one instance, the "image" of the society of the spectacle yet another.

The replication of these narrative forms that tell over and over the tale of the transformation of the particular into the formal and universal, of the presented into the representative, informs and circulates through every sphere of a still-dominant modernity. Grounded in the epistemological and the aesthetic, they disseminate through the political, the social, the economic, taking on the force of an unquestioned and discretely racializing self-evidence. These little narratives become the common sense of modernity. Indeed, the very commonsensicality of representation as the mode of our relation to the world is founded in the more or less Kantian logic by which common sense itself appears as the function of our modes of representation: All judgment passes by way of the movement from *Darstellung* to *Vorstellung*.

The coup of representation is to represent the regularity of that formalizing movement as the index of human subjecthood as such, to transform it from a contingent aspect of the phenomenology of perception into a decisive moment in a universalizing narrative.[28] The normalization of representation as *Vertretung* dissembles the foundational violence that institutes representation as a moment of displacement, a violence that continues to lurk throughout the operation of the legal and political system that claims legitimacy and civility. As Jacques Derrida puts it in relation to Benjamin's "Critique of Violence":

> The violence that founds or positions *droit* [law, right] need not be immediately present in the contract (*nicht unmittelbar in ihm gegenwärtig zu sein*: "it need not be directly present in it as lawmaking violence").
> . . . But without being immediately present, it is replaced (*vertreten*, "represented") by the supplement of a substitute. And it is this *différance*, in the movement that replaces presence (the immediate presence of violence identifiable as such in its *traits* and its spirit), it is in this *différantielle* representativity that originary violence is consigned to oblivion. This amnesic loss of consciousness does not happen by accident. It is the very passage from presence to representation.[29]

This amnesia that representation secures is the forgetting but not the abolition of violence, violence that continues to haunt both representation and the law.

Representation's Coup

Representation secretes and occludes the founding violence of the state, most obviously at the moment of a political coup or revolution when the apparent self-evidence of the forms of representation disintegrates. It substitutes what Kant called the "original compact" by which communicability grounds common or public sense for the violence that shadows even Thomas Paine's account of the origins of the social contract. In the *Eighteenth Brumaire*, representation continually flies in the face of common sense, and it is the disjunction between the moment of *Vorstellung* and that of *Vertretung*, rather than the regularity of the transition between them, that Marx emphasizes. As we have seen, the parodic mode of the text as a whole afflicts the concept of representation as *Vorstellung* with peculiar force, but it is ultimately the violence of the appropriation of representativity in the form of *Vertretung* that the text brings out. The *Brumaire* is obsessed with forms of representation, with theatrical as much as with political representation: Theatricality is its ubiquitous subtext and Shakespeare, and in particular *Hamlet*, is the mobile ghost in its cellarage.[30] This intertextual relation to Shakespeare's dramas, this alertness to dramatic genre—comedy, tragedy, farce—mimes the historical processes of repetition and reworking in a critically parodic mode. Rather than invoking the stage, in Schillerian fashion, as the institution that represents the eternal and universal image of Man and the exemplarity of political pasts, Marx stages the scene of representation so as to mark the breakdown of the commonsensical logic or self-evidence of the narrative structures. His invocation of the theatricality of revolution emphasizes not the transformation of some particular political struggle into a universal template but the failure of repetition, its debasement—"the first time as tragedy, the second as farce," as the *Brumaire's* opening sentences famously put it (10). Theatricality marks the disjunction between "phrase" and "content" (*Brumaire*, 13), the disproportion between the representation and what is represented. The moment of *Vorstellung*, which should be that at which a Louis Bonaparte is able to elevate himself into the dignity of the representative of the state, becomes rather that in which representation repeats the past as travesty— the lumpen army of lackeys, the Swiss vulture, Bonaparte as Nick Bottom as the parody of a parody. The moment of *Vertretung*, therefore, at which he seizes hold of the peasantry in order to appropriate representation from them, reveals its arbitrary and performative violence and casts its shadow over the more normative uses of the terms *Vertreter* and *Repräsentant*: all may legitimately be suspected of being merely *Ersatzmänner, remplaçants*.

Representation thus appears in the *Brumaire* as no more than a further coup. Seizing as its moment of analysis a crisis the bourgeois state faces in the prospect of a "social republic" after the 1848 rebellion, Marx demonstrates how that coup de main (unexpected stroke) of the 1848 socialist revolution is met by the reactionary bourgeois republic, which is in turn dissolved for good in the *coup de tête* (rash act) of December 1851

(*Brumaire*, 13), when an effective coup d'état establishes Louis Bonaparte's supremacy. But this coup d'état brings to light no less the coup of representation itself. The ideal time of representation, the movement of *Vorstellung* that presents itself as the adequate formalization into identity of the particular individuals or classes that compose a society, gives way to an act of *Vertretung* that imagines itself (*sich vorstellt*) as a standing- or speaking-for justified by that prior formalization. The representative is, in principle, identical with, equivalent to, the represented. In the *Brumaire*, however, the moment of *Vertretung* is captured in its arbitrary violence, as a moment of disproportion between represented and representative, a moment already inscribed in the abstraction and the suppression of difference that the act of *Vorstellung* entails. Denaturalized in those moments of parodic representation—the lackeys as the army, etc.—*Vorstellung* becomes the mark of a merely imaginary relation to social relations, a false universality.[31] Louis Bonaparte becomes a parody of representation no less than a "parody of Empire" (*Brumaire*, 112).

In the disjunction between the performance and the representation it repeats (for Napoleon Bonaparte himself merely played the role of Roman Emperor), both representation's coup and its absolute necessity to the state become apparent. In its longer historical trajectory, the *Brumaire* presents a narrative of state formation, of the emergence of the state in its centralization and separation out from society, a history that extends from the ancien régime through the French Revolution and Napoleon to the Revolution of 1848 and its aftermath: "All revolutions perfected this machine instead of smashing it. The parties that contended in turn for domination regarded the possession of this huge state edifice as the principal spoils of the victor. . . . Only under the second Bonaparte does the state seem to have made itself completely independent" (*Brumaire*, 105). According to this history, the state that had been supposed, from Burke to Hegel, to be the representative of society in fact separates itself from and takes the place of society, to which the state exists in a relation of *Vertretung* analogous to that of Bonaparte to the peasants. Marx emphasizes that since the restoration of 1815 "the material conditions that made the feudal peasant a smallholding peasant and Napoleon an emperor" have dissolved (*Brumaire*, 108). What has since emerged is a disjunction between contemporary relations of production and the state form that purports to represent them. As a feudal aristocracy has been replaced by bourgeois finance capital, indebting the vast majority of the peasantry, bourgeois and peasant interests cease to be aligned against the aristocracy and become instead antagonistic: "Hence the peasants find their natural ally and leader in the urban proletariat, whose task is to overthrow the bourgeois order. But strong and unlimited government—and this is the second '*idée napoléonienne,*' which the second Napoleon has to carry out—is called upon to defend this material order by force" (*Brumaire*, 110).[32] This disjunction between the peasantry and the Bonaparte who purportedly represents them thus leads to the establishment of an authoritarian relation of the state to society, finding "its final expression in the executive power subordinating society to itself" (*Brumaire*, 106).

The resultant antagonism between state and society is, for Marx, no more than a moment of clarification. The progressive outcome of the revolutions of the past half century reveals the state to be the false representation of society, "reducing it to its purest expression, isolating it, setting it up against itself as the sole reproach, in order to concentrate all its forces of destruction against it. And when it has done this second half of its preliminary work, Europe will leap from its seat and exultantly exclaim: well grubbed, old mole!" (*Brumaire*, 104). Marx believes that Bonaparte's coup will inaugurate the disenchantment of the representative state and its recognition as the antagonist of the proletariat and the peasantry alike. Whatever grounds he may have had for such optimism were to be radically undermined by factors that emerged in large part only in the second half of the nineteenth century. The first of these is the rise of the state form whose consolidation he relates in the *Brumaire*. What he was hardly in a position to forecast is the concurrent and gradual emergence of the institutions of civil society and the state whose ensemble Gramsci, working at a moment when its ideological consequences had become clearer, calls "the ethical state." His term nicely suggests how those institutions take charge of normalizing the subject's accession to representation, masking its implicit violence with the regularity of what we might call an "everyday coup." Within the framework of the ethical state, the work of the intellectual, including most specifically the teacher, is not confined to acts of what Spivak calls "mimetic representation" (*Darstellung*) but is directed principally at reproducing the function of representation (*Vorstellung*) as the disposition of the ethical subject. The function of the state intellectual is to naturalize the work of representation that prepares the moment of identity with the state in each individual, the work of making citizens. The citizen-subject formed in that process is the one who permits himself to be represented, *das vertretbare Subjekt*. And to be representable is, by the same token, to be human.

Accordingly, the function of the intellectual is not only to mediate and regulate for the state the becoming-representative of the subjects she or he oversees but to maintain a regime of representation that is fundamentally racial as well as political. As *Vorstellungsrepräsentant*, the representative of Representation, the intellectual stands in the place of whiteness or, in Denise Ferreira da Silva's terms, of the transparency by which access to universality is regulated. This is more than the contingent moral issue that, as Wynter notes, "we, as Western and westernized intellectuals, continue to articulate, in however radically oppositional a manner, the rules of the social order and its sanctioned theories."[33] As intellectuals, we are not merely the reluctant agents of the modern "racial descriptive statement"; we are constituted as the representative instances of representation through which the regime of representation is installed and reproduced.

Race is intrinsic to the other factor that would be crucial to the consolidation of the representative state and that Marx could scarcely have foreseen fully: empire itself. Numerous studies have shown the crucial role that imperialism played not merely in the capture and exploitation of resources for industrial capital and the provision of outlets for surplus finance capital but in the incorporation of the working classes into the European states domestically.[34] As Catherine Hall shows, the entry of the British working classes into representation and franchise depended on the differentiation of white male British subjects from both women and the colonized.[35] The other cost that franchise entailed was the submission of the working class in Britain to the pedagogical intervention of the state whose end was not merely their training in necessary skills but their disciplining as subjects capable of being represented.[36] Both demographically and economically, imperialism and its settler-colonial projects enabled the absorption of populations displaced by industrialization and enclosure through emigration, militarism, and increased production and consumption, while engaging them politically through identification with the whiteness of the citizen-subject. Louis Bonaparte's representation of the peasantry is generalized in the system of imperialism by the state's representation of its "whitened" populace: The racial state is the effect of representation's coup. At the same time, and in accord with the schema of the universal history of the state and representation outlined throughout this book, the colonized populations become by definition those who are not (yet) ready for representation and who are therefore in a state of perpetual tutelage. They are maintained, in John Stuart Mill's resonant phrase, in the "government of leading strings."[37] They cannot represent themselves, they must be represented.

What gradually emerged, then, in the colonial sphere as in the domestic sphere, was a system of rule that involved for a portion of the population their subjection to the state through and in pedagogy. The end of that pedagogy was to make of them subjects of representation through a process that, as Fanon's work so richly testifies, demanded of them a painful splitting: a splitting *from* all those elements of native culture that are inassimilable to the colonizer's culture and that become not signs of equivalence in difference but indices of underdevelopment; and a splitting *internal to their formation* entailed by the recognition that, however much they seek to represent themselves as subjects, their ineradicable difference will always leave them ultimately inassimilable and subjected to the colonizer. This is the burden of what I call in the previous chapter "race under representation" and what Fanon means by renaming assimilation as separation, dislocation, rupture, alienation.[38] It is the excruciating predicament of the colonial and the postcolonial intellectual, of those selected, in the terms of Lord Macaulay's infamous "Minute on Indian Education," to play the role of "intermediaries" between the colonizing power and the mass of the native people.[39] As they assume the function of representation "their privilege [becomes] their loss," to use Spivak's pithy formulation. And in this, as she asserts, "they are a paradigm of the intellectuals."[40]

But in neither case is this predicament that of the Subaltern. As we saw at the outset, the Subaltern stands in relation to the colonial apparatus both formally or logically and materially as the limit of representation. By definition never interpellated by the colonial state, the Subaltern never enters the system of representation. Moreover, the modes of living of subaltern formations are beyond representation in a double sense: They can only be grasped in the terms of colonial culture by an act of refractive translation that utterly alters their sense and their logic, while as cultural formations they stand outside of the logic of representation as that has emerged in and for the West.[41] The problem of the representation of the Subaltern is, therefore, not only an epistemological or methodological one. It is not a problem of the availability of archives and records or of "self-representations"—the difficulty does not evaporate with the recording of oral narratives.[42] Properly speaking, the Subaltern cuts across all these domains: It is a function of its differential relation to the social and cultural formations and the organizational modes of the colonial state with which it is constitutively incommensurable. This incommensurability makes the practices of the Subaltern recalcitrant and unreadable to the colonial state and to those formed in relation to it, including the historian. As Guha nicely shows, it is the impulse of the historian as it is of the colonial bureaucrat to rewrite the decentered, horizontal practices of the Subaltern as those of a subject operating as the more or less stable cause of its effects.[43]

Recalcitrant to discipline and assimilation, recalcitrant to representation, the Subaltern is equally recalcitrant in its incommensurability with
the moment of formalization that underwrites the possibility of the ethical
identification of the subject with the moment of universality that permits
representation at all. More even than the "element of matter" that must be
let go of in the act of representation that brings each subject into accord
with the universal Subject, to reinvoke Kant, the Subaltern defies representation. It is the *Unvorstellbar*, the unimaginable-unrepresentable, of the
regime of representation through which the modern subject comes into
being. As such, the Subaltern produces a crisis of identification that is read
from the place of the subject as an ethical crisis, from the perspective of the
state as an implicit violence.

This final observation allows us to comprehend the peculiar fact that
subalterns tend almost always to appear as violence, regardless of their actual practices. In this respect, their very existence appears analogous to
those nonviolent acts like the general strike that, as Benjamin notes in his
"Critique of Violence" (282), appear as violent to the state, even where
they avoid violence strictly speaking. The Subaltern, in other words, need
not actually engage in violence, commit or organize acts of violence to be
understood *as* violence. Its very recalcitrant existence in relation to the
state challenges the monopoly on violence that the state claims as its prerogative and as the foundation of the law: The Subaltern's mode of existence, its forms of life, appear to the state as a form of "counterlegality"
that defies the founding violence of the state on which the law itself rests.
At the same time, it challenges the monopoly on representation that is no
less claimed by the state and with it the assumption of representativity that
is the guarantee of the subject. The constitutive violence that the subalternity brings to light in the structure of representation that informs both the
state and its subjects is displaced back onto the Subaltern: The violence of
representation becomes cast as the violence of the unrepresentable.

Here, however, it is to the problem of a failure of identification that I
want to return, since that is what lies at the root of the ethical consternation that follows from the judgment that "the Subaltern cannot speak" or,
properly, that the intellectual cannot represent the Subaltern and therefore
ceases to be able to maintain the claim to be universally representative.
Precisely because the moment of *Vorstellung* must represent itself as an
intuition of universality, as a moment that formally reflects the identity of
the subject in all individuals, whatever their differences, the claim to represent and the claim to be representative are mutually founded in the neces-

sity of a possible identification with all humans. To be able to judge from the perspective of all humanity, which grounds the formal ethical moment of representation, presumes the moment of the subject, of representability, of all humans. That is not to say, as Kant clearly recognized, that all humans are at all moments capable of being represented; it is no more than a potentiality that must be developed and that, as we have seen in Chapter 3, requires the intervention of a pedagogy in order to be developed or cultivated. But the Subaltern is not the colonial subject under development. Rather, it appears as the absolute and constitutive limit of representation and it is around that instance of an *unvorstellbar* refusal to be represented that the Subaltern initiates a crisis in the intellectual's self-regard, a breakdown of the universal, representative Subject. That breakdown is generally expressed not as a moment of political insight leading to a genealogy of the intellectual's state function but as a pained frustration of the desire to identify with and incorporate the Subaltern.[44]

This failure of identification is not merely contingent, not merely that failure to empathize with another because of some accidental incompatibility, but a structural effect of the differential positioning of the Subaltern vis-à-vis the intellectual whose function it is to be representative, whose self-representation is to represent. Perhaps the Subaltern at first appears to be the lost possible object that instigates a form of melancholy paralysis in response.[45] However, it is not hard to conclude that the real lost object is—as always in melancholia—the self-image of the subject, its ego-ideal. The wound to the intellectual's narcissism is particularly profound, no doubt, in that it is a wound to the pleasurable investment in the idea of one's ethical universality. The Subaltern operates against the secondary mirror-stage of intellectual formation with a similar abyssal force as that with which the sight of the black body assaults the corporeal schema of the white subject. It is no less possible to see the destructive subtext, equally characteristic of melancholia, underlying the paralysis into which the Subaltern plunges the intellectual. Precisely insofar as the intellectual is shaped in and for the state as its representative moment, the intellectual shares with the state—even in disavowal—the realization that, faced with an instance of absolute recalcitrance to representation, its only course is to extirpate it, directly by violence or by the mediated violence of assimilative transformation—that is, by what is called "development." The well-meaning intellectual cannot admit such violent longings and falls instead into a kind of bitter crisis that resembles profoundly the condition Memmi describes in "The Colonizer Who Refuses": "an unenviable dilemma" in which "he no longer recognizes himself," a dilemma based in the contradiction between an ethical desire to identify with the colonized and the constitutive impossibility of doing so.[46]

As I shall elaborate in the final section of this essay, that conflicted, inwardly redirected, melancholic violence is ultimately suicidal: If the intellectual cannot identify with, cannot represent, the Subaltern, then the intellectual finds herself obliged to destroy herself, perceived now as the obstacle to a representativity that is valued more than the self who fails at representation.[47] That may be why "Can the Subaltern Speak?" must end with an instance of suicide, and not the suicide of a person who could in any sense be construed as a subaltern but that of an intellectual, a member of the Indian elite caught up in the nationalist struggle: a native woman indeed, but not a subaltern.[48] Bhubaneswari Bhaduri's suicide, this "woman's resistance in extremis," appears to have emerged from an ethical dilemma with regard to her capacity to represent the nationalist movement, and if it remained "unrecognized," it is not by the same token an unrepresentable act.[49] Yet this moment is so often taken in readings of the essay to represent the moment of female subalternity, as if it rendered momentarily possible, however perilous, an identification with the Subaltern. Such an identification is a guilty pleasure, a flirtation with the self-destruction of the intellectual. It does not give rise to critique; still less does it open onto political agency.

The dilemma that confronts the reader of "Can the Subaltern Speak?," then, the fact that it tends to induce guilt rather than further critical analysis, may lie in the essay's own short-circuiting of the question of representation into that "double session" of *darstellen* and *vertreten*. Its partial analysis of the system of representation has the unintended effect of posing the unrepresentability of the Subaltern as a problem of the individual positioning of the intellectual and therefore as an ethical or an epistemological rather than a political matter. The predicament of the intellectual registers as subjective ethical discomfort and melancholy, or even resentment, rather than enabling a critical genealogy of the intellectual's constitutive role in the representative formations against which the subaltern emerges differentially. To recognize the crisis of representation as an effect of its own structure might, to the contrary, give rise to a politically transformative critique rather than a guiltily affective reaction. Rather than seek to overcome the ethical dilemmas posed by the Subaltern's exteriority to representation by seeking the means to re-enter the Subaltern into some form, even provisional, of representation, the challenge of subalternity should rather return us to the critique of the regime of representation. That would, of course, entail the dismantling, critical rather than melancholic, of the intellectual's own formation and its relation both to the state, in which it is captured, and to the Subaltern, with which it differentially rather than developmentally unfolds. The work of the intellectual would then be not representation and the desire to develop and cultivate identity but a differential political practice, devoted, on the one hand, to deconstructing the self-evidence of the state-civil society formation—a task all the more urgent in this era of "failed states" and imposed democratization—and, on the other, to making space for the emergence of alternatives, illegible and unrepresentable to us as they may yet be. Inevitably, such a task would require a real disturbance of the regime of representation, to what Fanon calls, in characterizing the movement of decolonization, "a program of complete disorder."[50]

The Mirror of the Subaltern

I end by concretizing the "unenviable dilemma" of the intellectual in the face of the Subaltern by way of a literary example—"a literary representation" not so much "of the female subaltern" but of the Subaltern as she appears to the settler colonial's emerging self-consciousness.[51] Jean Rhys's novel *Wide Sargasso Sea* stages not the moment of identification pursued by the realist novel but its foundering, and does so precisely across the distance that separates the metropole from the colony and the white creole colonial from the colonized subject.[52] It relentlessly refuses to propose a resolution to the dilemma of the colonial subject in the form of a narrative of ethical development, precisely by weaving its own texture into the fabric of one of the nineteenth century's most celebrated novels of female *Bildung, Jane Eyre.* Like Marx's *Brumaire, Wide Sargasso Sea* foregrounds its intertextual and repetitive structure, reconstructing the story of Antoinette, the "Bertha Mason" of its ur-text. As with the *Brumaire,* the function of repetition in representation aims not at a successively higher degree of integration and generalization of the particular instance but at a parodic critique of the dominant textual structure on which the novel is parasitic.[53] The "emancipation" of the former slaves and the advent of a new mode of capitalist plantation ownership based on the exploitation of "free" black labor leave the older planters suspended historically and socially between the abolished slaveholding practices and the new mode that has bankrupted them, between the new white settlers and the black and mixed-race population they can no longer dominate. Finding herself thus stranded, Antoinette's mother, Annette, repeatedly complains that they are "marooned," appropriating the term from black *marronage* in a way that frames Antoinette's discovery that she is no more than—in the oxymoronic phrases—a "white nigger" or a "white cockroach."[54] This at first unwilling identification with the black population nonetheless becomes a willed, desirable identification for Antoinette, representing an imaginary way of resolving the contradictions of her life as the offspring of settler colonialism.

At a crucial moment of the text, in terms of the narrative's unfolding and of its symbolic structures, the new plantation regime provokes a riot in which the former slaves—a subaltern population both in their violent irruption into visibility and in their externality to the new forms of colonial rule and exploitation—burn down the plantation house that Antoinette has loved as a kind of wild Eden. As the white family and their servants flee, Antoinette catches sight of her black former playmate Tia:

> Then, not so far off, I saw Tia and her mother and I ran to her, for she was all that was left of my life as it had been. We had eaten the same food, slept side by side, bathed in the same river. As I ran, I thought, I will live with Tia and I will be like her. Not to leave Coulibri. Not to go. Not. When I was close I saw the jagged stone in her hand but I did not see her throw it. I did not feel it either, only something wet, running down my face. I looked at her and I saw her face crumple up as she began to cry. We stared at each other, blood on my face, tears on hers. It was as if I saw myself. Like in a looking-glass.[55]

In this moment where the mirror cracks, the desire for identification—"I will be like her"—is held in suspension with the violence of its shattering. The face that stares back is not identical but a reverse mirror stage that resembles that moment in which Fanon recognizes that the black body shatters the corporeal schema of the white man and does so "absolutely as the not-self—that is, the unidentifiable, the unassimilable."[56] The moment of reflection that shatters the desire for identification differentially produces the white subject and the black Subaltern, Tia, who henceforth disappears from the novel's action, recurring only in Antoinette's imaginary as the ambiguous mark of threat and desire.

This scene of violence becomes the kernel of a narrative that insistently undoes the narrative work of *Jane Eyre*. That novel moves from a similar moment of inaugural violence and mirroring, in the ten-year-old Jane's rebellion at Gateshead, to her gradual reintegration into a female narrative of self-formation that famously culminates in her assumption of "proper" female social identity: "Reader, I married him." *Wide Sargasso Sea*, fractured by the scar that might "spoil [Antoinette] on [her] wedding day," refuses to recuperate the moment of inaugural violence into a developmental narrative: It will not "heal nicely."⁵⁷ Rather, Rhys insistently repeats moments in which the mirror of identification shatters, multiplying such instances of disrupted reflection through the novel. A series of increasingly lengthy dreams reiterates a complex of more or less traumatic associations forged at the plantation Coulibri, constellating them around the motifs of courtship and marriage. Within these dreams the image of Tia is at first dispersed or disseminated as a figure of mirroring, blackness, and threat: "We are under the tall dark trees and there is no wind. 'Here?' He turns and looks at me, his face black with hatred."⁵⁸ Rhys fragments Tia's image precisely in order to associate it with the law as it impinges on Antoinette in the form of marriage and property rights and, therefore, of her necessary whiteness. The law constitutes Antoinette as the marriageable white woman, whose place is literally taken by her husband and who can no longer speak in her own name, even as it constitutes Tia differentially as the Subaltern beyond the pale of representation. The "Letter of the Law" that replaces slavery with the disciplines of colonial capitalism that "mash up people's feet," as Christophene, the obeah woman, puts it just before Antoinette's first nightmare, equally precludes any identification between the white, creole woman it interpellates as subject and the Subaltern.⁵⁹ As the dreams' urgent and terrifying trajectories suggest, the law also emerges as at once coercive and desired. The disturbing emergence of the Subaltern as violence in the same moment that the Subaltern is the desired object of identification draws Antoinette to desire the protection of a law that is nonetheless coercive and hostile to her desire. If Tia drops entirely from representation after this critical moment of broken mirroring, she in turn survives as the object of a loss that haunts Antoinette's dreams, both the violent cause of the law and the figure for the law's violence.⁶⁰

At the very end of the novel Antoinettte—renamed Bertha—is incarcerated in the attic of Mr. Rochester's mansion, reduced in her turn to a nonperson. There, the figure of Tia, posed over against the hate-filled man and his summons, once more appears to haunt and taunt her in the final recurrence of her dream:

> I saw my doll's house and the books and the picture of the Miller's Daughter. I heard the parrot call as he did when he saw a stranger, *Qui est là? Qui est là?* And the man who hated me was calling too, Bertha! Bertha! The wind caught my hair and it streamed out like wings. It might bear me up, I thought, if I jumped to those hard stones. But when I looked over the edge I saw the pool at Coulibri. Tia was there.

She beckoned to me and when I hesitated, she laughed. I heard her say, You frightened? And I heard the man's voice, Bertha! Bertha! All this I saw and heard in a fraction of a second. And the sky so red. Someone screamed and I thought, Why did I scream? I called "Tia!" and jumped and woke. . . . Now at last I know why I was brought here and what I have to do.[61]

It is a perplexing passage. In one respect, as the dream unfolds back into Antoinette's past, undoing all that has forced her into the confines of her present prison, returning her to Coulibri and Tia, it is an intensely liberating moment, a moment of the unravelling of the ties of coercion and of being represented or summoned by others. It is "a program of complete disorder." But the fabric of this dream is woven into a narrative already prescribed, that of the earlier novel that stands as a figure for the history that precedes Antoinette. Her fate is always already out of her hands and we know that this dream and her decision will culminate in her self-immolation. Her liberation is her suicide. To retrieve and to act "in her own name," to cease having to be represented by another, it is necessary to destroy herself.

How do we read this ending to a novel that stands as the counterhistory of *Jane Eyre* and as the trace of the Subaltern in the archive? It is, of course, a moment characteristic of the negativity of Rhys's work in general, of its refusal of easy exits from the toils of the patriarchal and colonial narratives within which her characters are framed. In this, her oeuvre is insistent on the difficulty of dismantling the structures that appear as desirable as they are coercive. In doing so, it returns to us the question as to what must be destroyed in order that the failed desire of the intellectual to identify with the Subaltern is not replaced by the melancholy desire for the law. Let there be no mistake: The white creole Antoinette is *not* the Subaltern, however abused she may be; she is, rather, the subject suspended between the desire for the Law, for the Name given by the Father, and the desire to identify with, to be in the place of, the Subaltern. But the Subaltern retreats from representation, is there only as the trace of a different opening, a different possibility, that cannot be realized from the place of the Law.

As I have hoped to show, the Subaltern emerges in the moment of the founding of the regime of representation that legitimates the state and its law even as it masks its violence. The Subaltern is not the name for that which is prior to the state or to representation but for that which emerges differentially in relation to and in time with it. As such, it is constitutively unavailable for representation, for identification, for development from primitive immediacy to self-conscious identity. It thus resists categorically the desire of the intellectual to subsume everything into representation. That desire is no less constitutive of the intellectual and of the intellectual's ethical self-regard. Hence, we can read the culmination of Antoinette's desire for Tia in suicide not as the act of a Subaltern denied any other mode of agency or of self-expression but rather as a figure for the necessity for the intellectual to take on (in every sense) the system of representation and to seek its deconstruction as a deconstruction of the intellectual's own formation and desires. This is no less than the task of self-destruction insofar as it demands the abandonment of the intellectual's deep and narcissistic investment in representation as the very form of our pedagogy and our practice heretofore. It is the task of delinking from the state as our representative and our end in the hope that, in a practice of differential engagement rather than representation or identification, we might make a space for the Subaltern to appear even as we make the space for our own thinking otherwise.

Thus, if I have chosen to end with *Wide Sargasso Sea* as an allegory for the predicament that has afflicted us as intellectuals, that is because, while the trajectory of the narrative turns obsessively to and is structured by this traumatic moment of failed identification, the very deliberate, parodic inscription of that narrative within the constraints of a major, canonical, and representative text at every point prevents the desire for identification beyond difference from succumbing to an ethical fantasy of achieved identity. If Rhys's work appears relentlessly, even despairingly, negative, that is surely because even now the institutions of the colonial state, that at once set on and frustrate such desires, have by no means dissolved but have, as Christophene remarks of the moment of Emancipation, taken on new and more rigorous forms. Neither a work of mourning or of melancholy, *Wide Sargasso Sea* is rather a molework that bores through the attic of our narratives of representation much as the parodic ghost of Hamlet's father mines the cellarage of the rotten state of Denmark, revealing what is out of joint.

CHAPTER 5

The Aesthetic Taboo: Aura, Magic, and the Primitive

If the aesthetic realm originally emerged as an autonomous sphere from the magic taboo which distinguished the sacred from the everyday, seeking to keep the former pure, the profane now takes its revenge on the descendant of magic, on art.

—THEODOR W. ADORNO

Aesthetics as Universal Anthropology

The foregoing chapters of *Under Representation* have circulated around and elaborated a set of propositions about the structure and function of the aesthetic. First, the inaugural texts of modern aesthetics—those, indeed, that give us the very terms by which we now understand the aesthetic as a distinct discursive formation—oversee a shift from the idea of an aesthetic judgment directed at natural objects and physical sensations to one predicated on artworks. But aesthetic discourse and its effects are by no means confined to the sphere of art. On the contrary, aesthetic philosophy establishes a regime of representation that grounds both the condition of possibility of the public sphere on which the modern conception of the political rests and the developmental trajectory along which distinct modalities of human being are distributed according to their distance from representative or universal subjecthood. If the former regulates the formation of the political subject for the state, the latter governs the conception of the human around which modern racial judgment—or discrimination—is organized. Second, within that regime of representation the formalism of aesthetic judgment describes the movement of the subject's apprehension of the object from its material qualities to its form, thereby cultivating the

124

moment of the universal in that subject. It also normalizes at the very heart of subject formation itself the decisive distinction between the emancipated human Subject and "pathological" subjects that are still subjected to nature, either through external force or through internal impulses such as desire, fear, or gratification. It is the dubious achievement of the aesthetic to have rendered such distinctions definitive of a scale of development along which whole human groups—races, ethnicities, or what would come to be called "cultures"—are distributed. This deeply implicit racial structure of a narrative of representation is constitutive of aesthetic philosophy rather than a contingent limit determined by the accidental historical biases and perspectives of its inaugural thinkers. The aesthetic regime of representation must therefore be understood as constitutive simultaneously of the terms of the modern political sphere and of a culturally determined racial order of the human. The two domains of representation cannot easily be prized apart.

Accordingly, the aesthetic is a historically situated regulative discourse in two associated domains: the political and the anthropological in the broadest senses. Aesthetics belongs to a constellation or a cluster of discourses—including law, politics, political economy, geography, and philology—that have together determined and differentiated the space of the human. Indeed, in its initial articulation, aesthetics was understood to be a subset of anthropology in precisely this sense: a science devoted to the determination of a universal form of the human. As Kant put it in the lectures published as *Anthropology from a Pragmatic Point of View*: "A systematic treatise comprising our knowledge of man (anthropology) can adopt either a *physiological* or a *pragmatic* point of view.—Physiological knowledge of man investigates what *nature* makes of him; pragmatic what *man* as a free agent makes, or can and should make, of himself."[1] It is the pragmatic point of view, however, that ultimately defines the human as opposed to merely describing different kinds of human being. The human as self-determining subject is, therefore, the concern of anthropology, rather than the physiological human as a natural creature, because, as Kant goes on to affirm, "man is his own final end." Physiology studies only "what nature makes of him"—that is, man as an object of necessity, subject to the heteronomy of natural laws or physical limitations—while pragmatic philosophy considers man as the subject of freedom—that is, as the Subject for itself.

Nonetheless, in *Anthropology from a Pragmatic Point of View*, the aesthetic remains a subset for Kant of the actually lived modalities of being human rather than a regulative discourse of the human. Thus, he analyzes the distinct feelings of pleasure and displeasure produced by the sublime and the beautiful rather than regarding either as indications of the capacity for formal judgment that grounds any subject's capacity for universality. "Feelings," as Chapter 2 shows, remain in the domain of what Kant designates the "pathological": Being predicable only on the individual human body and its subjection to need, desire, or fear, feeling cannot furnish the basis of a universal judgment. Thus, only in *The Critique of Judgement* does the aesthetic become the ground for the determination of the very possibility of any idea of the human Subject in general, the subject at once of freedom and of moral law. Only then does the aesthetic become anthropological in the fullest sense of "regarding man as his own final end."[2]

This anthropology is, as the foregoing chapters argue, no less a fundamental political theory. The possibility of a disinterested formal judgment of taste that allows a claim to universal consensus on subjective rather than objective grounds enables the idea of what Kant calls common or public sense. Even before it is articulated with the sphere of politics strictly conceived, this public sense, predicated on the formal identity of the reflective judgment in all humans—*Vorstellung* or representation—furnishes the condition of possibility for the public sphere in which each and every human subject represents humanity in and for others.[3] Here the possibility of the political intersects with the distribution of the racial. For the possibility of such a formal judgment and the disinterest that it presupposes is not itself given as an a priori faculty of every human subject but requires the supposition of a developmental narrative that leads from the Savage— Kant's Iroquois or Carib for whom "charm" or interested aesthetic feeling still dominates—to the civil subject. This narrative establishes the distribution of racialization along a temporal axis. Along that axis, the Savage marks the limit point of the human, occupying the threshold that determines the differentiation of the human from the nonhuman and, as such, is at once interior and exterior to human being. In other terms, the Savage, defined as the highest degree of subjection to nature and necessity, is the pathological subject to the fullest extent. As the antithesis of the political or civil subject, it represents what Denise Ferreira da Silva, in *Toward a Global Idea of Race*, designates the "subject of affectability," consigned to the external domain of need or force ("what nature makes of him") and accordingly always already the object of what legal discourse defines as "the state of necessity" (*Notstaat*). Insofar as inhabiting the state of necessity is that which defines the Savage as pathological subject, this is a constitutively and inescapably racial schema that subtends any racial judgment based on supposedly empirical grounds such as phenotype or color. Not to have crossed the threshold from subordination to nature into a consciousness of freedom is, as Hegel notoriously remarked of the black African, what defines racial inferiority.[4] The Savage, degree zero of the racial subject, occupies always that racialized state of emergency that is the norm for the oppressed and the perpetual condition of the colonial sphere.[5]

This developmental schema, first outlined in the Third Critique, enabled Friedrich Schiller's reinscription of the aesthetic in his *Aesthetic Education* as a fundamentally pedagogical project.[6] For Schiller, aesthetic contemplation instantiates the possibility of the subject's noncoercive or "liberal" relation to its objects, furnishing what he terms "the archetype of the human" whose canonical form is found to be the State. That archetype, which corresponds to Kant's universal Subject, is no more than a potentiality in each individual, only gradually realized through an aesthetic pedagogy that defers the institution of the state of freedom that the aesthetic state anticipates. The process of aesthetic formation through which each individual must pass in order to be prepared for the ultimate state of freedom corresponds to the universal history of humanity. This history is also predicated on a typological schema of human development: Schiller offers a systematic developmental history of humanity's evolution from the Savage, subjected to the state of necessity, through the barbarian despotism of the state of might or force, to civilization and the state of rights. The aesthetic state prefigures, though it cannot actualize, an ultimate state of freedom. Obviously, this schematic racial history maps onto an equally ideal history of political state formation that likewise leads from the state of necessity to the state of force to the state of freedom. For Schiller, universal history takes the form of a typological anthropology of development regulated by aesthetic formation.

In his introduction to the *Aesthetics: Lectures on Fine Art*, Hegel casts forward from Kant and Schiller the general "economic" implications of this typological anthropological schema that undergirds aesthetic philosophy. Here, the aesthetic first explicitly becomes the discourse on the formation of Man, and of Man as fundamentally both alienated and as such self-producing:

> Things in nature are only *immediate and single*, but man as spirit *duplicates* himself, in that (i) he *is as* things in nature are, but, (ii) he is just as much *for* himself; he sees himself, represents himself to himself, thinks, and only on the strength of this active placing himself before himself is he spirit. . . . Man brings himself before himself by *practical* activity, since he has the impulse, in whatever is directly given to him, in what is present to him externally, to produce himself, and therein equally to

recognize himself. . . . This need runs through the most diversiform
phenomena up to the mode of self-production in external things which
is present in the work of art.[7]

Hegel's emphasis on production, albeit reflective or spiritual production,
suggests that aesthetics is an anthropology that views the human as the
historical result of its own "auto-production." This universal anthropology
affirms that the realization of the universal requires the development of a
latent capacity from its subordination to need and gratification in the state
of necessity into a reflective capacity for representation. It thus distributes
the gradations of humanity along the axis that separates necessity from
freedom according to the development of a capacity for reflexive judgment that definitively produces the subject as human. Aesthetics becomes,
then, the discourse that knits together the political concept of human freedom attained through the production of one's own representativity with
a racialized distribution of the human within which certain subjects fall
short of humanity precisely insofar as they are deemed not yet capable of
representation.

Aesthetics after Anthropology

So far, we have been considering an aesthetic anthropology that postulates
a universal form of the human and grounds the philosophical project of
establishing the possibility of both the subject and its universality. This
aesthetic anthropology, I have argued, forges the very possibility of thinking the political and the concept of representation in the modern episteme.
The question then arises as to what happens to the anthropological claims
of the aesthetic (and therefore to it as a regulative discourse of the human)
when the "anthropological" no longer refers principally to the general form
of the human that is at once the ground and end of Kantian philosophy.
At least in common understandings of the term, the notion of an anthropology no longer assumes the universality of the form of the human but
describes and analyzes the highly differentiated forms of living that constitute the spectrum of possibilities of human being. Anthropology came to
designate the objects and procedures of a distinct disciplinary formation
that emerged in the 1860s as the study of what founding practitioner E. B.
Tylor terms "primitive culture" or what Franz Boas would later designate
"the primitive mind."[8] The emergence of a discipline devoted to the study
of culture, and in particular to the study of "primitive culture," consoli-
dated a division that had already discretely structured the aesthetic nar-

rative of development, even as the very concept of "culture" as a distinct aesthetic domain of human practice, that of self-cultivation (or *Bildung*), began to inform its own set of disciplinary practices, including literary criticism and art history.[9] That consolidation inaugurates a splintering of the idea of an unfolding, differentiating, but fundamentally unitary process of human self-cultivation in keeping with "final ends," even if initially—as in the work of Tylor—a historicist schema of stages of development continued to structure the concept of "primitive culture."

The task here is not to recapitulate the genealogy of the modern discipline of anthropology but to ask a number of more basic questions as a way of recasting and rethinking the ways in which aesthetics as an anthropology and as a regime of representation continues to regulate our thinking about the human, the political, and the racial. The discourse on the aesthetic directly and indirectly informed art practice and criticism across the terrain of European art throughout the nineteenth century, from Romanticism through to Symbolism and Realism. It gave shape to a notion of representation that determined not only the conceptions of mimesis in the realist novel and in successive schools of painting but also the more esoteric theories of the relation of part to whole that structured the idea of the symbol and its intricate relation to a political sphere in which the notion of representation was ever more dominant.[10] As Chapter 4 points out, it found material instantiation in the emerging pedagogical institutions that linked aesthetic cultivation to the formation of the citizen and became critical to the identification and education of colonial subjects as intermediaries within the structures of colonial governmentality. Not only the terms but even the underlying structures and assumptions of aesthetic philosophy live what we might call a casual afterlife in the least systematic statements of nineteenth-century thinkers, from Lord Macaulay's infamous judgment of the inferiority of Hindu and Sanskrit literatures to John Stuart Mill's remarks on the interest of children and Arabs in narrative forms as being symptomatic of their underdevelopment.[11]

The function of aesthetics as a key element in the network of discourses that regulated the conception and representation of the human raises the question of how its terms transform in relation to the explicit reframing of the idea of the human that anthropology undertakes in its study of the "primitive." It seems clear that an idea of development and cultivation initially framed in aesthetic terms continued to influence Tylor's conception of primitive culture and the evolution of human civilization, giving shape to the comparative framework within which he assigned both contemporary and historical peoples their distinct place in an overarching developmental schema.[12] The gradual emergence of a relativist approach to the diversity of human cultural practices, stemming from Johann Gottfried Herder and finding its first full disciplinary articulation in Franz Boas, clearly affects the idea of any possible universal standard for aesthetic value, resurrecting the problem of culturally different ideals of beauty that Kant had wrestled with in §17 of the Third Critique. There he resolved the impasse by distinguishing the empirical "normal idea" of beauty, which allows for cultural variation, from the ideal of beauty, which, in its emancipation from "sensuous charm," has regard only to "the form of finality" in its object.[13] If it is no longer possible to think of humanity as a whole governed by a single "rational idea" after anthropology's emergence as a distinct discipline, what becomes of the idea of the Savage in modernist reformulations of aesthetic theory? How does the aesthetic theory of modernism relate to and (re)structure itself around the disciplinary objects and practices of anthropology—that is, around an idea of the indigenous or the primitive as defined by a set of practices that are at once prior to and coeval with modernity? In turn, since aesthetics grounds its claim to be a universal anthropology on the idea of a general representative capacity that modernism and its aesthetic statements critique, can we map a correlated shift in the relation of representation to anthropology, or at least in aesthetic uses of anthropology? What then would become of the function of the Subaltern, which we have seen in the last chapter to mark a deconstructive relation to the representative projects of the state and the disciplines? Could the thinking of the Subaltern converge with an aesthetic theory critical of representation to suggest the outlines of a postcolonial or a race critical aesthetics?

The Aesthetic Taboo

The findings of "primitive" or "cultural anthropology" notoriously exerted their influence very broadly on Anglophone modernist writing, from T. S. Eliot's use of J. G. Frazer's *Golden Bough* in *The Wasteland*, through Ezra Pound's invocations of the Africanist Leo Frobenius, or J. M. Synge's training in French anthropological method under the Celticist Henri de Jubainville.[14] It is a similar commonplace that modernist visual art from Gauguin through Picasso and down to Surrealism was utterly transformed by its absorption of the forms and motifs of "primitive" artwork from ritual masks to bronze sculptures. Simultaneously, the work of predominantly French anthropologists—Bronisław Malinowski, Marcel Mauss, Lucien Lévy-Bruhl, Michel Leiris, and Claude Lévi-Strauss—was a for-

mative influence on French modernist writers and theorists like Georges
Bataille, André Breton, and Roger Caillois.[15] Possibly less well known is
the degree to which German culture of the late nineteenth and early twen-
tieth century was saturated with a similar interest in both "primitive culture" and myth. In its longer duration, this fascination stems from a range
of writers as various as Johann Jakob Bachofen (whose celebrated *Mother
Right [Mutterrecht*, 1861] was a crucial influence on—and disseminated
by—Friedrich Engels's writings on the family), Max Müller, or Edward
Westermarck, all of whose work was an interdisciplinary mix of mythology, philology, aesthetics, and anthropology. Interest was no less stimu-
lated by the German tradition of cultural anthropology and folklore that
descended from Herder and Alexander von Humboldt to Boas.[16]

The most famous and influential synthesis of this tradition in German
thought is Sigmund Freud's extended essay of 1913, *Totem and Taboo*. A
psychoanalytic extrapolation of the findings of primitive anthropology
from Tylor through Frazer and Boas, it is, more generally, a reading of
anthropology and myth for the light that he believed primitive cultural
practices shed on the etiology of mental life.[17] *Totem and Taboo* would remain a fundamental touchstone in his work and particularly in the later
metapsychological works like *Group Psychology and Ego Analysis* or *Moses
and Monotheism*. Through all these works, Freud located the primordial
origins of the modern Oedipus complex and of both infantile and neurotic
"totems and taboos" in the hypothetical primal horde that was dominated
by the tyrannical primal father. In Freud's myth of origins, the sons gather
to murder the primal father and their subsequent guilt becomes internal-
ized as a racial memory, displaced onto the totemic animal who is ritually
and recurrently sacrificed in an ambivalent expiation and commemoration
of the deed. Following Freud's guiding formulation that "ontogeny repeats
phylogeny," both the primal sense of guilt at their murder of the father
and their modes of expiation survive in the beliefs and practices of modern
children and in the neurotic compulsions of adults. These, he observes,
often take the form of superstitious convictions, ritual avoidances or "pro-
hibitions," and protective, quasi-magical behaviors.

In deriving apparently inexplicable contemporary conduct from "primitive" practices whose systematic if irrational foundations *Totem and Taboo*
purports to explain, Freud explicitly draws on the concept of the "survival"
developed first by Tylor and extended by Boas and other anthropologists.
The survival is a practice or belief that was initially part of a larger system
of magical or religious thought and that now only persists as a residual
fragment into "modern" times. Thus, apparently idiosyncratic neurotic or

infantile compulsions can be interpreted as survivals of a culturally shared
"racial memory" of those primordial systems of belief and ritual. Crucial
to Freud's thinking is a more or less Tylorian assumption that the practices of contemporaneous "primitive peoples" furnish evidence of those of
prehistoric and primordial humans, even if complicated by accretions of
ritual over time and the loss of any original memory of the primal crime.
Contemporary primitives—"savages or half-savages" (*TT*, 1)—are coeval
at once with modern civilizations and with their and our primordial forebears. They represent in themselves undeveloped "survivals," cross sections
of the past in our present epoch, "a well-preserved picture of an early stage
of our own development" (*TT*, 1). The difference is that whereas, by and
large, anthropologists had seen survivals as remnants of obsolete systems
of belief that were destined to wither away, Freud understands the primal
history of the race as something that continues to exert a determining
influence on modern consciousness as much as on primitive mentalities.
It operates as an unworked-through repressed stratum or unconscious element that continues to inform practices that range from neurotic compulsions to "those great social institutions, art, religion and philosophy" (*TT*,
73). The Savage thus occupies the same threshold space in *Totem and Taboo*
as in Kant's Third Critique. It stands at the point of origin for the dialectic between freedom or self-determination and universal accord that the
aesthetic regulates as it stands for Freud as that in which law emerges at a
stroke from the primal murder. The Savage is at once within the trajectory
of development and its excluded if defining moment. As Peter Fitzpatrick
puts it in his extensive commentary on the relation between Freud's myth
of origins and modern law: "Savagery may lend its violent force to law, but
it is law which constitutes and contains that force within itself. And whilst
savagery may provoke a civilizing law into being, it is law which delineates
that savagery by separating civilization from it."[18] The difference is that
for Freud, that threshold remains not a starting point that mankind has
left behind in its development but as an enduring moment of the modern,
manifest significantly in its pathologies, in the persisting affectability of
those subjected to the civilizing process.

Accordingly, much of *Totem and Taboo* is concerned with the origins and
practice of magic and with the forms of "primitive thought," categories
and classifications that Freud believes survive most evidently in infantile
thought and in neurotic compulsions. Magic is a "technique" that derives
from "the practical need for controlling the world," whether protectively
or proactively, and whose general mode of operation or "principle" Freud
defines, citing Tylor, as "mistaking an ideal connection for a real one"

(*TT*, 78–79). As a technique, magic operates either across distance through the principle of sympathy (in Frazer's terms, through imitation) or through touch or "contagion." As Freud recognizes, magic, in other words, occupies the axes of similarity and contiguity, "the two essential principles of processes of association" (*TT*, 83), that *The Interpretation of Dreams* (1900) had already identified in the dream logic that depends on condensation and contiguity, metaphor and metonymy.[19]

Since magical influence can be exerted by contact, whether actual or remotely produced by symbolic acts, the taboo serves to protect the sacralized object, whether through respect and awe or disgust and horror: The tabooed object is fundamentally the untouchable. Freud understands the taboo, which is simultaneously or alternately "sacred" and "unclean," to be the product of "an emotional ambivalence," one he sees as peculiarly manifest in the primitive mind and deducible from the love-hate relationship to the primal father (*TT*, 66–67). This ambivalence is the origin of the conscience and of the dread associated with its violation. Indeed, the fundamental traits of both magic and the taboo are projected in sublimated forms into the institutions of civilization: Where taboo is the origin for Freud of the superego and even of the Kantian categorical imperative, "which operates in a compulsive fashion and rejects any conscious motives" (*TT*, xiv), art originates as a sublimation of the mimetic impulses through which magic seeks to exert the power of similitude in warding off or influencing natural or human phenomena (*TT*, 90). Art, Freud claims, is the one domain of modern life that retains a sense of "the omnipotence of thoughts," achieving the realization of desire through illusion. Its primordial relation to magic remains active in it: "There can be no doubt that art did not begin as art for art's sake. It worked originally in the service of impulses which are for the most part extinct to-day. And among them we may suspect the presence of many magical purposes" (*TT*, 90).

Freud's instrumental and characteristically "philistine" assumptions about art—resting in large part on Salomon Reinach's reading of prehistoric cave paintings and their relation to supposed magical projections of the human will—would be difficult to reconcile with an aesthetic tradition that asserts the noninstrumental, disinterested quality of the artwork, as his somewhat polemical reference to "art for art's sake" indicates. Nonetheless, the complex that *Totem and Taboo* forges between magic, art, compulsion, and the taboo itself turns out to be surprisingly decisive for the unfolding of aesthetic theory in German thought, an unfolding that will return us to the question of magic and eventually to the topos of the cave paintings themselves.

Aura and Taboo

Freud's influence on the Frankfurt School's critical theory, which attempted to synthesize psychoanalysis methodologically with Marxism, is well known. Indeed, Freud's writings on primitive culture and on its survival in contemporary civilization saturate the aesthetic thought of both Walter Benjamin and Theodor Adorno, especially the metapsychological writings of the 1920s like *Group Psychology and the Analysis of the Ego* or *Civilization and Its Discontents* that draw so extensively on the arguments of *Totem and Taboo*. To a remarkable extent, we can trace the resonances of Freud's thinking through a complex or constellation of topoi in their work: myth, magic, compulsion—or the "spell" in Adorno's language—and, in particular, the concept of aura. Despite their interest in other theorists of myth or cultural anthropologists, tracking their engagement with Freud offers the "royal road" for any consideration of their relation to historical anthropology and ethnography.[20]

The traces of Benjamin's reading of Freud are clearest in his late aesthetic theory, written in the midst of his most intense engagement with Adorno and alongside the extended work on the *Arcades Project* that explicitly elaborates his notions of the collective unconscious, primitive survivals, and the phantasmagoria, or the contemporary magic of capitalism.[21] At the heart of Benjamin's aesthetic theory is his twofold meditation on the transformation—or "crisis"—of perception induced by modern technologies and mass consumption and by the concomitant effect of what he terms "the decay of aura" in "The Work of Art in the Age of Its Technological Reproducibility."[22] According to Benjamin, the aura of the traditional work of art is determined by two related conditions that stem from its uniqueness and particularity: its distance from the viewer and its untouchability. As he puts it succinctly, if somewhat enigmatically: "We define the aura . . . as the unique apparition of a distance, however near it may be" (WATR, 255). In the more or less contemporaneous "On Some Motifs in Baudelaire," he clarifies this apparent paradox of distance being a property of something near at hand by remarking: "The essentially distant is the unapproachable, and unapproachability is a primary quality of the ritual image."[23] Initially, the artwork is "an object of worship" (WATR, 256) originating in cult and ritual and, therefore, is essentially something that may not be approached or touched. In its origins, the artwork and its aura are thus cognate with the object of a taboo. Benjamin's terms here seem strikingly like a citation from Freud's *Totem and Taboo*, where the latter observes that "'taboo' has about it the sense of something unapproachable" (*TT*, 18).[24] Like any cultic object, the artwork succumbs to the taboo against touching of which its aura is the index. Indeed, the prototype of the aura or halo in this sense may be the light that surrounded Moses on his descent from Mount Sinai, venerable and untouchable in consequence of having been in the presence of the Lord. In this respect, the notion of aura intersects with the taboo on touching or approaching as well as on representation, forbidden in the Commandments with which Moses descended from Sinai.

I will return shortly to the complex ways in which the notion of aura mobilizes the contradictory complex of magic and art, similitude and contiguity, mimesis and its prohibition. For the moment it is sufficient to note that aura—as Freud's analysis of the taboo and its afterlife implied—belongs with a set of sublimating aesthetic metaphors whose function is the prohibition of precisely what they invoke. Thus taste, aesthetically the lowest of the senses insofar as it involves the dissolution of the object in the subject, gives rise to the concept-metaphor of Taste that is so central to aesthetic judgement, as if honoring the commandment "Thou shalt not taste." Similarly, the sense of "Tact" crucial to evaluation and the aesthetic order rests on the prohibition on actually touching the artwork. The emphasis placed on these prohibitive concept-metaphors is by no means age-old, either in the sphere of ritual or in that of art, but is intimately bound up with the emergence of the autonomous artwork that is the necessary counterpart of aesthetic theory itself. In the sphere of ritual, it is by no means clear that every cult object is embraced by a taboo on touching—the rich history of popular practices of healing and invocation by "contiguity," by touching the statue or relic, would belie that assumption. In the sphere of art, on the contrary, the reciprocal relation between the emergence of the autonomous work of art for reception in a Schillerian contemplative mode and the commodification of the artwork as the condition of its freedom from the patronage system culminates in what Benjamin calls "exhibition value" (WATR, 257), though far earlier than he allows. In that exhibition value—really the "exchange value" of a work of art that "can be sent here and there"—the aura of the work of art, according to Benjamin, gradually decays. A dialectical relation thus opens between the very condition of the auratic artwork as such—its autonomy—and its negation in the commodity form that it must assume in order to achieve that condition.

Although Benjamin nowhere notes that this contradiction and its consequent dialectic are constitutive of the auratic or autonomous work, commodification of the artwork is central to Benjamin's understanding of its ongoing transformation "in the age of its technological reproducibility." For Benjamin, the "decay of aura" is predicated on two phenomena that

radically undermine the "unique apparition of a distance." The first of
these is the emergence of the masses, or the urban crowd that is the social
manifestation of the commodification of human beings themselves in the
form of labor. This crowd, that in pressing in on and "jostling" the poet
Baudelaire confronts him with the perpetual experience of being touched,
gives rise to the decisive experience of urban shock and to the "the disintegration of the aura in immediate shock experience [*Chockerlebnis*]."[25]
Closeness is the very medium of the masses, and "*the desire of the present-
day masses to 'get closer' to things spatially and humanly*" is inseparable from
their "*overcoming each thing's uniqueness*" by embracing its reproducibility
(WATR, 255; italics in original): "The stripping of the veil from the object,
the destruction of the aura, is the signature of a perception whose 'sense
for sameness in the world' has so increased that, by means of reproduction,
it extracts sameness even from what is unique" (WATR, 255–56). The decay of aura and the emergence of the masses as the instruments of its decay
are thus equally predicated on the tendency under capitalism toward the
universalization of exchange or equivalence subjectively and objectively:
the fate of the masses, their own reduction to equivalence, is projected in
turn onto things, including the artwork that has fallen subject to reproduction and the laws of exchange.

The second phenomenon of capitalist modernity that brings about the
"destruction of aura" is that the effects of exchange and equivalence are
counterpointed by a corresponding will to penetrate the object that likewise destroys distance and brings things ever closer. Mass society thus
abolishes the "pathos of distance" of which Adorno wrote in his essay on
jazz.[26] If aura corresponds to magic, which affirms the unapproachability
of the tabooed or cult object, modern technologies of reproduction correspond to the work of the surgeon: "The surgeon represents the polar
opposite of the magician. The attitude of the magician, who heals a sick
person by laying-on of hands, differs from that of the surgeon, who makes
an intervention in the patient. The magician maintains the natural distance between himself and the person treated; more precisely, he reduces it
slightly by laying on his hands, but increases it greatly by his authority. The
surgeon does exactly the reverse; he greatly diminishes the distance from
the patient by penetrating the patient's body" (WATR, 263).[27] Benjamin
extends this analogy to the industrial process of the cinema that dismantles
action into discrete sequences and reassembles them in its montage: "Magician is to surgeon as painter is to cinematographer" (WATR, 263). The
mystique of the organic integrity of the artwork, its conformity to a sub-

jectively final end that its suspension within an ideal distance preserves as mere *Schein* (semblance), is thus abolished.

Both the abolition of distance and the profaning penetration of the object tend to destroy the residues of the cultic function of the art object in its origins. Like Freud, Benjamin assumes that the primitive work of art was "an instrument of magic" (WATR, 257): "Originally the embeddedness of an artwork in the context of tradition found expression in a cult. As we know, the earliest art works originated in the service of rituals—first magical, then religious. And it is highly significant that the artwork's auratic mode of existence is never entirely severed from its ritual function" (WATR, 256). The process of secularization that establishes the autonomy of the artwork separates it from its cultic function, as eighteenth-century aestheticians already discerned, but it retains those elements of its initial "cult value" that preserve its auratic quality: "Unapproachability is, indeed, a primary quality of the cult image; true to its nature, the cult image remains 'distant, however near it may be'" (WATR, 272n11). Unapproachability is a function of the uniqueness of the art object, a quality that determines the specific form of fetishism that attaches to the work and that requires the contemplative relation that aesthetics since Schiller had prescribed. We might question, then, whether aura is not in fact a relatively new phenomenon, a historical effect of the emancipation of art, rather than a remnant of the cultic function onto which Benjamin back-projects it. But in any case, the mode of contemplation proper to the emancipated artwork, which preserves the aura of the artwork precisely by not appropriating or "touching" it, is displaced in Benjamin's larger argument by the relation of "distraction" (*Zerstreuung*) that typifies the proletarian cinema-goer as consumer.[28]

Benjamin finds a model for distraction, which seeks to redeem the new mode of participation of the masses from the still familiar charge that it is merely the pursuit of diversion, in architecture. The experience of architecture—"the prototype of an artwork that is received in a state of distraction and through the collective"—takes place through a mode of perception that is both "optical" and, significantly, "tactile." The traditional visual mode of apprehension of the auratic artwork is supplemented by one of touch or "use": "On the tactile side, there is no counterpart to what contemplation is on the optical side. Tactile reception comes about not so much by way of attention as by way of habit" (WATR, 268). Against every formalist claim for the aesthetic destruction of habitual modes of perception in estrangement, Benjamin links the tactile formation of habit to the masses' capacity to master the new tasks "which face the human apparatus of perception at historical turning points," of which his moment was manifestly one (WATR, 268). The very casualness of the masses' relation to the reproducible work of art, by analogy with the everydayness of architectural space in use, accordingly constitutes a new relation of intimate indifference to the postauratic work. The capacity for reproduction, in destroying both the work's uniqueness and its distance from the masses, thus equally destroys any remaining cult value that has survived secularization. Insisting on that survival of cultic value, Benjamin dates the emancipation of art to the present, declaring that "technological reproducibility emancipates the work of art from its parasitical subservience to ritual" (WATR, 256).

In this transitional moment of auratic decay in the face of new technologies, Benjamin discerns an absolute demystification or disenchantment, driven by capitalism's technological innovation and relentless rationalization, of what remains of the magical and its taboos in the work of art. These claims provoked some of Adorno's critiques of the political claims of the essay, to which I will return momentarily. Meanwhile, the disenchantment of the aura by the development of capitalist technologies conforms surprisingly well to the emancipatory trajectory away from the primitive or Savage in its subordination to enchantment and toward the Subject of freedom that I argue structures the developmental and regulative narrative of Enlightenment aesthetic theory.

Aura thus becomes the residual mark of a pre-Enlightenment human condition of heteronomy, or subjection to external forces, that Benjamin elsewhere nominates "fate." As such, it ceases to define the contemplative or "liberal" (*frei*) relation to the aesthetic object that in turn makes it a "common property" in the double sense of an object whose essence is inappropriable and of a subject whose aesthetic judgment formally corresponds to that of all possible human subjects. The untouchability of the aesthetic object, which was the mark of its uniqueness and incapacity for consumption in use, becomes merely a remnant of mythic thought. In consequence of that reconception of the auratic artwork, Benjamin imposes a taboo on the taboo: Where Freud holds that the mental structures of the "savage or half-savage" survive in the pathologies of the modern subject, Benjamin regards their survival as a residue to be overcome in the name of a progressive emancipation.[29]

Benjamin could, of course, stand accused here of short-circuiting the dialectic, envisaging a mere inversion of the terms of the critique of reification. Massification becomes immediately—without mediation—the condition of a restored and positively valued proximity, even in the form of commodification. The endless reproduction of things for exchange paradoxically restores social relations among humans and between humans and demystified things. Moreover, his argument seems so strikingly at odds with other of his more or less contemporaneous formulations—including his emphasis elsewhere on the auratic quality of artworks and profane things in general—that it may feel at moments that the essay were written *à contrecoeur*, as if Benjamin in the effort to engage the cultural struggle against Nazism were brushing himself against his own grain.[30] The very passages in which he describes aura—which he clearly valued enough to draw almost verbatim from the earlier "Little History of Photography" where aura is far less negatively evaluated—are, as many note, among the most lyrical and affecting, even auratic, passages of the essay.[31] More significantly, the very form of the argument seems to fly in the face of his own critiques of historicism, in both the late theses of "On the Concept of History" and the *Arcades Project*, devoted to "a historical materialism which has annihilated within itself the idea of progress."[32] The "Work of Art" essay may then be one outer reach of the ellipse that Benjamin's mature work constantly described between cultural Marxism and theologically inspired reflection. But its peculiarly strenuous antagonism to the auratic is as much drawn along in the wake of idealist aesthetics and its developmental narrative of disenchantment as it is burdened by its failure to grasp fully the contradiction internal to the artwork: that the auratic work is simultaneously a commodity form, already subject in principle to the laws of exchange even before its conditions of production were transformed by new techniques of reproduction.

The Dialectic of Magic and Aura

Adorno's initial response to the draft of "The Work of Art in the Age of Its Technological Reproducibility" offers a version of all of the critiques sketched above and in some ways anticipates all of the criticisms that Benjamin's essay would face. In a letter dated March 18, 1936, Adorno writes:

> I now find it somewhat disturbing—and here I can see a sublimated remnant of certain Brechtian themes—that you have now rather casually transferred the concept of the magical aura to the "autonomous work of art" and flatly assigned a counter-revolutionary function to the latter. I do not need to assure you just how aware I am of the magical element that persists in the bourgeois work of art. . . . However, it seems to me that the heart of the autonomous work of art does not

itself belong to the dimension of myth—forgive my topical manner of speaking—but is inherently dialectical, that is, compounds within itself the magical element with the sign of freedom.[33]

Though Adorno too passes over the contradiction that the "sign of freedom" in the artwork is inseparable from its commodity form, the pertinence of his critique is hard to gainsay. Benjamin does indeed not merely perceive the residual trace of the magical or cultic function in the auratic, but he effectively reduces the auratic to the magical. Affirming, to the contrary, the artwork's dialectical nature, Adorno is no less trenchant in his criticism of Benjamin's hypostatization of a revolutionary proletarian subject, his positing of a direct relation between the transformation of perception in "distraction" and the political potential it might embody. Adorno goes on: "If you legitimately interpret technical progress and alienation in a dialectical fashion, without doing the same in equal measure for the world of objectified subjectivity, then the political effect of this is to credit the proletariat (as the cinema's subject) directly with an achievement which, according to Lenin, it can only accomplish through the theory introduced by intellectuals as dialectical subjects, although they belong themselves to the sphere of works of art which you have already consigned to Hell."[34]

As his reference to "the magical element that persists in the bourgeois work of art" suggests, Adorno's work from *Dialectic of Enlightenment* to *Aesthetic Theory* occupies a very similar terrain of thinking about the relation of art to its magical antecedents, especially in relation to mimesis and aura. No less saturated with references to *Totem and Taboo* than Benjamin's essay, his work is more explicit in its borrowings and engages quite extensively with a range of other anthropological works. Adorno's aesthetic theory, often assumed to be free of the esoteric reference points that form a kind of "red thread" through Benjamin's work, is in fact as persistently in dialogue with the anthropology of primitive culture, magic, and sorcery as it is with the better-known issue of "myth" that the *Dialectic of Enlightenment* takes on. The invocation of magic, however, moves Adorno in a rather different direction.

For Adorno, the critical function of psychoanalysis lay in the effort of theory to defetishize the subject's relation to the mystified world of "administered society." In that respect, he was generally sympathetic to Benjamin's larger project, believing it to be indispensable to understanding what each called the "phantasmagoria" of capitalist commodity culture and thus a major elaboration of Marx's chapter on commodity fetishism. Benjamin's "Work of Art" essay is a fragment of that common project and the decay of aura part of his complex address, composed at once of fascination and repulsion, to the phantasmagoric scene. Nonetheless, Adorno constantly returns to that essay in later work and with increasing force critiques it in the name of a dialectical preservation of aura. His references to it in *Aesthetic Theory* are characteristically caustic:

> The simple antithesis between the auratic and the mass-produced work, which for the sake of simplicity neglected the dialectic of the two types, became the booty of a view of art that takes photography as its model and is no less barbaric than the view of the artist as creator. . . . What slips through the wide mesh of this theory . . . is the element opposed to the cultic contexts that motivated Benjamin to introduce the concept of aura in the first place, that is, *that which moves into the distance* and is critical of the ideological superficies of life.[35]

Adorno's critique of "the simplification that made the essay on reproduction so popular" (*AT*, 56) could be summed up in the request he made of Benjamin in the same letter: "*more* dialectics."[36] As he proceeds, it becomes clear that the dialectical approach is not to be confined to the dialectic "between the auratic and the mass-produced work" or between artwork and commodity. Rather, Adorno's account of art and aura entailed a dialectical if speculative account of the origination of the work of art in primitive magical practice.

Adorno does not reproduce the tale whereby the practice of magic is superseded historically, first by the work of art and then by technology or science, as both Freud and Benjamin (in the "Work of Art" essay) tend to do. Rather, in his account of the "origin of the work of art," art emerges from and against the primitive practices of magic that represent the primarily mimetic or, as Freud puts it, "sympathetic" warding off of an overwhelmingly threatening and irrational nature. Freud had understood magic, in keeping with his anthropological sources, to be an instrument of wishful thinking, seeking to effect in the world whatever the subject willed. Art, in turn, is an active survival of that impulse: "In only a single field of our civilization has the omnipotence of thoughts been retained, and that is in the field of art. Only in art does it still happen that a man who is consumed by desires performs something resembling the accomplishment of those desires and that what he does in play produces emotional effects—thanks to artistic illusion—just as though it were something real. People speak with justice of the 'magic of art' and compare artists to magicians" (*TT*, 90). Committed as he remains to the Schillerian notion of aesthetic *Schein* or semblance—the aesthetic appearance that does not pretend to be or affect reality—Adorno makes short of work of Freud's simpleminded and habitual reduction of art to the illusory satisfaction of desire or to its sublimation. Yet his critique accommodates the force of the impulse to compensate. Alluding to this passage from *Totem and Taboo* in *Aesthetic Theory*, he remarks:

> Expression is a priori imitation. Latently implicit in expression is the trust that by being spoken or screamed all will be made better: This is a rudiment of magic, faith in what Freud polemically called "the omnipotence of thought." Yet expression is not altogether circumscribed by the magic spell. That it is spoken, that distance is thus won from the trapped immediacy of suffering, transforms suffering just as screaming diminishes unbearable pain. . . . Stumbling along behind its reification, the subject limits that reification by means of the mimetic vestige, the plenipotentiary of an undamaged life in the midst of mutilated life, which subverts the subject to ideology. (*AT*, 117)

The historical dialectic of magic and artistic expression here embraces an astonishing temporal arc, from participation in the archaic spell, even if it is no more than a survival or relic of the past stranded in our present, to the reification of the present-day subject of ideology. What subtends that arc is, of course, the ahistoricity of the "pathological subject," subordinated to nature and necessity in "the trapped immediacy of suffering." Already in repeating the wishful—or hopeful—gesture of magic, which is seen as a repetition or mimesis of what the subject fears or is hurt by, even the rudimentary artwork introduces a distance between the pathological subject and its subordination, whether to nature or to the "second nature" of ideology. This distance is at once spatial, invoking the notion of the sorcerer's circle that the spell "circumscribes," and temporal, introducing an irrevocable mediation of suffering: "What has once been said never fades away completely, neither the evil nor the good, neither the slogan of 'the final solution' nor the hope of reconciliation" (*AT*, 117).

Adorno thus simultaneously distinguishes art from magic and from the pathological; it is neither an illusory wish-fulfillment nor a mere reflex scream of pain. Precisely through the moment of auratic distance that Benjamin dismisses, art cancels and preserves (*aufhebt*) its magical "antecedents." It introduces a moment of the rational—of mediation—into the supposedly irrational mimesis or "sympathetic" practice of magic, but it retains a moment of mimetic play in the midst of a rationalized world:

"Art's disavowal of magical practices—its antecedents—implies participation in rationality. That art, something mimetic, is possible in the midst of rationality, and that it employs its means, is a response to the faulty irrationality of the rational world as an overadministrated world" (*AT*, 53). In contradistinction to Benjamin, Adorno's art does not simply assume the tools of rationalization as the means to furthering disenchantment. It preserves and opposes the irrational moment of rationality itself.

Art may have originated as a kind of mimetic homeopathy that obeyed what Freud describes as the process of association, a "sympathetic magic" whose "principles" are "similarity and contiguity"—likeness or imitation and touch or contagion (*TT*, 83). But art is, as the *Dialectic of Enlightenment* puts it, a deinstrumentalized magic precisely by virtue of its status as mere *Schein*, "aesthetic semblance":

> The work of art still has something in common with enchantment: it
> posits its own, self-enclosed area, which is withdrawn from the context
> of profane existence, and in which special laws apply. Just as in the
> ceremony the magician first of all marked out the limits of the area
> where the sacred powers were to come into play, so every work of art
> describes its own circumference which closes it off from actuality. This
> very renunciation of influence, which distinguishes art from magical
> sympathy, retains the magical heritage all the more surely. It places the
> pure image in contrast to animate existence, the elements of which it
> absorbs. It is in the nature of the work of art, or aesthetic semblance, to
> be what the new, terrifying occurrence became in the primitive's magic:
> the appearance of the whole in the particular. In the work of art that
> duplication still appears by which the thing appeared as spiritual, as the
> expression of *mana*. That constitutes its aura. As an expression of totality, art lays claim to the dignity of the absolute.[37]

With great economy this passage condenses the whole tradition of idealist aesthetics within which Adorno continues to work. The Kantian disinterest of the aesthetic work—its finality without ends—that lies in its "renunciation of influence" makes of the artwork, in contradistinction to the spell, a "pure image," a Schillerian "aesthetic semblance." Its function is "duplication," the moment of reflective *Vorstellung* in which—as in Hegel—the human can appear as its own representation, by way of the distinction of the spiritual moment from its mere animate being in nature. Thus, the formerly terrifying manifestation that the magical invocation summons becomes the symbolist particular in which the whole is translucent: Aura lies in the capacity of the artwork to produce the human as the subject distanced from its extra-historical (rather than prehistorical) pathological subordination.

The aesthetic distance that preserves aura is nomothetic, insofar as the term *nomos* originally denoted "a constitutive act of spatial ordering," a measure that divides. The original aesthetic gesture is already a judgment (*Urteil*) of the world that divides (*teilt*) it between the human and the natural, "as in the ceremony [when] the magician first of all marked out the limits of the area where the sacred powers were to come into play."[38] The appropriation and determination of a specific proper space or "circumference" for the artwork is critical to the institution of that distance in which it can become and remain auratic. Though absent from almost all the anthropological texts that he cites on the subject of magic, this concept-metaphor of drawing a magical circle plays a peculiar and fundamental role in Adorno's aesthetic theory. The image of the sorcerer or magician beginning by drawing a protective spell round himself or his petitioner before beginning to summon the spirits or demons has become so iconic in Western popular culture as to seem almost definitive of the practice of magic, but it is not especially significant in the sources Adorno cites.[39]

However, one likely source for Adorno's consistent assertion that the drawing of a circle was fundamental to primitive magic underscores how formative for him such conceptions were. An aside in a brief essay on Ernst Bloch's *Geist der Utopie* recalls an object that drew his fascination in childhood: "The dark brown volume of over 400 pages [Bloch's book], printed on thick paper, promised something of what one hopes for from medieval books, something I had felt, as a child at home, in the calf's leather *Heldenschatz* [Treasury of the heroic], a belated eighteenth-century book of magic full of abstruse instructions many of which I am still pondering."[40] The temporal structure of this brief and somewhat enigmatic anecdote is in itself symptomatic, moving from the youthful Adorno's reading of Bloch around 1921 back to the boy's naive fascination for a "belated" work of magic and forward to his continuing "pondering" of that work. The archaic fascination of the child is still at work in the theoretical musings of the adult. As Adorno remarks toward the end of the essay, "Like all thought worthy of the name, Bloch's thrives on the edge of failure, in close proximity to sympathy for the occult."[41] Occult Johannes Staricius's *Geheimnisvoller Heldenschatz oder Der vollständige ägyptische Magische Schild* (Mysterious treasury of the heroic or complete Egyptian magic shield) (1750) certainly is. Claiming on its black-letter title page to be "*voll wunderwürdiger Verborgenheiten und reicher Schätze*" (full of marvelous hidden things and rich treasures) and to be "*genau aus der Pergamenthand-schrift einer Klosterbibliothek*" (accurately copied from the parchment manu-script in a monastery library), the Gothic text is a compendium of spells, mostly of a folkloric nature but including some for summoning up spirits. A number of the latter diagram the required movement of the magician through the room and the cruciform protective space it circumscribes — the *Kreis* (circle) that either wards against the appearance of demons or binds spirits to appear in human rather than fearsome form and to do no harm to body or soul.[42] In this curious text from his childhood, we find richly exemplified the peculiar relation that Adorno later invokes between the magical effort to exert power over the world and the fear that attends both that world and the exercise of power itself.

Magic thus occupies a field of tension between the fear of the subject utterly subjected to necessity and the unknown in nature and the same subject's will to exert power over that nature or, at the least, to ward off the danger of its unknown forces. Magic represents not simply an irrational, superstitious response to the overwhelming state of force or unfreedom that the pathological human inhabits but the irrational kernel of rational-ity itself. Magic is not merely representation or mimesis; it is "a praxis meant to influence nature" (*AT*, 139). As Mauss succinctly puts it, magic is performative in nature: "Rites are eminently effective; they are creative; they *do* things."[43] The magician thus stands at the threshold between mi-mesis and science out of which the dialectic of Enlightenment emerges. Science's rationalizing relation to the world unfolds precisely in time with its abandonment of the mimetic element that was the core of magic's op-eration through similitude: "Reason and religion deprecate and condemn the principle of magic enchantment. . . . Nature must no longer be influ-enced by approximation, but mastered by labor."[44] This implies also the inadequacy of Freud's one-sided identification of magic with the illusion of "the omnipotence of thought": "Like science, magic pursues aims, but seeks to achieve them by mimesis—not by progressively distancing itself from its object. It is not grounded in the 'sovereignty of ideas,' which the primitive, like the neurotic, is said to ascribe to himself; there can be no 'over-valuation of mental processes as against reality' where there is no radical distinction between thoughts and reality. The 'unshakeable con-fidence in the possibility of world domination' which Freud anachronisti-cally ascribes to magic, corresponds to realistic world domination only in terms of a more skilled science."[45] The urge to "world domination" unfolds out of only one side of magic—its will to exert influence on the world. Its other, mimetic dimension is what art retains.

An alternative dialectic, that of art rather than science or enlightenment, unfolds here. Art emerges from magic precisely in relinquishing that dimension of the magical performance that seeks to "influence nature" while retaining a vestige of the mimetic impulse. Artworks originally "shared in a praxis meant to influence nature, separated from this praxis in the early history of rationality, and renounced the deception of any real influence" (*AT*, 127). Adorno's logic critiques Freud's account and rewrites and reverses Benjamin's account of the survival of the cultic dimension in the auratic artwork. Insofar as it is mimesis without a practical function, imitation without ends, art actually separates itself from or exceeds any remaining subordination to cult. This, not just its recession into tabooed space, is what preserves its aura: "Aura is not only—as Benjamin claimed—the here and now of the artwork, it is whatever goes beyond its factual givenness, its content; one cannot abolish it and still want art. Even demystified artworks are more than what is literally the case" (*AT*, 45).

Still, the movement of the dialectic immediately takes up the contrary dimension of the artwork, its participation in rationality that culminates in the reduction of every thing to equivalence or exchange: "The 'exhibition value' that, according to Benjamin, supplants 'cult value' is an *imago* of the exchange process" (*AT*, 45). As we have seen, the price of art's autonomy is its commodification and subordination not only to exchange but also to the mediation of the equivalence of all subjects in the name of a premature universality. Adorno goes beyond this insight, however: Art is permeated with rationality, which is the mark of its form and of its techniques, and in the movement by which it disavows magical functions it also embraces and retains the tendency of magic, fulfilled in science, to reduce its objects to equivalence. Science oversees the transformation of magic's "specific representations"—its substitution of the similar or analogous for the thing to be influenced or protected—into the nonspecific representations that prepare the way "for the fungible—universal exchangeability."[46] But aesthetic philosophy, the science of the auratic artwork, transforms the sensuous particularity of the mimetic artwork into the image of a universal equivalence of subjects that is the end of its narrative of representation. This is for Adorno the defining limit of aesthetics heretofore, its inability to grasp at the same time art's negation of identity:

> Art is a stage in the process of what Max Weber called the disenchantment of the world, and it is entwined with rationalization; this is the source of all art's means and methods of production; technique that disparages its ideology inheres in this ideology as much as it threatens

it because art's magical heritage stubbornly persisted throughout art's transformations. Yet art mobilizes technique in an opposite direction than does domination. The sentimentality and debility of almost the whole tradition of aesthetic thought is that it has suppressed the dialectic of rationality and mimesis immanent to art. . . . The aporia of art, pulled between regression to literal magic or surrender of the mimetic impulse to thinglike rationality, dictates its laws of motion; the aporia cannot be eliminated. (*AT*, 54)

That aporia spells not the end of aura but precisely the "conflict" by which the auratic artwork challenges the very conditions that produced that "sense for sameness in the world" that for Benjamin was the condition of its withering.

Precisely by virtue of that moment that is "an afterimage of enchantment" rather than a mere commodity, art confronts the spell of a "disenchanted" world that takes the form of the fetishism of commodities:

Art is motivated by a conflict: Its enchantment, a vestige of its magical phase, is constantly repudiated as unmediated sensual immediacy by the progressive disenchantment of the world, yet without its ever being possible finally to obliterate this magical element. Only in it is art's mimetic character preserved, and its truth is the critique that, by its sheer existence, it levels at a rationality that has become absolute. Emancipated from its claim to reality, the enchantment is itself part of enlightenment: Its semblance disenchants the disenchanted world. This is the dialectical ether in which art today takes place. The renunciation of any claim to truth by the preserved magical elements marks out the terrain of aesthetic semblance and aesthetic truth. . . . Though it will not acknowledge it, for the disenchanted world the fact of art is an outrage, an afterimage of enchantment, which it does not tolerate. (*AT*, 58)

Art's resistance to the rationalized world, at the very edge of its failure, lies in its capacity to "cancel the spell that this world casts by the overwhelming force of its appearance, the fetish character of the commodity" (*AT*, 58–59). This notion of the "spell" of modernity is one that Adorno mobilizes with striking regularity both to denote the reifying power of contemporary capitalism and to designate the residual critical function of the artwork that persists in the trace of the magical that it perforce retains. The auratic—the "qualitatively modern"—work of art, precisely by its distance, or its "step back" from the empirical world, dispels the spell or—to echo the *Communist Manifesto*—the "sorcery" of an ideology that has taken the place of a fearsome and mystified nature (*AT*, 145).

In the dialectic of enlightenment, rationalization reverts to unreason: "The more the machinery of thought subjects existence to itself, the more blind its resignation in reproducing existence. Hence enlightenment returns to mythology, which it never knew how to elude."[47] The meaning of the spell also reverses, being no longer the performance that protects the subject but that which subjugates and entrances humans and things in the reifying power of domination: "It is not merely that domination is paid for by the alienation of men from the objects dominated: with the objectification of spirit, the very relations of men—even those of the individual to himself—were bewitched. The individual is reduced to the nodal point of the conventional responses and modes of operation expected of him. Animism spiritualized the object, whereas industrialism objectifies the spirits of men."[48] The "spell" (*Bann*) is the subjection of the modern subject to a "fate" that returns in the form of a necessity imposed on the individual by a thoroughly rationalized world. As Adorno puts it in *Negative Dialectics*, "Human beings, individual subjects, are under a spell now as ever. The spell is the subjective form of the world spirit, the internal force of its primacy over the external process of life. Men become that which negates them, that with which they cannot cope."[49] In the dialectic of rationality, the ineluctable force of "things as they are" takes the place of an alien and dominating nature, assuming an absoluteness no less terrorizing than myth itself: "The mythical spell has been secularized into compactly dovetailed reality. The reality principle, which the prudent heed in order to survive in it, captures them as black magic: they are unable and unwilling to cast off the burden, for the magic hides it from them and makes them think it is life."[50]

Adorno's conception of magic in such passages is more than a mere metaphor. Where Freud posits the permanent recurrence of psychic formations established primordially in human history and sees art merely as a sublimation of primal compulsions or contemporary neurotic traits, Adorno recasts that repetition—the survival of the irrational—as a dialectical critique of rationalization by what the latter has expunged. Like Benjamin, he assumes the origins of art in magical instrumentality, but he insists on the difference in art that remains after its cultic function has been exhausted: "Art is what remains after the loss of what was supposed to exercise a magical, and later a cultic, function" (*AT*, 127). This "cultic function" is not merely exhausted by technological advances; it is what art renounces in order to emancipate itself from magic. While initially artworks "shared in a praxis meant to influence nature," in their distantiation from magic they "separated from this praxis in the early history of rationality, and renounced the deception of any real influence" (*AT*, 139).

Accordingly, as Adorno puts it in the section of *Aesthetic Theory* on the origins of art (perhaps the richest evidence of his ambivalent debt to historical anthropology), art is both defined by and derives its remaining critical effect from its constitutive refusal of instrumentality: "An irrevocable necessity of art and preserved by it, aesthetic comportment contains what has been belligerently excised from civilization and repressed, as well as the human suffering under the loss, a suffering already expressed in the earliest forms of mimesis. This element should not be dismissed as irrational. Art is in its most ancient relics too deeply permeated with rationality. . . , What marks aesthetic comportment as irrational according to the criteria of dominant rationality is that art denounces the particular essence of a *ratio* that pursues means rather than ends" (*AT*, 330). Homeopathically, a magical residue in art in which rationality retains the memory of its irrational antecedents confronts the reifying magic of a rationality that has forgotten or disavows its irrationality. Aura, the effect of a distance, is for Adorno that in which the critical power of serious art is preserved against the brutal factuality of the existent. In this affirmation, Adorno supplies the "speculative theory" that breaks the spell of the "crossroads of magic and positivism," the "bewitched" place that he believed Benjamin's work occupied in the late 1930s.[51] At the same time, he restores to the concept of aura that uncanny dimension that Benjamin himself so strikingly figured in the "gaze" that nonhuman things return to the one who perceives them.[52] In this auratic reanimation of the thing, a residual magical projection still seeks to liberate phenomena from the cold grip of their reification. Magic is redeemed precisely insofar as the longings it embodied retain a redemptive force.

But what is it to be redeemed if the price of redemption is to be consigned irredeemably to a place of deficit with regard to the human? There where at the opening of *Black Skin, White Masks* Fanon discovered the racialized being as "the 'not-yet-human,'" magic continues to figure the response of the "mutilated," the ur-condition of the human figured as an aboriginal (and therefore *ano*riginal) damage, suffered even prior to that which rationalization inevitably comes to inflict. The condition of the primitive remains that of need, lack, and terror, of subjection to an as yet unmastered and uncomprehended world, the correlative of the perpetual condition of scarcity in which capitalist political economy perforce imagines both its antecedents and its marginalized sectors. The arts of the primitive—they are still "not yet" Art—can only be those determined by an abject state of heteronomy, akin to that which for Adorno famously haunts the origins of jazz, "the domesticated body in bondage."[53] As Denise Ferreira da Silva has shown, the trajectory that leads from the heteronomy of the Savage—subject to the laws of necessity—to the racialized body—subject to the "state of necessity" of suspended law—is fundamentally ahistorical: It is a conceptual folding of the one upon the other.[54] Similarly, in Adorno the primitive, again like jazz, is not historical. The appearance of the archaic in jazz indexes the "mutilated instinctual structure" where the unfreedom of commodity culture appears in the faux spontaneity by which the consuming public—"whose sovereign freedom of choice is legitimated by their social status"—mimics the "original and primitive" only by repeating its subjection.[55] However, the oppressed from whom the forms and inventions of jazz have been appropriated have only the lesson of their own mutilation and their "identification with their own oppression" to offer the not yet fully mutilated liberal subject. Even the regression that the desire for the primitive appears to represent is the return not to an origin but to a very contemporary, colonial state of domination that reproduces itself in commodity culture.[56] Adorno's language of regression remains revealing. The difference between him and Fanon, facing the call of "a magical Negro culture," is manifest: For the latter, it is not out of subjection to necessity but out of "the necessities of my struggle" that he chooses "the method of regression."[57]

The locus of the magical, in other words, the space of the primitive, is thus still distributed between art's potential "regression to literal magic" and its status as an analogical remainder, two directions along the axis of development that so insistently, if immanently, propel the law of aesthetic form for Adorno (*AT*, 54). The aesthetic is properly the historical, defined precisely by its "separation" from an ur-historical primitive that turns out to be the a-historical. Indeed, it still generates the historical from the threshold condition of prehistory by inaugurating the development of the human out of the Savage though reflective representation, as if under the sway of Kant's inaugural moment of *Vorstellung*. The primitive's magic may linger as resistance to necessity once it has been appropriated into the aesthetic, but it never attains to the self-doubling, reflective awareness that defines the human. The primitive never escapes the conditions of an anthropology that, even at its most enlightened, continues to divide the world between having and being, between those who have culture, in the sense of a reflective and historical capacity for self-representation, and those who *are* culture, for whom culture is a state without outside and without history.

For all his commitment to preserving the irrational moment in the aesthetic against the dead hand of reason-as-domination, Adorno only invokes the magical as the substrate of art's resistance to its complete rationalization. He thus appropriates what he assumes to be the primitive as example while liquidating—to use his recurrent term—the human cultures for which magic may denominate the outlines of an alternative epistemology and aesthetic, the possibilities of whose autonomous unfolding he nowhere considers. So-called primitive culture, for which magic is the figure, becomes itself no more than a figure, a projection of a state of unchanging or "perennial" stasis onto the paralyzed condition of the modern subject under the "spell" of ideology and of technological domination. Quite as much as in Kant's Third Critique, analogy here furnishes the bridge from the lower to the higher: As organic nature was to the work of art for Kant, so the primitive is to art for Adorno. "Magic" remains a name for the domain of human subordination to necessity, from which art separates itself in order to fulfill its own concept and inaugurate its own essential historicity. Critical aesthetic theory thus reproduces the logic in which, as we have seen, the foundations of aesthetic thought are lodged: the opposition of the subject of culture to the pathological subject, the human creature subordinated to the state of necessity.

For Adorno, "primordial history" (*Urgeschichte*) is not, as in Freud, a transhistorical template for modern consciousness but the necessary inaugural moment of the dialectic of an enlightenment to which it remains external. Just as much as Benjamin or even Kant, he relegates the practitioners of the magical to the threshold of history itself, where history is understood as the dialectical movement of domination and freedom. The perennial denizens of a-history never manage to escape their peculiar incorporation as the excluded of the fundamental historical schema of aesthetics, the transition from a state of necessity in which they reside, through the state of domination to the ideal state of freedom or reconciliation.[58] Insofar as the state of necessity is that which defines the Savage as pathological subject, the aesthetic remains not contingently but immanently a racial schema. It is not the product of any contingent distaste for, say, black music or performance, for indigenous ornament or aboriginal painting. Rather, it is an intrinsic effect of the fundamental distributions of the human that aesthetic philosophy institutes and reproduces at every moment. Even at their most critical, even with the deepest sympathy for and insight into "damaged life" and "the tradition of the oppressed," both Adorno and Benjamin remain within the enclosure that both enlightenment and the dialectic establish, whose threshold divides the Savage into the latent or proto-human and the outcast, the being discarded to the realm of mere affectability. They think, therefore, with the immanently racial grain of the aesthetic, rather than thinking at or across its limit.

The End of Representation

What follows is not so much a conclusion to this chapter or to this book but the unfolding of two distinct sets of observation in the spirit of opening.

First, I argue throughout this book that an "aesthetic anthropology," in establishing the grounds of common or public sense, founded modernity's racial regime of representation in the assumption of a universal form of the human. In so doing, it regulated the racial judgment of humanity along a developmental axis that divided the subject subjected to nature—to gratification, fear, and desire—from the reflective subject of aesthetic judgment. This aesthetic thus anticipated and shaped the form of the modern political sphere of representation; it also inaugurated a mode of pedagogical formation of the subject of representation. That pedagogical formation continues through what we still denominate the humanities, those disciplines that Kant subsumed under philosophy. In so doing, Kant gave to philosophy the task of critiquing superstition and dogma in the name of an enlightened *Mündigkeit* (maturity/autonomy). More consequentially, he entrusted to the humanities the critique of those disciplines (religion, medicine, and law) whose instrumentality for the state made their practitioners no more than *Werkzeuge* (tools) whose thinking was necessarily constrained by their service to domination. The critical subject, whose exemplary model is the Kantian critical philosopher, the disinterested subject as spectator, prefigures the model citizen that "aesthetic education" will be charged with forming.[59]

From one angle, Adorno's *Aesthetic Theory* could be read as the last gasp of that critical subject as of the whole tradition of aesthetic philosophy on whose inaugural moments these essays focus. Almost relentlessly, *Aesthetic Theory* extends and performs the work of the critique of instrumentality, of domination, and the "administered society" that has proven to be the end of enlightenment. It does so precisely by marking the incapacity of the aesthetic to fulfill any longer—either in its formal capacities or in its exemplary prefiguration of political freedom—the function of representation that an older tradition had defined as its domain. In the dissolution of that representative capacity, as in the decay of aura, the artwork of modernity can no longer counteract the collapse or regression of the subject under the "spell" of an immediate relation to the reconstituted sovereign power of the "overadministrated world." On the contrary, the artwork itself either simulates the effects of domination in the mass-produced commodities of the culture industry or it withdraws into an ever-more restricted circle from which it maintains its "magical" banning of heteronomy. Deprived of its self-legitimating function as the stand-in for a universality and a freedom that had yet to be realized and that it claimed to prefigure, the aesthetic and its exemplary works fall apart into a condition of mutual redundancy. What remains of an aesthetic theory without a formative function is its repetitive protest against the conditions of its own desuetude. What remains of the autonomous artwork and of its anticipatory representation of freedom and universality is the perpetual assertion of its autonomy in the form of an almost obligatory investigation and reconstitution of the terms of its own emergence. The mimetic element that remains to it is the repetition of the inaugural circumscription by which the work excises itself from the world.

It is not only aura but the pedagogical function of the humanities in the educational apparatus that has entered into its decay. The regime of representation that once sought to legislate the formation of the subject survives only in the automatisms of a pedagogy whose compulsive performance of the routines of aesthetic education marks all the more plangently its loss of social use value. The only coherent opposition that a critical aesthetic can pose to the conditions of domination that have dispensed with it is the proclamation, in a defiant resurrection of the slogans of *l'art pour l'art*, of the value of the useless. Its protest only confirms the redundancy to which it has already been consigned: "Expression, the true bearer of aesthetic protest, is overtaken by the might against which it protests."[60] At best, that redundancy is a distorted image of and a refusal to endorse the disposability of an economically discarded humanity that is likewise expelled from the consideration of the humanities. The illiberal corporate university can quite easily and brutally dispense with what was for Kant the critical and is now the traditional function of the humanities, producing subjects for the state. Serviceability and adaptation rather than autonomy and critical thinking are what best serve the neoliberal economy. And yet, their function in decay and their survival in the corporate institution hard to justify, the humanities persist in the material forms and protocols of the university, in the shape of the classroom as of the curriculum, and continue to serve at least to mask if not to legitimate the unexhausted agenda of race. The regime of representation continues to perform its work of differentiating the proper human subjects of freedom as capacity from the objects of necessity and scarcity in the new neoliberal logic of disposability.

Adorno's and Benjamin's aesthetic theories quite lucidly anticipated these conditions of the neoliberal state that has discarded the biopolitical care of the subject in the name of a new regime of accumulation. There, the subject is again exposed to the state of necessity, incorporated only by the compulsions of need, fear, and desire and subjected to the sovereign power of a perpetual state of exception. The pathological is a generalized condition of subjecthood now, if to varying degrees of violent subjection or willing conformity, in face of the increasingly explicit dismissal of even that conception of autonomy whose real meaning was already found in the universal fungibility of equivalence. Now, if ever, it may be true—if not quite in the sense Adorno means it—that the "not yet adequately mutilated liberals" have something to learn from the traditions of the oppressed for whom, as Benjamin notoriously remarks, "the state of exception in which we live is not the exception but the rule."[61] Those who have inhabited the state of exception are those who have been excised from the law and no less from the aesthetic. Where Hegel proclaims the "end of art" as the general condition of the modern age, paradoxically designating the era in which art emerged in its autonomy, our own moment may be that of "the end of an aesthetic" that has already been lived by the oppressed. The question remains whether that end is to be conceived as the death or the emancipation of the aesthetic. The fading of the regime of representation in our time, sustainable neither as a pedagogical project nor as a regulative concept for political formation, might release aesthetic theory into other possibilities even as it abolishes the thought of the Subject as the proper destiny of the barred, pathological, and racial other. The aesthetic might then return to its roots, in an elaboration of the conditions of justice and solidarity from the needs and desires, the fears and the griefs, of the feeling human thing.

My second set of observations concerns Adorno's genealogy of the artwork. To this point, I have read Adorno's derivation of the artwork from and against primitive magic as an instance of the systemic or immanent racial subtext of aesthetic philosophy that is inscribed in the regime of representation. However, Adorno's insistence on the nonrepresentational character of the late modern artwork also reads as a critique of the system of representation that aesthetic philosophy grounded. Is it possible to read Adorno against his own grain here and to retrieve from the place of that magic, against which the aesthetic initially stands out, the anticipation of an alternative that thinks through rather than against the pathological condition of the subject? That condition, evidently, Adorno for the most part considers as one of regression, by which he implies not a movement of return to an anterior condition but a falling away of the subject from the promise of autonomy that constituted it. But regression is finally inseparable from the movement of thought that, in gradually assuming the primacy of representation as identity over the immediacy of "specific representation," prepares the conditions of "universal exchangeability" to which autonomy succumbs. Magic is thus subsumed in the dialectic of representation. In *Dialectic of Enlightenment*, Horkheimer and Adorno directly address that ambiguity in magic that opens out into the emergence of a system of representation:

> It is the identity of the spirit and its correlate, the unity of nature, to which the multiplicity of qualities falls victim. . . . In magic there is specific representation. What happens to the enemy's spear, hair or name, also happens to the individual; the sacrificial animal is massacred instead of the god. Substitution in the course of sacrifice marks a step towards discursive logic. Even though the hind offered up for the daughter, and the lamb for the first-born, still had to have specific qualities, they already represented the species. They already exhibited the non-specificity of the species. But the holiness of the *hic et nunc*, the uniqueness of the chosen one into which the representative enters, radically marks it off, and makes it unfit for exchange. Science prepares the end of this state of affairs. In science there is no specific representation: and if there are no sacrificial animals there is no god. Representation is exchanged for the fungible—universal exchangeability.[62]

In terms I use in earlier chapters, the capacity for *Vorstellung* becomes nothing more than *Vertretbarkeit*. Commodity fetishism, which places a taboo on approaching the social relations that underlie production, is the secret culmination of the system of representation, just as the autonomous artwork in Schiller cannot escape the logic of commodification secreted in its status as ideal "common property." In light of this analysis, magic's play of contiguity and similarity, its logic of substitution, can only prefigure both the systems of representation and of exchange. Here the logic of the aesthetic converges fatally with that of political economy, leading to the ultimate demise of the former.

At the same time, magic, like the Savage, also stands outside those systems, occupying the differentiating threshold that divides reason from that which escapes subsumption to reason. Designated here as "the multiplicity of qualities," magic is the obverse of Kant's conceptual "unity of the manifold" that is the object of a representation (*Vorstellung*). The relation of "incorporation as the excluded" is not merely passive. Something in magic resists incorporation into representation and therefore points toward a domain that exceeds representation as it is historically structured. We can rethink this dimension of magic through its transposition into a figural schema familiar to formalist criticism and to subaltern historiography alike, considered in Chapter 3. From Tylor through Mauss, anthropology construes magic's reliance on similarity and contiguity and on the substitution of part for whole in formalist terms. Magic's formal structure repeats the tropological triad metonymy-synecdoche-metaphor, where metonymy occupies the axis of contiguity (e.g., crown for monarch), synecdoche the part for the whole (e.g., sail for ship), and metaphor that of the axis of identity that supervenes over difference (e.g., for all that they differ, the warrior and the lion are alike in strength and courage). Mauss, who considers magical ritual to be "extraordinarily formal," insists on this recurrent substructure but considers each mode of representation as distinct and equivalent: "Like produces like; contact results in contagion; the image produces the object itself; a part is seen to be the same as the whole."[63] In the progressive narrative Horkheimer and Adorno tell, however, that structure is mapped as a developmental schema: magic's reliance on contiguity—the spell cast on the victim's hair or weapon—gives way to the idea of the part standing for the whole—the victim's hair or weapon *is* the victim. In turn, the substitution of that part for the whole allows for the substitution of something that resembles the victim—the sacrificed first-born lamb takes the place of the first-born child, different as they may be. Hence emerges a naturalization of representation—one that translates into figural terms the narrative implied in Kant's formalization of immediate presentation (*Darstellung*) into representation (*Vorstellung*). As Chapter 4 shows, this is the parabolic narrative of reason and science, and of civil society also. Accordingly, Adorno and Horkheimer offer as a historical schema what is actually a recursive reading of the practice of magic from within the narrative of representation that seeks to make sense of it.

Read from the perspective of science, reason, or civility, magic occupies the domain of the irrational or of the human subject still subjected to nature and necessity. The definitive practice of "the savage mind," magic marks the threshold of the human and the nonhuman. From another perspective, however, magic emerges in *Aesthetic Theory* less as the positive practice of the primitive than as the negation of representation. It partakes of that dimension of the artwork that is the ineluctable materiality that resists formalization, that sensuous remnant that withstands rationalization. From this vantage we can rethink a moment already cited from *Aesthetic Theory*: "Its enchantment, a vestige of its magical phase, is constantly repudiated as unmediated sensual immediacy by the progressive disenchantment of the world, yet without its ever being possible finally to obliterate this magical element. Only in it is art's mimetic character preserved, and its truth is the critique that, by its sheer existence, it levels at a rationality that has become absolute. Emancipated from its claim to reality, the enchantment is itself part of enlightenment: Its semblance disenchants the disenchanted world" (*AT*, 58). Where art turns its face away from the progressive narrative of reason and enlightenment, its resistance to the domination always secreted in rationality resides in its refusal to enter into the system of representation, its insistence on remaining with the particularity and materiality that operates through difference and metonymy rather than identity and similitude. In this moment of the artwork, Adorno may find an intimation of that "togetherness of the diverse" that is the utopian quality of a state of justice that reverts self-consciously to "the multiplicity of qualities" that magic initially respected.[64] There, art is no longer, as Hegel defines it in the wake of Kant and Schiller, "the sensuous presentation of the idea" in which the sensuous is always subsumed by its representation. It is always the trace or "vestige" of the singular thing or event that remains after representation, inassimilable to representation, in movement rather than just a moment of the dialectic.[65] Its figures are found throughout Adorno's aesthetic and critical writings, especially in his reflections on Samuel Beckett and Paul Celan that present a vista of the impotence and denudation of the subject that challenges any possibility that the aesthetic could still be the vehicle for the declaration of sovereign subjecthood.

In this contrapuntal reading of Adorno's aesthetic theory, a reading that pushes against the limits or boundaries of his conceptions, the fate of the aesthetic and the possibilities of the work of art in the face of an ever-advancing rationalization of the world converge not with political economy but with the counterfigure of the Subaltern. As Chapter 4 proposes, the Subaltern is the name we give to those social formations and practices that stand beyond the possibility of entering into representation, those the state relegates to the place of the Savage as the constitutive others of its rationality. In this convergence, the artwork—like the Subaltern—appears as the performance of the violence and unreconciled affectivity of the pathological subject. This would not be a consolatory, aestheticizing conjunction but requires the intellectual clarity and honesty with which Fanon, observing the pervasive inhibitory violence of a colonized culture that is inscribed on the bodies and musculature of the native, remarks: "The atmosphere of myth and magic frightens me and so takes on an undoubted reality."[66] For this anticolonial intellectual, separated by his formation from the people whose conditions he would theorize, this is a pathological state of paralysis from which he hopes that this people, "lost in an imaginary maze, prey to unspeakable terrors yet happy to lose themselves in a dreamlike torment," might awaken, become "unhinged," and organize themselves to take "real and immediate action."[67] It is also the impulse toward a disarticulation of the "racializing assemblages," in Alex Weheliye's term, in which colonial relations trap them.[68] The counterpoint between his own visceral affect- ability, his vital apprehension of the corporealization of colonial violence that issues "in the form of a muscular orgy," and the intellectual's desire for them to "discover reality and transform it" is the mark of a deep and enduring ambivalence.[69] This is the ambivalence that Fred Moten so well captures: "Fanon shares Du Bois's Kantian ambivalence toward the tumul- tuous derangements that emerge from imagination and that are insepara- ble from the imaginative constitution of reason and reality. The ambiguity is shown in what elsewhere appears as a kind of valorization of the depths that are held and articulated in the surface of actual events, as the call for intellectuals to linger in the necessarily rhythmic and muscular music of the '*lieu de déséquilibre occulte*' (which Constance Farrington translates as "zone of occult instability")."[70] This is, precisely, the ambivalence of the intellectual suspended between the will to represent and the desire for an impossible identification with that "muscular music" in which another, very social relation to the world is discovered and set in motion.

Moten goes on to ask: "How can the struggle for the liberation of the pathological be aligned with the eradication of the pathological?"[71] I want to suggest that the convergence of the artwork and the Subaltern describes the countermovement within the system of representation whose very in- sistence appears as the destruction of the law and as the possible inaugu- ration of another conception of life in common, predicated on the pains and pleasures of the suffering, desiring, necessitous subject. This moment of convergence, not of identification—above all not the displacement by aesthetic representation of the Subaltern—does not entail the death of the subalterns. Nor is it the aesthetic *of* the Subaltern or the Subaltern *as* the aesthetic. Rather, both concepts, both material instances of the threshold, approach the crisis of representation along different trajectories, each de- termined by a different relation to the state and to the function of repre- sentation for the state. They converge from different but mutually consti- tutive orbits: The Subaltern is a category unthinkable without the regime of representation that the aesthetic regulated; the Subaltern remains as the ineluctable moment of the irrepresentable that spells the limit of the aesthetic's unilateral promise of universality.

In this time of generalized redundancy, of ever-increasing and unneces- sary subjection to necessity, the difficult task is to think again the history of the present *from* the place of the subaltern subject of affectability and *with* the irreducible element of art that is its abundance even in the poverty of means. This abundance of art, "beyond its factual givenness," is its excess over ends, over instrumentality, over representation. Through its own abundance, art meets with the abundance of possibilities already embedded in the history of human and nonhuman beings and in the unexhausted repertoire of their practices, an abundance of differences without identity. That history and those practices are inevitably entwined with the effects of the racial regime of representation that they have always countered. To think from within the multiple countercultures of a modernity that has been shaped by representation is to assert the possibility of a living in and through difference that does not seek simply to erase race in the name of another cosmopolitan conception of humanity. It is to recognize that even in the violent trajectory of that modernity possibilities were imagined and realized whose examples remain for us even as that violence continues to demand our resistance, here and now.

INTRODUCTION: UNDER REPRESENTATION

1. Zygmunt Bauman, *Modernity and the Holocaust* (Ithaca, N.Y.: Cornell University Press, 2001), cited in David T. Goldberg, *The Racial State* (Malden, Mass.: Blackwell, 2002), 87.

2. See Paul Gilroy, *Against Race: Imagining Political Culture beyond the Color Line* (Cambridge, Mass.: Belknap, 2000), 30. The resources of liberal thinking "have been tainted by a history in which they were not able to withstand the biopolitical power of the race-thinking that compromised their boldest and best ambitions." Jodi Melamed persuasively argues that the neoliberal moment has mobilized what she terms "the trick of racialization"— that is, "a process that constitutes differential relations of human value and valuelessness according to specific material circumstances and geopolitical conditions while appearing to be (and being) a rationally inevitable normative system that merely sorts human beings into categories of difference." See Jodi Melamed, *Represent and Destroy: Rationalizing Violence in the New Racial Capitalism* (Minneapolis: University of Minnesota Press, 2011), 2.

3. See Nahum Dimitri Chandler, "Of Exorbitance," chap. 1 in *X: The Problem of the Negro as a Problem for Thought* (New York: Fordham University Press, 2014).

4. Rei Terada, "The Racial Grammar of Kantian Time," *European Romantic Review* 28, no. 3 (2017): 268, an essay that focuses primarily on the *Critique of Pure Reason*. See also Ronald A. T. Judy, "Kant and the Negro," *Surfaces* 1, no. 8 (1991): 4–70.

5. See Emmanuel Chukwudi Eze, ed., *Race and the Enlightenment: A Reader* (Oxford: Blackwell, 1997). See also Jon M. Mikkelsen's important collection *Kant and the Concept of Race: Late Eighteenth-Century Writings* (Binghamton: State University of New York Press, 2004).

6. Robert Bernasconi, "Will the Real Kant Please Stand Up: The Challenge of Enlightenment Racism to the Study of the History of Philosophy," *Radical Philosophy* 117 (2003): 14.

7. See, for example, Robert Bernasconi, "Kant's Third Thoughts on Race," in *Reading Kant's Geography*, ed. Stuart Elden and Eduardo Mendieta

(Albany: SUNY Press, 2011). See also Robert Bernasconi, "Kant and Blumenbach's Polyps: A Neglected Chapter in the History of the Concept of
Race," in *The German Invention of Race*, ed. Sara Eigen (Binghamton: State
University of New York Press, 2006), on the persistence and consistency of
Kant's racial statements throughout his career. Simon Gikandi remarks on
how "the idea of Kant as a pure philosopher rests on an institutional separation of his critical philosophy from his work in anthropology and physical
geography, work concerned, one might say obsessed, with questions of race."
See Simon Gikandi, "Race and the Idea of the Aesthetic," *Michigan Quarterly
Review* 40, no. 2 (2001): http://quod.lib.umich.edu/cgi/t/text/text-idx?cc
=mqr;c=mqr;c=mqrarchive;idno=act2080.0040.208;g=mqrg;rgn=main;view
=text;xc=1. No less an authority than the Oxford *Encyclopedia of Aesthetics*
bears out Gikandi's remark, contending that a reference to the African ideal
of beauty in the section on the "normal idea of beauty" is "Kant's only reference to race in the *Critiques* and suggests that he no longer sought to integrate his critical theory with his study of anthropology, and it foreshadows
a general separation between aesthetics and race in the nineteenth century."
Michael Kelly, ed., *Encyclopedia of Aesthetics*, 2nd ed., s.v. "Race" (Oxford:
Oxford University Press, 2014).

8. The volume of such work is by now too vast to cite exhaustively.
I note here a tiny selection of race critical texts that have proven indispensable to me over the years in their approach to thinking artworks as reper-
toires of alternative social and affective possibilities: Alfred Arteaga, *Chicano
Poetics: Heterotexts and Hybridities* (Cambridge: Cambridge University Press,
1997); Saidiya Hartman, *Scenes of Subjection: Terror, Slavery, and Self-Making
in Nineteenth-Century America* (Oxford: Oxford University Press, 1997); Lisa
Lowe, *Immigrant Acts: On Asian American Cultural Politics* (Durham, N.C.:
Duke University Press, 1997); Toni Morrison, *Playing in the Dark: Whiteness
and the Literary Imagination* (Cambridge, Mass.: Harvard University Press,
1992); Fred Moten, *In the Break: The Aesthetics of the Black Radical Tradition* (Minneapolis: University of Minnesota Press, 2003); Cedric Robinson,
*Forgeries of Memory and Meaning: Blacks and the Regimes of Race in American
Theater and Film before World War II* (Chapel Hill: University of North Caro-
lina Press, 2007); Sarita Echavez See, *The Decolonized Eye: Filipino American
Art and Performance* (Minneapolis: University of Minnesota Press, 2009);
Hortense J. Spillers, *Black, White and in Color: Essays on American Literature
and Culture* (Chicago: University of Chicago Press, 2003); Alexander G.
Weheliye, *Habeas Viscus: Racializing Assemblages, Biopolitics, and Black Feminist
Theories of the Human* (Durham, N.C.: Duke University Press, 2014).

9. Gikandi, "Race and the Idea of the Aesthetic." Regrettably, despite
such observations, Gikandi's own argument continues to separate the body of

Enlightenment observations on race from the "pure" philosophical systems
that the former "contaminate."

10. Gayatri Chakravorty Spivak, *A Critique of Postcolonial Reason: Toward
a History of the Vanishing Present* (Cambridge, Mass.: Harvard University
Press, 1999). My hesitancy about the extent of her critique of the aesthetic
as a regime of representation will become clear in later chapters, although I
continue to regard her work in that book as indispensable.

11. Chandler, "The Figure of the X," chap. 2 in *X*, 72.

12. Eric Williams, *Capitalism and Slavery* (Raleigh: University of North
Carolina Press, 1994); Cedric Robinson, *Black Marxism: The Making of the
Black Radical Tradition* (Raleigh: University of North Carolina Press, 2000);
Aníbal Quijano, "Coloniality of Power, Eurocentrism, and Latin America,"
Nepantla 1, no. 3 (2000): 533–80; Patrick Wolfe, *Traces of History: Elementary
Structures of Race* (London: Verso, 2016).

13. Sylvia Wynter, "Unsettling the Coloniality of Being/Power/Truth/
Freedom: Towards the Human, After Man, Its Overrepresentation—An
Argument," *CR: The New Centennial Review* 3, no. 3 (Fall 2003): 264.

14. Wynter, 265–66.

15. Wynter, 318.

16. Wynter, 282.

17. Sylvia Wynter, "On Disenchanting Discourse: 'Minority' Literary
Criticism and Beyond," in *The Nature and Context of Minority Discourse*, ed.
Abdul JanMohamed and David Lloyd (Oxford: Oxford University Press,
1990), 460. I return to the notion of a "universal declaration of universality,"
paraphrased from Fanon, at the end of this Introduction.

18. Katherine McKittrick, "Yours in the Intellectual Struggle: Sylvia
Wynter and the Realization of the Living," in *Sylvia Wynter: On Being Human
as Praxis*, ed. Katherine McKittrick (Durham, N.C.: Duke University Press,
2015), 3.

19. This is not to say that efforts to root racial difference in biological
evidence have entirely disappeared. Stuart Hall's assessment is rightly nuanced: "Biological conceptions of race have greatly receded in importance,
though they have by no means wholly disappeared (for example: the revival of
bio-sociology, and the reintroduction of biologically-based theories, through
the genetic principle)." See Stuart Hall, "Race, Articulation and Societies
Structured in Dominance," in *Sociological Theories: Race and Colonialism* (Paris:
UNESCO, 1980), 306. See Richard Purcell, "Trayvon, Postblackness, and
the Postrace Dilemma," *boundary* 2 40, no. 3 (2013): 142–43, for some cau-
tions on declaring prematurely the death of biological racism given the rise of
"the instrumental use of genetic research."

20. Wynter, "On Disenchanting Discourse," 460.

21. Throughout this book, I am in continual dialogue with Denise Ferreira da Silva's equally important *Toward a Global Idea of Race* (Minneapolis: University of Minnesota Press, 2007), but note that despite its close attention to the critical tradition in philosophy from Descartes to Hegel, the aesthetic is not a category with which she engages in that work.

22. Robinson, *Forgeries of Memory*, 3; Wolfe, *Traces of History*, 271.

23. Hortense J. Spillers, "Interstices: A Small Drama of Words," in *Black, White and in Color*, 155.

24. The term *subject of affectability* is introduced by da Silva in *Toward a Global Idea of Race* (xxxix) and elaborated throughout that work. I explain below why I have retained the Kantian notion of the "pathological" rather than adopting her usage.

25. Frantz Fanon, *The Wretched of the Earth*, with a preface by Jean-Paul Sartre, trans. Constance Farrington (New York: Grove, 1968), 51–55. The boundary stone alludes to Walter Benjamin's use of this figure in his "Critique of Violence" to signal the instituting violence that founds a new regime of law. Walter Benjamin, "Critique of Violence," trans. Edmund Jephcott, in *Selected Writings*, vol. 1, *1913–1926*, ed. Marcus Bullock and Michael W. Jennings (Cambridge, Mass.: Belknap, 1996), 248.

26. See Denise Ferreira da Silva, "No Bodies," *Griffith Law Review* 18, no. 2 (2009): 213–36.

27. The classic statement of this view is that of Hegel: "Negroes are enslaved by the Europeans and sold to America. Nevertheless, their lot in their own country, where slavery is equally absolute, is almost worse than this; for the basic principle of all slavery is that man is not yet consciousness of his freedom, and consequently sinks to the level of a mere object or worthless article." In Eze, *Race and the Enlightenment*, 134–35.

28. See, in particular, Jacques Rancière, *The Politics of Aesthetics*, trans. Gabriel Rockhill (London: Verso, 2004).

29. Most immediately pertinent to this study has been the continuing investigation of the relation of the aesthetic to politics and ideology, from Georg Lukács through the Frankfurt School down to Fredric Jameson's numerous works on ideology, postmodernism, and the culture of late capitalism. Some relevant texts are gathered in Jameson's *Aesthetics and Politics* (London: New Left, 1977). Other significant landmarks in this tradition have been Terry Eagleton's *The Ideology of the Aesthetic* (Oxford: Blackwell, 1990) and the essays from the 1980s collected in Paul de Man's *Aesthetic Ideology*, ed. Andrzej Warminski (Minneapolis: University of Minnesota Press, 1996). George Hartley's *The Abyss of Representation: Marxism and the Postmodern Sublime* (Durham, N.C.: Duke University Press, 2003) valuably returns recent ideological critique to its foundations in aesthetic theory. More recently, as

I discuss further below and in Chapter 1, the work of Jacques Rancière has given a new life to reflections on the aesthetic, together with other French thinkers like Alain Badiou, whose *Handbook of Inaesthetics*, trans. Alberto Toscano (Stanford, Calif.: Stanford University Press, 2005), and *The Age of the Poets and Other Writings on Twentieth-Century Poetry and Prose*, ed. and trans. Bruno Bosteels (London: Verso, 2014) explore the relation of the aesthetic to philosophy as a discipline. Likewise, a series of books by Jean-Luc Nancy, from *The Muses*, trans. Peggy Kamuf (Stanford, Calif.: Stanford University Press, 1996), to *Listening*, trans. Charlotte Mandell (New York: Fordham University Press, 2007), have extended the terrain of the aesthetic back into that of the question of feeling, of "pathological" pleasure and displeasure. Nonetheless, despite some efforts to think a queer aesthetics, notably Sianne Ngai's *Ugly Feelings* (Cambridge, Mass.: Harvard University Press, 2005) and *Our Aesthetic Categories: Zany, Cute, Interesting* (Cambridge, Mass.: Harvard University Press, 2012) or José Esteban Muñoz's Marcusean *Cruising Utopia: The Then and There of Queer Futurity* (New York: New York University Press, 2009), no work to my knowledge has extensively addressed the aesthetic tradition in terms of its constitutive relation to modern racial categories as *Under Representation* seeks to do.

30. See, for some very different examples, Elaine Scarry, *On Beauty and Being Just* (Princeton, N.J.: Princeton University Press, 2001); Peter de Bolla, *Art Matters* (Cambridge, Mass.: Harvard University Press, 2001); Denis Donoghue, *Speaking of Beauty* (New Haven, Conn.: Yale University Press, 2003). Muñoz's *Cruising Utopia* seems to me the most persuasive reassertion of the traditions of affirmative aesthetics.

31. I borrow this term from Jonathan Loesberg, *A Return to Aesthetics: Autonomy, Indifference, and Postmodernism* (Stanford, Calif.: Stanford University Press, 2005).

32. Herbert Marcuse, *The Aesthetic Dimension: Toward a Critique of Marxist Aesthetics* (Boston: Beacon, 1978).

33. See Nada Elia et al., "Introduction: A Sightline," in *Critical Ethnic Studies: A Reader*, ed. Nada Elia et al. (Durham, N.C.: Duke University Press, 2016), 1.

34. For a critique of multiculturalism's "unity-in-diversity" strategy, see Jared Sexton, *Amalgamation Schemes: Antiblackness and the Critique of Multiracialism* (Minneapolis: University of Minnesota Press, 2008), 32.

35. Wynter, "Unsettling the Coloniality," 307.

36. Denise Ferreira da Silva, "Extraordinary Times: A Preface," *Cultural Dynamics* 26, no. 1 (2014): 5. For an analysis of the impact of struggles to diversify the university in the 1980s and 1990s that addresses this crisis felt by liberal professors, see David Lloyd, "Foundations of Diversity," in *"Culture"*

and the Problem of the Disciplines, ed. John Carlos Rowe (New York: Columbia University Press, 1998).

37. Elia et al., "Introduction," 3. For an extended genealogy of the notion of excellence and its racial overtones, see Roderick A. Ferguson, "The Racial Genealogy of Excellence," chap. 3 in *The Reorder of Things: The University and Its Pedagogies of Minority Difference* (Minneapolis: University of Minnesota Press, 2012).

38. Alexander Weheliye's comments are apt: "If demanding recognition and inclusion remains at the center of minority politics, it will lead only to a delimited notion of personhood as property that zeroes in comparatively on only one form of subjugation at the expense of others, thus allowing for the continued existence of hierarchical differences between full humans, not-quite-humans, and nonhumans." See Weheliye, *Habeas Viscus*, 81.

39. Ferguson, *The Reorder of Things*, 7.

40. Fred Moten, "The Case of Blackness," *Criticism* 50, no. 2 (Spring 2008): 180. See also Ronald A. T. Judy, "Fanon's Body of Black Experience," in *Fanon: A Critical Reader*, ed. Lewis R. Gordon, T. Denean Sharpley-Whiting, and Renée T. White (Oxford: Blackwell, 1996), 54; for Judy, Fanon's analysis of white "negrophobia" "reveals a pathology that is co-terminous with the very symbolic order of modernity, and not just colonialism." Pathologization cuts both ways.

41. For Fanon's definition of decolonization as "a program of complete disorder," see *Wretched of the Earth*, 36.

42. My argument here diverges both from Gilroy's assertion that "the comfort zone created in the fading aura of those wonderful cultures of dissidence is already shrinking" and from his desire for an "emphatically postracial humanism." His eagerness to stand off from "the cheapest pseudo-solidarities" that others might disparage as "identity politics" leads him into an all too uncritical Arendtian understanding of the political as "the exercise of power in a reasoned public culture capable for simultaneously promoting both self and social development." Gilroy, *Against Race*, 14, 37, 41.

43. Fanon, *Black Skin, White Masks*, 138.

44. David Lloyd, *Irish Culture and Colonial Modernity, 1800–2000: The Transformation of Oral Space* (Cambridge: Cambridge University Press, 2011).

45. I paraphrase this expression from Frantz Fanon, "Racism and Culture," chap. 2 in *Toward the African Revolution: Political Essays*, trans. Haakon Chevalier (New York: Grove, 1988), 31.

1. THE AESTHETIC REGIME OF REPRESENTATION

Some of the material in this essay, since entirely recast, was originally published as "Analogies of the Aesthetic: The Politics of Culture and the Limits of Materialist Aesthetics," *New Formations* 10 (1990): 109–26.

1. On the historical emergence of that tradition of cultural pedagogy, see David Lloyd and Paul Thomas, *Culture and the State* (New York: Routledge, 1997).

2. For some of the debates alluded to here, see Ernst Bloch et al., *Aesthetics and Politics*, afterword by Frederic Jameson (London: New Left, 1977); Jean-François Lyotard, "Answering the Question: What Is Post-Modernism," in *The Postmodern Condition: A Report on Knowledge*, trans. Geoff Bennington and Brian Massumi, foreword by Frederic Jameson (Minneapolis: University of Minnesota Press, 1984), 71–82; Jürgen Habermas, "Modernity: An Incomplete Project," in *The Anti-Aesthetic: Essays on Post-Modern Culture*, ed. Hall Foster (Port Townsend, Wash.: Bay, 1983); Kumkum Sangari, "The Politics of the Possible," in *Politics of the Possible: Essays on Gender, History, Narratives, Colonial English* (London: Anthem, 2002), 1–28; Asha Varadharajan, *Exotic Parodies: Subjectivity in Adorno, Said, and Spivak* (Minneapolis: University of Minnesota Press, 1995); Neil Lazarus, *The Postcolonial Unconscious* (Cambridge: Cambridge University Press, 2011).

3. For Marx's commentary, see *Grundrisse: Foundations of the Critique of Political Economy*, trans. and foreword by Martin Nicolaus (Harmondsworth, England: Penguin, 1973), 110–11. Among the numerous discussions of this passage, see especially Michael McKeon, "The Origins of Aesthetic Value," *Telos* 57 (Fall 1983): 63–82; and Michael Sprinker, *Imaginary Relations: Aesthetics and Ideology in the Theory of Historical Materialism* (London: Verso, 1987). On the antinomial character of aesthetics in general, see especially Ference Fehér and Agnes Heller, "The Necessity and Irreformability of Aesthetics," in *Reconstructing Aesthetics: Writings of the Budapest School*, ed. Agnes Heller and Ference Fehér (Oxford: Blackwell, 1986).

4. See Immanuel Kant, *Critique of Pure Reason*, trans. Norman Kemp Smith (London: Macmillan, 1978), 435; cited hereafter as *CPR*.

5. Karl Marx, "A Contribution to the Critique of Hegel's Philosophy of Right: Introduction," in *Early Writings*, trans. Rodney Livingstone and Gregor Benton (New York: Vintage, 1975), 250. For a theoretically invaluable summary of those conditions and the genesis of a "German ideology," see Rebecca Comay, *Mourning Sickness: Hegel and the French Revolution* (Stanford, Calif.: Stanford University Press, 2011).

6. See Sylvia Wynter, "Unsettling the Coloniality of Being/Power/Truth/Freedom: Towards the Human, After Man, Its Overrepresentation—An Argument," *CR: The New Centennial Review* 3, no. 3 (Fall 2003): 60.

7. See Reinhardt Koselleck's *Kritik and Krise: Ein Beitrag zur Pathogenese der bürgerlichen Welt* (Freiburg, Germany: Alber, 1959) for a sustained account of the foundation of the liberal hegemony in a critical common sense, which, emerging in the private sphere, comes increasingly to form a public sphere in conflict and eventually crisis with the autocratic states. Critiques of the abstraction of this "figure of Man" range politically from Edmund Burke's *Reflections on the Revolution in France*, ed. Conor Cruise O'Brien (Harmondsworth, England: Penguin, 1968) to Karl Marx, "On the Jewish Question," in *Early Writings*, ed. Quintin Hoare, trans. Rodney Livingstone and Gregor Benton (New York: Vintage, 1975), 211–41. The notion of hegemony as a form of socially disseminated "common sense" is crucial to Antonio Gramsci's writings in the Prison Notebooks. See especially *Selections from the Prison Notebooks*, ed. and trans. Quintin Hoare and Geoffrey Nowell Smith (New York: International Publishers, 1971), 323–43. For a discussion of the Marxist tradition of critiquing abstract citizenship in liberal theory, see Paul Thomas, "Alien Politics: A Marxian Perspective on Citizenship and Theory," in *After Marx*, ed. Terence Ball and James Farr (Cambridge: Cambridge University Press, 1984).

8. See Jacques Derrida, "Déclarations d'indépendence," in *Otobiographies: l'enseignement de Nietzsche et la politique du nom proper* (Paris: Galilée, 1986), 13–32, for a discussion of the paradox of the constitution of states. For a critique of the genealogy and political functioning of the abstract figure of man as a crucial ideological element of racialist humanist culture, see, among other essays, Sylvia Wynter, "On Disenchanting Discourse: 'Minority' Literary Criticism and Beyond," in *The Nature and Context of Minority Discourse*, ed. Abdul JanMohamed and David Lloyd (Oxford: Oxford University Press, 1990).

9. See Thomas Paine, *Rights of Man*, ed. Henry Collins (Harmondsworth, England: Penguin, 1969), 87–89.

10. A historically useful account of the place of property in political theory is Alan Ryan's *Property and Political Theory* (Oxford: Blackwell, 1984). On the colonial templates for the modern conception of property as abstraction, see Brenna Bhandar, *Colonial Lives of Property: Regimes of Ownership* (Durham, N.C.: Duke University Press, 2018).

11. Paine, *Rights of Man*, 90–91. Marx comments on this splitting of the liberal subject in "On the Jewish Question," *Early Writings*, 220–22, and in "Critique of Hegel's Philosophy of Right," *Early Writings*, 250: "The German conception of the modern state, which abstracts from *real man*, was only possible because and in so far as the modern state itself abstracts from *real* man or satisfies the *whole* man in a purely imaginary way."

12. On this relation between the representative human Subject and the State, see Lloyd and Thomas, *Culture and the State*, 46–53.

13. Immanuel Kant, *Critique of Judgement*, trans. James Creed Meredith (Oxford: Clarendon, 1952), §60, 226–27, referred to in the text hereafter as *CJ*. Citations in German from the Third Critique are from *Kritik der Urteilskraft*, ed. Wilhelm Weischedel (Frankfurt, Germany: Suhrkamp, 1974), cited throughout the text as *KU*. The allusions to Georg Lukács and Mikhail Bakhtin are, of course, to Georg Lukács's *Theory of the Novel*, trans. Anna Bostock (Cambridge, Mass.: MIT Press, 1971), esp. chaps. 1 and 3; and to Mikhail Bakhtin's *The Dialogic Imagination: Four Essays*, ed. Michael Holquist, trans. Caryl Emerson and Michael Holquist (Austin: University of Texas Press, 1981). Bakhtin remarks typically in the essay "Epic and the Novel" that "the epic world knows only a single and unified world view, obligatory and indubitably true for heroes as well as for authors and audiences" (chap 1. in *Dialogic Imagination*, 35). For Kant, as we shall see, the organic nature of such a community is always already the product of an art, dependent on the form of the "as if" that governs all aesthetic productions. It is not, therefore, a primal condition of the human disrupted by the advent of modernity as, with varying affect, it appears for Lukács and Bakhtin. These paragraphs are modified from my essay "Kant's Examples," *Representations* 28 (Autumn 1989): 34–35.

14. For a critique of the misprision of Kant's analogy that leads to a more substantive claim to organic form, in the literary critical as well as the political tradition, see Jonathan Loesberg, *A Return to Aesthetics: Autonomy, Indifference, and Postmodernism* (Stanford, Calif.: Stanford University Press, 2005), 15–26.

15. Jacques Derrida has emphasized the crucial function of analogy in the Third Critique in "Le Parergon," in *La vérité en peinture* (Paris: Flammarion, 1978), 19–168, esp. 43. Where the present essay differs in its emphasis from Derrida's is in finding in the figure of the analogy the rhetorical structure of the *Critique* and the site of a certain mise en abyme and, more importantly, the very formality that provides the political efficacity of the discourse of aesthetic culture.

16. On the intrinsically pedagogical investments of the Third Critique, see my essay "Kant's Examples." For an excellent account of the workings of symbolic analogy in Kant, see George Hartley, *The Abyss of Representation: Marxism and the Postmodern Sublime* (Durham, N.C.: Duke University Press, 2003), 38–42. Throughout, however, my account of the relation of *Darstellung* (presentation) and *Vorstellung* (representation) differs in significant ways from Hartley's in his book.

17. Kant is here dispensing with the notion that beauty lies in the perfection of the object. Since the perfection of the object entails a conception of the end for which it is perfect (i.e., a concept of the object itself), this would

imply that beauty lay in the object itself, in which case it could not be the representation of an autonomous subjective judgment but would be a logical judgment subordinated to understanding.

18. See again Derrida, "Le Parergon," *La véritié en peinture*, 42, for comments on this crux of *Critique*. I fill out here his undeveloped remark that "On pourrait montrer que ce suspens assure la complicité d'un discours moral et d'un culturalisme empirique. Nécessité permanente."

19. Richard E. Aquila, "A New Look at Kant's Aesthetic Judgments," in *Essays in Kant's Aesthetics*, ed. Ted Cohen and Paul Guyer (Chicago: University of Chicago Press, 1982), provides an excellent discussion of the way in which aesthetic judgment works by analogy with predication. See especially 107–10.

20. Koselleck, in *Kritik and Krise*, 42–45, discusses the development of a modern bourgeoisie in the continuous interchange between rational critique and moral censure, with specific reference to Locke's "Philosophical Law," or law of opinion and reputation.

21. Comay, *Mourning Sickness*, 34.

22. As Spivak comments, "He is only a *casual* object of thought, not a paradigmatic example. He is not only not the subject as such; he also does not quite make it as an example of the thing or its species as natural product. If you happen to think of him, your determinant judgment cannot prove to itself that he, or a species of him need exist." See Gayatri Chakravorty Spivak, *A Critique of Postcolonial Reason: Toward a History of the Vanishing Present* (Cambridge, Mass.: Harvard University Press, 1999), 26. Such figures may be in themselves only "throwaway names" (35), but their systemic and necessary place within the system of the aesthetic as figures is indubitable. See also Robert Bernasconi, "Kant's Third Thoughts on Race," in *Reading Kant's Geography*, ed. Stuart Elden and Eduardo Mendieta (Albany: SUNY Press, 2011), 301, 310–12, for more extended discussion of Kant's questioning of the necessity for various peoples to exist.

23. J. Kameron Carter, *Race: A Theological Account* (Oxford: Oxford University Press, 2008), 89.

24. See Loesberg, *Return to Aesthetics*, 104, for an account of the latter passage that clarifies the distinction between a moral or political judgment and one subordinated to sensual gratification but that is strikingly casual about the racial implications. I discuss the manner in which the formal constitution of the public sphere structures the assimilative discourse of aesthetic culture in Chapter 3, "Race under Representation."

25. This political subtext has long been recognized. Hans-Wolf Jäger comments on the penetration of political concepts into the very structure of the description and definition of literature in the late eighteenth century

in Germany; see *Politische Kategorien in Poetik und Rhetorik der zweiten Hälfte des 18. Jahrhunderts* (Stuttgart, Germany: J. B. Metzler, 1970), 6. Hannah Arendt's late *Lectures on Kant's Political Philosophy*, which astutely takes the *Critique of Judgement* as its primary text, focuses on the importance of "communicability" to Kant and its relation both to public or common sense and to disinterest. Her account of Kant differs fundamentally from mine, however, in endorsing Kant's account of the conditions for the public sphere without noting their full political and racial implications. See Hannah Arendt, *Lectures on Kant's Political Philosophy*, ed. Ronald Beiner (Chicago: University of Chicago Press, 1982).

26. See Odo Marquard, "Kant und die Wende zur Ästhetik," *Zeitschrift für philosophische Forschung* 16 (1962); repr. in *Zur Kantforschung der Gegenwart*, ed. Peter Heintel and Ludwig Nagl (Darmstadt, Germany: Wissenschaftliche Buchgesellschaft, 1981). *"Ästhetik wird angesichts der Aporie des emanzipierten Menschen gebraucht als Ausweg dort, wo das wissenschaftliche Denken nicht mehr und das geschichtliche Denken nicht trägt"* (242). On the importance of the "as if" in this movement, see 247. This article is probably the most succinct account of the logical necessity by which the aesthetic becomes a "Fundamentalphilosophie."

27. In "Kant's Examples" I have argued that this aporia of common sense is practically overcome in the ironic and ethical form of liberal pedagogy that seeks to produce a subject of ideology in the form that aesthetic judgment indicates.

28. Philip Pettit argues that what emerges from the late eighteenth century as liberal political philosophy is required to displace an older republican tradition of political thought that had become a threat inasmuch as its principles were increasingly being invoked by men (and women) of no property. See Philip Pettit, "Non-Domination as a Political Ideal," in *Republicanism: A Theory of Freedom and Government* (Oxford: Oxford University Press, 1997), 80–109.

29. Friedrich Schiller, *On the Aesthetic Education of Man, in a Series of Letters*, ed. Elizabeth M. Wilkinson and L. A. Willoughby (Oxford: Clarendon, 1982), 215. That "common property" we enjoy precisely by way of what makes us common, "as representatives of the human genus" (217).

30. The phrase is Karl Marx's, who refers to *"political* man" as "simply abstract, artificial man, man as an *allegorical, moral* person" in "On the Jewish Question," *Early Writings*, 234.

31. Schiller, *Aesthetic Education*, 219. See also Marquard, "Kant und die Wende zur Ästhetik," 247–48.

32. See Herbert Marcuse, "The Affirmative Character of Culture," chap. 3 in *Negations: Essays in Critical Theory*, trans. Jeremy J. Schapiro

(Boston: Beacon, 1968), 120–21, where, of course, the utopian moment of even "affirmative culture" is the merest of moments. In later work, such as *The Aesthetic Dimension: Toward a Critique of Marxist Aesthetics* (Boston: Beacon, 1978) and *An Essay on Liberation* (Boston: Beacon, 1968), the utopian moment of art receives far more emphasis from Marcuse. The aesthetic dimension of Western Marxism has a remarkable persistence, recurring not only, in its most articulate and nuanced form, in T. W. Adorno's aesthetic writings but also, more unexpectedly, in such essays as Louis Althusser's "A Letter on Art in Reply to Andre Daspar," in *Lenin and Philosophy and Other Essays*, trans. Ben Brewster (New York: Monthly Review, 1971), 221–27, where even such central concepts of liberal aesthetics as inner distancing are valorized. For a persuasive attempt to reanimate the German idealist tradition with a queer utopianism that may be productively against its grain, see José Muñoz, *Cruising Utopia: The Then and There of Queer Futurity* (New York: New York University Press, 2009).

33. Grimm's *Deutsches Wörterbuch*, 33 vols. (Munich: Deutscher Taschenbuchverlag, 1984), 1982–94, supports this implicit history of the usage of *Vertreten*. Its initial meaning appears to have been to tread underfoot or to misstep (as in *zertreten* and *ver-treten*); thereafter, "einem den Weg vertreten" (*versperren*). Although early instances of the usage of *vertreten* in the sense of "represent" are given, the vast majority are from the modern period, while its political usage meaning "eine Richtung, Körperschaft, Autorität repraesentieren, in sich darstellen" emerges only in the nineteenth century. See Chapter 4, "Representation's Coup," for further discussion of *vertreten* and its synonyms.

34. See Hannah Arendt's lengthy discussion of Kant's response to the French Revolution, where the properly philosophical position of the spectator rather than the agent allows for the interpretation of the event as a sign of a progress perpetually in process. Arendt, *Lectures on Kant's Political Philosophy*, 45–58. See also Comay, *Mourning Sickness*, 32–33.

35. See again, Lloyd and Thomas, *Culture and the State*, especially chapter 2.

36. On the historical, political, and social background to the German late Enlightenment, an excellent general source is still W. H. Bruford, *Germany in the Eighteenth Century: The Social Background of the Literary Revival* (1935; repr., Cambridge: Cambridge University Press, 1959). See also Nicolao Merker's excellent *An den Ursprüngen der deutschen Ideologie: Revolution und Utopie im Jakobinismus*, ed. and trans. Manfred Buhr (Berlin: Akademie-Verlag, 1984), especially chapters 2 and 3. On the development of the "moral weeklies" in Germany throughout the eighteenth century, see Wolfgang Martens, *Die Botschaft der Tugend. Die Aufklärung im Spiegel*

der deutschen moralischen Wochenschriften (Stuttgart, Germany: J. B. Metzler, 1968), especially 441–60. Poetry is seen to develop taste and virtue simultaneously, foreshadowing the later philosophical analysis of taste and morality. Bruford, in *Germany in the Eighteenth Century* (279–80), comments at length on the upsurge in journal publication through the century. For a discussion of the debate on the moralizing effects of reading, see Martha Woodmansee, "Towards a Genealogy of the Aesthetic: The German Reading Debate of the 1790s," *Cultural Critique* 11 (Winter 1988–1989): 203–21.

37. Schiller, *Aesthetic Education*, 43.

38. For an extensive account of the place of the sublime in the theorization of ideology, representation, and ethics, see Hartley, *Abyss of Representation*. See also Jacques Rancière's critique of the emergence of a negative ethics of the sublime in "The Ethical Turn of Aesthetics and Politics," in *Dissensus: On Politics and Aesthetics*, trans. Steven Corcoran (London: Bloomsbury Academic, 2015), 192–210.

39. See, for example, Schiller, *Aesthetic Education*, 31–43; and for commentary, Georg Lukács, "Zur Ästhetik Schilllers," in *Probleme der Ästhetik*, *Werke*, vol. 10 (Berlin: Luchterhand, 1969), 17–106, 32, and W. H. Bruford, *The German Tradition of Self-Cultivation: "Bildung" from Humboldt to Thomas Mann* (Cambridge: Cambridge University Press, 1975), 98.

40. I borrow the image of the unemployment line from Ron Silliman, "Disappearance of the Word, Appearance of the World," in *The L=A=N=G=U=A=G=E Book*, ed. Bruce Andrews and Charles Bernstein (Carbondale: Southern Illinois University Press, 1984), 127: "Serialization . . . places the individual as a passive cypher into a series of more or less identical units, Whitman's 'simple separate persons.' Its apotheosis is to be found in the modern unemployment line." For *das vertretbare Subjekt*, see Marquard, "Kant und die Wende zur Ästhetik," 244.

41. Marx, "Introduction" to the *Grundrisse*, 85. See also Rastko Močnik, "Toward a Materialist Concept of Literature," *Cultural Critique* 4 (Fall 1986): 172–73, to whom I owe this understanding of the category of the aesthetic. Insofar as Sprinker espouses an Althusserian division of the object of aesthetics, "one in its specifically aesthetic modality; the other in its function with the formal structure of particular historical ideologies" (*Imaginary Relations*, 272), he is open to the charge of an ideological misrecognition of the category of the aesthetic.

42. See Walter Benjamin, "Critique of Violence," trans. Edmund Jephcott, in *Selected Writings*, vol. 1, *1913–1926*, ed. Marcus Bullock and Michael W. Jennings (Cambridge, Mass.: Belknap, 1996), 240.

43. As Alexander Weheliye tersely puts it, "Legal personhood is available to indigenous subjects only if the Indian can be killed—either literally or

figuratively—in order to save the world of Man (in this case settler colonialism and white supremacy)." See Alexander G. Weheliye, *Habeas Viscus: Racializing Assemblages, Biopolitics, and Black Feminist Theories of the Human* (Durham, N.C.: Duke University Press, 2014), 79.

44. Jacques Rancière, *The Politics of Aesthetics*, trans. Gabriel Rockhill (London: Verso, 2004), 21–22. Page numbers given in the text hereafter.

45. Jacques Rancière, "The Aesthetic Revolution and Its Outcomes," chap. 9 in *Dissensus*, 139.

46. Jacques Rancière, "L'esthétique comme politique," chap. 1 in *Malaise dans l'esthétique* (Paris: Éditions Galilée, 2004), 48. My translation, here and elsewhere.

47. Rancière, 48.

48. Rancière, 49–50.

49. Jacques Rancière, "Ten Theses on Politics," chap. 1 in *Dissensus*, 44.

50. Jacques Rancière, "Lyotard et l'esthétique du sublime: une contre-lecture de Kant," chap. 4 in *Malaise dans l'esthétique*, 132.

51. On the historical difficulty state institutions faced in actually making the disposition to representation seem self-evident, see Lloyd and Thomas, *Culture and the State*, chapters 2 and 3.

52. Schiller, *Aesthetic Education*, 17.

53. Rancière, "Ten Theses on Politics," *Dissensus*, 44.

2. THE PATHOLOGICAL SUBLIME: PLEASURE AND PAIN IN THE RACIAL REGIME

This chapter is revised from an essay originally published in *Postcolonial Enlightenment: Eighteenth-Century Colonialism and Postcolonial Theory*, ed. Daniel Carey and Lynn Festa (Oxford: Oxford University Press, 2009), 71–102.

1. Ranajit Guha, "The Prose of Counter-Insurgency," in *Selected Subaltern Studies*, ed. Ranajit Guha and Gayatri Chakravorty Spivak (New York: Oxford University Press, 1988).

2. J. Kameron Carter, *Race: A Theological Account* (Oxford: Oxford University Press, 2008), 6. It is also to this moment that Sylvia Wynter dates the rupture between the early modern Man as political subject of the state and the modern Man as a bioeconomic subject. See Sylvia Wynter, "Unsettling the Coloniality of Being/Power/Truth/Freedom: Towards the Human, After Man, Its Overrepresentation—An Argument," *CR: The New Centennial Review* 3, no. 3 (Fall 2003): 265, 318.

3. Karl Marx, *A Contribution to the Critique of Political Economy*, ed. Maurice Dobb, trans. S. W. Ryazanskaya (Moscow: Progress, 1970), 210–13. On the antecedents of capital that are understood to be part of its own prehistory,

see Dipesh Chakrabarty, "The Two Histories of Capital," in *Provincializing Europe: Postcolonial Thought and Historical Difference* (Princeton, N.J.: Princeton University Press, 2000), 47–71. I discuss the aesthetic as a "rational abstraction" in this sense of Marx's in Chapter 1.

4. For an overview of the prior taste-forming institutions of the eighteenth-century journals and coffeehouses, which produced not a universal claim but a "consensus" among "all respectable social ranks," see Terry Eagleton, *The Function of Criticism: From the Spectator to Post-Structuralism* (London: Verso, 1984), 9–27. As I discuss in Chapter 1, German bourgeois writers sought to emulate this emergent public sphere behind which they felt they lagged through producing their own "moral weeklies."

5. For further elaboration of the relation between aesthetic and anthropological understandings of culture, see Chapter 5.

6. See especially Frantz Fanon, *The Wretched of the Earth*, with a preface by Jean-Paul Sartre, trans. Constance Farrington (New York: Grove, 1968), 51–55.

7. See, in particular, Hortense J. Spillers's classic essay "Mama's Baby, Papa's Maybe" in *Black, White and in Color: Essays on American Literature and Culture* (Chicago: University of Chicago Press, 2003), 203–29. Alexander G. Weheliye, *Habeas Viscus: Racializing Assemblages, Biopolitics, and Black Feminist Theories of the Human* (Durham, N.C.: Duke University Press, 2014), builds compellingly on Spillers's (and Wynter's) arguments. On mimicry and hybridity in postcolonial theory, the seminal text is Homi Bhabha, *The Location of Culture* (London: Routledge, 1994), while the most extensive study of postcolonial melancholy is Ranjana Khanna, *Dark Continents: Psychoanalysis and Colonialism* (Durham, N.C.: Duke University Press, 2003).

8. Ronald A. T. Judy has made a comparable critique of African diaspora studies, which "identifies and analyzes tendencies of art, social organization, linguistic and religious practice, and customs among select populations and invests them with symbolic significance in order to identify a collective or group memory." See Ronald A. T. Judy, "Beside the Two Camps: Paul Gilroy and the Critique of Raciology," *boundary* 2 28, no. 3 (2001): 210.

9. See Guha, "The Prose of Counter-Insurgency," and Gayatri Chakravorty Spivak, "Subaltern Studies: Deconstructing Historiography," in *Selected Subaltern Studies*, ed. Ranajit Guha and Gayatri Chakravorty Spivak (Oxford: Oxford University Press, 1988).

10. For an excellent account of the distinction between Kant and the British aesthetic tradition and from Burke in particular, see Vanessa L. Ryan, "The Physiological Sublime: Burke's Critique of Reason," *Journal of the History of Ideas* 62, no. 2 (2001): 265–79. As she remarks, "At the point where the British tradition seems to come closest to the Kantian, namely, in the

writings of Burke, it also most clearly marks its distance from it. Burke is in some ways the least Kantian of eighteenth-century British thinkers. Whereas Kant holds that the sublime allows us to intuit our rational capacity, Burke's physiological version of the sublime involves a critique of reason" (266).

11. See further on this in Chapters 1 and 3.

12. Terry Eagleton, *The Ideology of the Aesthetic* (Oxford: Blackwell, 1990); Hannah Arendt, "The Crisis in Culture: Its Social and Political Significance," in *Between Past and Future: Six Exercises in Political Thought* (New York: Viking, 1961), 218.

13. Immanuel Kant, *Critique of Judgement*, trans. James Creed Meredith (Oxford: Clarendon, 1952), 104–5, §26; cited hereafter in the text as *CJ*. See the previous chapter for a full elaboration of the ramifications of Kant's painstaking insistence that the disinterest of the aesthetically judging subject is derived from the fact that its reflection is on the mode of its representation as a form rather than on the object represented. Describing Kant's analytic of the sublime as "an intuition of that part of the self that exceeds intuition by means of an immolating failure of intuition," Nick Land grasps succinctly the dissimulated violence of the aesthetic against the "pathological" human subject: "It would be difficult to delineate the violent desire to consummate the purity of reason in the annihilation of animality more starkly." See his essay "Delighted to Death," in *Fanged Noumena: Collected Writings, 1987–2007*, ed. Robin MacKay and Ray Brassier (New York: Sequence, 2011), 135, 140.

14. Although, as Daniel Carey shows, the conundrum posed by the desire to establish the grounds for universal human taste and moral feeling in the face of manifest diversity in each sphere exercises British thinkers throughout the eighteenth century, Kant's mode of posing the question sets quite different terms than theirs. From the outset, he rejects the deduction of common sense from experience rather than predicating it, as the British tradition (whatever its conclusions) tended to, on nature and the frame of the human senses. See Daniel Carey, *Locke, Shaftesbury, and Hutcheson: Contesting Diversity in the Enlightenment and Beyond* (Cambridge: Cambridge University Press, 2006).

15. Gayatri Chakravorty Spivak, *A Critique of Postcolonial Reason: Toward a History of the Vanishing Present* (Cambridge, Mass.: Harvard University Press, 1999), 4–6. See Hortense Spillers, "Interstices: A Small Drama of Words," chap. 6 in *Black, White and in Color*, 155.

16. See Denise Ferreira da Silva, *Toward a Global Idea of Race* (Minneapolis: University of Minnesota Press, 2007), xxxix. This distinction also marks the philosophical difference between Kant's narrative of development and Scottish Enlightenment historicism, influential though the latter may have been on German thought and on Kant himself. For Scottish thinkers, as Carey argues in *Locke, Shaftesbury, and Hutcheson*, "Difference emerged as a

feature of historical predicament, a conclusion that did not militate against the notion of a unified human nature but rather placed societies on a continuum from savagery to civilisation" (193). Kant's argument is grounded rather in the trajectory of the Subject and its emergence into autonomy out of heteronomy than in empirical history. On the influence of the Scottish Enlightenment in mid-eighteenth century Germany, and especially in Göttingen, see John H. Zammito, *Kant, Herder and the Birth of Anthropology* (Chicago: University of Chicago Press, 2002), 28.

17. As Meg Armstrong points out, Kant's account of the sublime in the Third Critique also departs from his own earlier empirical, and more Burkean, accounts in his *Observations on the Feeling of the Beautiful and Sublime* (1763), where the sublime is considered in relation to specific national types, and both in relation to gendered divisions. The Third Critique, on the contrary, is concerned only with a universal subject representative of humanity. See Meg Armstrong, "'The Effects of Blackness': Gender, Race and the Sublime in Aesthetic Theories of Kant and Burke," *Journal of Aesthetics and Art Criticism* 54, no. 3 (Summer 1996): 221–26.

18. For comments on Kant's response to the French Revolution and its very circumspect republicanism, as well as its place in his narrative of development, in *The Conflict of the Faculties*, see my "Foundations of Diversity," in *"Culture" and the Problem of the Disciplines*, ed. John Carlos Rowe (New York: Columbia University Press, 1998), 32, and Rebecca Comay, *Mourning Sickness: Hegel and the French Revolution* (Stanford, Calif.: Stanford University Press, 2011), 26–50. Philip Pettit offers an important theorization of republicanism as a political philosophy of nondomination in his *Republicanism: A Theory of Freedom and Government* (Oxford: Oxford University Press, 1997), 80–109.

19. Edmund Burke, *A Philosophical Enquiry into the Origin of Our Ideas of the Sublime and Beautiful*, facsimile of the 2nd ed. (1759; Menston, England: Scholar, 1970), 288; hereafter cited in the text as *OSB*.

20. Srinivas Aravamudan, *Tropicopolitans: Colonialism and Agency* (Durham, N.C.: Duke University Press, 1999), 198–202.

21. As Seamus Deane puts it, "Burke's weakness, to others his strength, is his capacity to find in subjectivity a universal dimension." *Foreign Affections: Essays on Edmund Burke* (Cork: Cork University Press, 2005), 5.

22. If, as James Engell suggests, Burke is on the cusp at this point of endowing the Imagination with active creative powers, as opposed to regarding it merely as the faculty that bears images from the senses to the reason, the principal point of these passages is to assert that the universality of Taste is predicated on the universal conformity of the senses in humans. This is where Burke most profoundly differs from Kant, for whom that universality

can only be grounded in a transcendental account of the subject. See James Engell, *The Creative Imagination: Enlightenment to Romanticism* (Cambridge, Mass.: Harvard University Press, 1981), 71–72.

23. As Aravamudan points out, Burke does suppress the outcome of the anecdote that he tells here, as to the Turkish Emperor's superior empirical knowledge of the anatomical effects of execution: He demonstrates his point by actually having a slave beheaded (see *Tropicopolitans*, 202). However, the point remains that the anecdote is introduced by Burke to emphasize the common ground of aesthetic taste despite other differences. This, of course, places Burke at some distance from either of his immediate British forebears, Shaftesbury and Hutcheson. Shaftesbury's definition of the society that would be the community of taste where consensus is formed is that of "polite society," that is, "an elevated collective," as Carey puts it, but one that has "something selective or restrictive about it." Burke is closer to his country-man Hutcheson in the universalizing and more democratic streak that leads the latter to reject Shaftesbury's "hierarchical notion of full access to the sociable and disinterested affections." But even Hutcheson "attempted to exclude from consideration those 'unfortunates' . . . living in rude circum-stances without the benefit of arts and proper human conditions. Hutcheson's traditional affiliations, based on innateness and a restrictive *consensus gentium*, become clearer in this context" (*Locke, Shaftesbury and Hutcheson*, 172; see also 127–28, 187). The limit on Burke's own capacity to include all human subjects will become clear later.

24. Cf. Zammito, *Kant, Herder and the Birth of Anthropology*, 256: "Kant emphatically condemned the impulses associated with empirical psychol-ogy as an obtuse 'naturalism.'" Although Zammito is speaking here mostly of anthropology rather than aesthetics, in the broader sense, Burke's analysis of taste is anthropological. Indeed, as Zammito elsewhere puts it, for Kant, aesthetics is rather "the key to anthropology" insofar as anthro-pology is considered not as accumulating empirical data but as concern-ing the ends of man. See John H. Zammito, *The Genesis of Kant's Critique of Judgment* (Chicago: University of Chicago Press, 1992), 292–305. For Kant, to project the awe felt in the face of an object onto nature involves a "subreption" that signals "a misplacement of the actual ground of the feeling, which authentically betokened the supersensible destination in the subject" (301).

25. Spivak, *Critique of Postcolonial Reason*, 14.

26. David Lloyd, "Kant's Examples," *Representations* 28 (Autumn 1989): 34–54.

27. In this respect, the Savage stands in Kant's Third Critique precisely as an example—that material remainder of particularity that cannot finally be

formalized out of existence precisely because it is a requirement of the system. For an elaboration of this predicament of Kant's aesthetics, see Lloyd, "Kant's Examples."

28. Though, of course, in those celebrated passages, Burke seeks to counter the popular and immediate appeal of revolution with the no less immediately affecting spectacle of a tragedy befalling the French monarchs. Indeed, one could say that Burke has learned his own lesson well, as the *Reflections on the Revolution in France* maintains the argument against the abstract theorizing of the radicals through the appeal of immediate affective rhetoric and through the invocation of familiar associations and the sublimity of power as the grounds for the legitimacy of monarchical government. On the theatrical rhetoric of the *Reflections* and other of his writings on the revolution, see Deane, *Foreign Affections*, 64–65 and 75–76.

29. For a full version of this argument, see David Lloyd and Paul Thomas, *Culture and the State* (London: Routledge, 1997), chapter 1.

30. William Godwin, *Enquiry Concerning Political Justice*, ed. Isaac Kramnick (Harmondsworth, England: Penguin, 1976), 183.

31. See Shelley Streeby, *American Sensations: Class, Empire, and the Production of Popular Culture* (Berkeley: University of California Press, 2002), for one study of such a popular tradition rooted in sensationalism. In my *Irish Culture and Colonial Modernity, 1800–2000: The Transformation of Oral Space* (Cambridge: Cambridge University Press, 2011), I track the persistence of subaltern forms based on collectivities predicated on pleasure and pain that Kant would have dubbed "pathological."

32. Cf. Weheliye, *Habeas Viscus*, 1–2, on the concepts of biopolitics and necropolitics and bare life: "These concepts, seen individually and taken as a group, neglect and/or actively dispute the existence of alternative modes of life alongside the violence, subjection, exploitation, and racialization that define the modern human."

33. Luke Gibbons, *Burke and Colonial Ireland: Aesthetics, Politics and the Colonial Sublime* (Cambridge: Cambridge University Press, 2003), especially chapters 1, 2, and 5. See also Deane, *Foreign Affections*, 22–27.

34. See Frantz Fanon, *Black Skin, White Masks*, foreword by Homi Bhabha, trans. Charles Lam Markmann (London: Pluto, 1986), 109–10 (cited hereafter in the text as *BSWM*), and *Wretched of the Earth*, 53. See also Fred Moten's brilliant commentary on both the limits of and the possibilities for rereading these formulations of Fanon's in his "The Case of Blackness," *Criticism* 50, no. 2 (Spring 2008): 177–218.

35. Fanon, *Wretched of the Earth*, 38, contrasts the interpellative function of Western civil society with the direct confrontation of the colonized with police violence. Following Fanon, Frank Wilderson argues for the complete

antipathy between civil society and blackness: "The Prison Slave as Hegemony's (Silent) Scandal," *Social Justice* 30, no. 2 (2003): 18. Insofar as the construction of civility requires—as Chapter 3 will explore further—the constitutive barring of the black subject from representation, Wilderson's assertion seems correct. See also Lewis R. Gordon, "Lived Experience, Embodying Impossibility," chap. 3 in *What Fanon Said: A Philosophical Introduction to His Life and Thought* (New York: Fordham University Press, 2015), 48: "Blacks live, at best, on the level of the particular, not the universal. Thus, black experience suffers from a failure to bridge the gap between subjective life and the world." My emphasis of the collapse of subjectivity back into the body does differ from Ronald A. T. Judy's assertion that for Fanon:

> there is no *nègre* body, only the *nègre imago*, and it is an object in-itself only for the consciousness that is human. . . . If it is this paradoxical moment in the becoming of consciousness that must be overcome in order to gain freedom, then why does Fanon insist that what must be remembered is the fact of the *nègre* body? Precisely because the *nègre* is a symptom of the repression of the repression of the experience of the body. What Fanon calls "corporeal scheme" is arguably the expression (*Darstellung*) of the essence of consciousness *along with* "the residual sensations and perceptions primarily of a tactile, vestibular, kinesthetic, and visual character."

See Ronald A. T. Judy, "Fanon's Body of Black Experience," in *Fanon: A Critical Reader*, ed. Lewis R. Gordon, T. Denean Sharpley-Whiting, and Renée T. White (Oxford: Blackwell, 1996), 54.

36. Frantz Fanon, "Racism and Culture," chap. 2 in *Toward the African Revolution: Political Essays*, trans. Haakon Chevalier (1964; New York: Grove, 1988), 31. The whole passage merits citation:

> The unilaterally decreed normative value of certain cultures deserves our careful attention. . . .
>
> There is first affirmed the existence of human groups having no culture; then of a hierarchy of cultures; and finally the concept of cultural relativity.
>
> We have here the whole range from overall negation to singular and specific recognition. It is precisely this fragmented and bloody history that we must sketch on the level of cultural anthropology.

37. See Armstrong, "Effects of Blackness," 228, where she also compares Burke and Fanon, arguing both that Fanon's anecdote "can be used as an effective counterexample to Burke's claim that the 'effects of blackness' are entirely natural" and that the aesthetic gaze's power is "masked, and possibly occluded, in the innocent terror of the boy blind since birth."

38. Armstrong considers the suggestion that the female body can be at once "(safely) beautiful and, as in the case of a body which is both black *and*

female, sublime and threatening" as a contradiction, whereas I would regard it rather as profoundly coherent with the logic of Burke's analysis. See Armstrong, "Effects of Blackness," 215.

39. Aravamudan comments extensively on this passage, remarking that "the African woman seems in a strange structural equivalence to the despot" (*Tropicopolitans*, 201; for the full discussion, see 192–201). My point is rather that, while Burke finds the source of the sublime to be some "modification of power," in this singular case of blackness, there is a convergence of the power of the sublime with the "passive" power of the feminine/beautiful.

40. Hortense Spillers, "'All the Things You Could Be By Now, If Sigmund Freud's Wife Was Your Mother': Psychoanalysis and Race," in *Black, White and in Color*, 390.

41. For alternative readings of Fanon's misogyny and of his overdetermined "infernal circle" (*BSWM*, 116), see Rey Chow, "The Politics of Admittance: Female Sexual Agency, Miscegenation, and the Formation of Community in Frantz Fanon," in *Ethics after Idealism: Theory, Culture, Ethnicity, Reading* (Bloomington: Indiana University Press, 1998), 55–73; Diana Fuss, "Interior Colonies: Frantz Fanon and the Politics of Identification," chap. 5 in *Identification Papers* (New York: Routledge, 1995), 142–44, 157–58; and Françoise Vergès, *Monsters and Revolutionaries: Colonial Family Romance and Métissage* (Durham, N.C.: Duke University Press, 1999), 209–11.

42. Armstrong, in her extended discussion of this passage, notes that in Burke, the presence of the black female "threatens the power or integrity of the boy's gaze" ("Effects of Blackness," 220). For a related reading of Fanon's analysis, see Robert Gooding-Williams's essay on the Rodney King trial, "Look, A Negro!," in *Look, A Negro! Philosophical Essays on Race, Culture and Politics* (New York: Routledge, 2006), 1–16. The demythification of the ahistorical figure of the black man as violent, threatening and "[incarnating] a wilderness chaos inimical to civilization" (11) can only be countered by strategies that invoke the "economic and historical" realities of racist structures of power and violence, as Fanon does.

43. Wilderson proceeds to argue that "the Black American subject does not generate historical categories," producing a "historical scandal" for liberal and Marxist historiographical assumptions and practices ("Prison Slave as Hegemony's (Silent) Scandal," 24–25).

44. Carter remarks of Kant's racial science: "If the white race exemplifies humanity on its way to perfection, the black race embodies the departure and failure to attain this perfection. In the Negro race, white flesh observes a race so mired in its particularity as never to be able to speak with universal force and, therefore, as never positioned to be an analogy or index of the universal. Black flesh lacks universal gravitas. It is trapped in its particularity in such a

way that it always needs to justify its existence before universal white flesh" (*Race*, 90).

45. On the dynamics of colonial rage, see Albert Memmi, *The Colonizer and the Colonized*, introduction by Jean-Paul Sartre, trans. Howard Greenfield (Boston: Beacon, 1967), 66–67.

3. RACE UNDER REPRESENTATION

1. Frantz Fanon, "Concerning Violence," in *The Wretched of the Earth*, preface by Jean-Paul Sartre, trans. Constance Farrington (New York: Grove, 1968), 38.

2. Among many such critiques, see Johannes Fabian, *Time and the Other: How Anthropology Makes Its Object* (New York: Columbia University Press, 1983); Andre Gunder Frank, *On Capitalist Underdevelopment* (Bombay: Oxford University Press, 1975); Majid Rahnema, "Under the Banner of Development," *Seeds of Change* 1–2 (1986): 37–46; Arturo Escobar, *Encountering Development: The Making and Unmaking of the Third World* (Princeton, N.J.: Princeton University Press, 1995); and the work of Dipesh Chakrabarty in *Provincializing Europe: Postcolonial Thought and Historical Difference* (Princeton, N.J.: Princeton University Press, 2000) and *Habitations of Modernity: Essays in the Wake of Subaltern Studies* (Princeton, N.J.: Princeton University Press, 2002).

3. "The logic of obliteration operates mostly unchallenged even in the markers of the end of race." Denise Ferreira da Silva, "Extraordinary Times: A Preface," *Cultural Dynamics* 26, no. 1 (2014): 4. Jodi Melamed similarly argues in *Represent and Destroy: Rationalizing Violence in the New Racial Capitalism* (Minneapolis: University of Minnesota Press, 2011) that "the shift away from white supremacy toward formal antiracism has enabled liberal modes of instituting power to expand and intensify as putatively antiracist social norms have saturated more domains of social life and interpellated racialized subjects previously disciplined primarily through overt applications of force" (11).

4. Sylvia Wynter, "Unsettling the Coloniality of Being/Power/Truth/Freedom: Towards the Human, After Man, Its Overrepresentation—An Argument," *CR: The New Centennial Review* 3, no. 3 (Fall 2003): 282.

5. See Michael Omi and Howard Winant, *Racial Formation in the United States: From the 1960s to the 1990s*, 2nd ed. (New York: Routledge, 1994), 59.

6. For an elaboration of the concept of aesthetic culture in its relation to representation and the state, see David Lloyd and Paul Thomas, *Culture and the State* (New York: Routledge, 1997).

7. I follow Omi and Winant in deriving this concept of sites from Herbert Gintis and Samuel Bowles: "A site is defined not by what is *done* there,

but by what imparts *regularity* to what is done there, its characteristic 'rules of the game.'" Cited from "Structure and Practice in the Labor Theory of Value," *Review of Radical Political Economics* 12, no. 4 (Winter 1981): 4, in Omi and Winant, *Racial Formation*, 166. As may be apparent from what follows, I would annex the notion of a regularity within sites to a quite Kantian concept of the "regulative idea" in order to indicate that it is the implicit teleology, and not merely the contingent practices, of social institutions that structures those institutions as reproducible at all levels, including that of the subjects formed by them.

8. See Paul de Man, "Kant and Schiller," in *Aesthetic Ideology*, ed. Andrzej Warminski (Minneapolis: University of Minnesota Press, 1996), where he comments that in Schiller and others, "there is a regression, an attempt to account for, to domesticate the critical incisiveness of the original" (130). In "Kant's Examples," *Representations* 28 (Autumn 1989), I argue for the fundamentally pedagogical ends of the Third Critique.

9. Friedrich Schiller, *On the Aesthetic Education of Man, in a Series of Letters*, ed. and trans. Elizabeth M. Wilkinson and L. A. Willoughby (Oxford: Clarendon, 1967), 195; cited hereafter as *AEM*. In an interesting extension of this narrative of the senses, the German philosopher and racial theorist Lorenz Oken would divide the races of man according to whichever of the five senses dominated a race. See Michael Banton, *Racial Theories* (Cambridge: Cambridge University Press, 1987), 18–19.

10. Immanuel Kant, *Critique of Judgement*, trans. James Creed Meredith (Oxford: Clarendon, 1952), I, 225, §59; cf. 65, §14. Cited in the text hereafter as *CJ*.

11. See my comments in Chapter 1 on the limits of an empirical deduction of racial logics.

12. Cf. Fanon's remarks on this aspect of colonial self-legitimation in "Concerning Violence," *Wretched of the Earth*, 41: "The native is declared insensible to ethics: he represents not only the absence of values, but also the negation of values." I have discussed Arnold's and Mill's racial assumptions more extensively in *Nationalism and Minor Literature: James Clarence Mangan and the Emergence of Irish Cultural Nationalism* (Berkeley: University of California Press, 1987), 6–13, and in "Genet's Genealogy: European Minorities and the Ends of the Canon," *Cultural Critique* 6 (Spring 1987): 162–70. On the conservative figures mentioned here, and others, see Banton, *Racial Theories*, 19–60. On Gobineau, see also Paul Gilroy, *Against Race: Imagining Political Culture beyond the Color Line* (Cambridge, Mass.: Belknap, 2000), 330.

13. See Colette Guillaumin, "Race and Nature: The System of Marks. The Idea of a Natural Group and Social Relationships," *Feminist Issues* 8, no. 2 (Fall 1988): 25–43; Fanon, "Concerning Violence," *Wretched of the*

Earth, 41. On the misfit between racism and imperialism, see Banton, *Racial Theories*, 62.

14. Guillaumin, "Race and Nature," 32–33. Guillaumin uses the expression *symbol* to describe arbitrary marks. I prefer to keep the term *symbol* for those signs that, in principle, "participate in what they represent," that have, that is, "an organic relationship" to the signified. It is a commonplace of literary critical history that the devaluation of allegory in favor of the symbol takes place in the late eighteenth century and early nineteenth century. A shift in aesthetics accordingly corresponds to a shift in racist discourse, confirming the congruence between relatively discrete spheres of cultural practice.

15. Guillaumin, "Race and Nature," 41.

16. On "Person and Condition," see Schiller, *AEM*, 73–77. Thomas and I discuss these concepts further in *Culture and the State*, 48–51. See also my discussion of *das vertretbare Subjekt* (the fungible or exchangeable subject) in Chapter 1.

17. J. Kameron Carter, in *Race: A Theological Account* (Oxford: Oxford University Press, 2008), sees this relation between global ubiquity and exemplary universality as central to Kant's scientific racism: "Functioning also as a teleologically structured philosophy of history, Kant's theory of race articulates an account of the destiny of the species as coinciding with the global perfection and spread of whiteness" (81).

18. See Robert Bernasconi's discussion of Kant's questioning of the "purpose" or need to exist of various ethnic groups in his "Kant's Third Thoughts on Race," in *Reading Kant's Geography*, ed. Stuart Elden and Eduardo Mendieta (Albany: SUNY Press, 2011), 310.

19. On the botanist Saussure, see Kant (*CJ*, I, 115–16, §29). Jacques Derrida discusses the complicity between a moral discourse and an empirical culturalism in relation to the Third Critique in "Le Parergon," in *La vérité en peinture* (Paris: Flammarion, 1978), 42. The anthropological subject is, as Gregory Schrempp puts it in a very valuable essay, "boundless." See Schrempp, "Aristotle's Other Self: On the Boundless Subject of Anthropological Discourse," in *Romantic Motives: Essays on Anthropological Sensibility*, ed. George W. Stocking Jr. (Madison: University of Wisconsin Press, 1989). In tracing anthropology's founding terms to Aristotle and, more immediately, to Kant, Schrempp most valuably demonstrates its indebtedness to the "principle of identity," a point that has interesting implications for the present essay. On the relation between scientific rationality, Western cultural hegemony, and anthropology, see Partha Chatterjee, *Nationalist Thought and the Colonial World: A Derivative Discourse* (London: Zed, 1986), 14–17. For a valuable study of the formation of the white colonial self as "ubiquitous," as "abstract,

unspecifiable in its contents," see Satya P. Mohanty, "Kipling's Children and the Colour Line," *Race and Class* 31, no. 1 (July/September 1989): 36.

20. Paul Ricoeur, "The Metaphorical Process as Cognition, Imagination, and Feeling," in *On Metaphor*, ed. Sheldon Sacks (Chicago: University of Chicago Press, 1979), 146.

21. The Abbé Étienne de Condillac, *Essai sur l'origine des connaissances humaines*, ed. Charles Porset (1746; repr., Paris: Galilée, 1973), bk. 1, sec. 2, 194, quoted by Paul de Man, "The Epistemology of Metaphor," in *On Metaphor*, ed. Sheldon Sacks (Chicago: University of Chicago Press, 1979), 20.

22. See Paul Ricoeur, "Metaphor and the Main Problem of Hermeneutics," *NLH* 6, no. 1 (Autumn 1974): 108–10. Cyrus Hamlin draws attention to this moment in Ricoeur's essay in order to develop his argument concerning the place of metaphor in the Romantic construction of selfhood; see "The Temporality of Selfhood: Metaphor and Romantic Poetry," *NLH* 6, no. 1 (Autumn 1974): 172. His argument has been very valuable for some of the contentions of the present essay. See also, on the relation between metaphor and implicit narrative, de Man, "Epistemology of Metaphor," *On Metaphor*, 21–22: "From the recognition of language as trope, one is led to the telling of a tale, to the narrative sequence I have just described. The temporal deployment of an initial complication, of a structural knot, indicates the close, though not necessarily complementary, relationship between trope and narrative, knot and plot."

23. Ricoeur, "Metaphorical Process," *On Metaphor*, 154.

24. Banton notes how the term *assimilation* transforms in meaning from "any process by which peoples became more similar" to a process by which one people "was expected to absorb another . . . without itself undergoing any significant change" in *Racial Theories*, ix. Fanon's comment is fittingly acerbic on the ideological bent of both understandings: "This event, which is commonly designated as alienation, is naturally very important. It is found in the official texts under the name of assimilation." Frantz Fanon, "Racism and Culture," chap. 2 in *Toward the African Revolution: Political Essays*, trans. Haakon Chevalier (1964; repr., New York: Grove, 1988), 38.

25. On the perdurability of simian metaphors for black people, see Tommy L. Lott, "Racist Discourse and the Negro-ape Metaphor," in *The Invention of Race: Black Culture and the Politics of Representation* (Oxford: Blackwell, 1999), 7–13.

26. I think here especially of Homi K. Bhabha, "The Other Question: Stereotype, Discrimination and the Discourse of Colonialism," in *The Location of Culture* (New York: Routledge, 1994), 66–92. The "four-term strategy" of colonial discourse that Bhabha posits (circulating between metaphor and metonymy, narcissism and aggression) seems to restore to the stereotype

the fixity that his analysis critiques, only in the form of an anxious oscillation between lack and the masking function of the fetish. This transfer from metonymy to metaphor in the process of assimilation is both irreversible and determinant for the forms that resistance to assimilation takes—a dialectic succinctly analyzed by Fanon in "Racism and Culture," *Toward the African Revolution*.

27. Sigmund Freud, "On Fetishism," in *On Sexuality: Three Essays on the Theory of Sexuality and Other Works* (Harmondsworth, England: Penguin, 1977), 352. For the theory of castration, see the essays "The Dissolution of the Oedipus Complex" (1924) and "Some Physical Consequences of the Anatomical Distinction between the Sexes" (1925), in *On Sexuality*, 313–22 and 323–344 respectively. Cited hereafter as *DOC* and *ADS* in the text.

28. In Sigmund Freud, "Infantile Sexuality" (1905), in *On Sexuality*, 116–19.

29. The subject of psychoanalysis, which is produced, as Lacan's Schema L illustrates, in suspension between the ego and the superego—that is, between the "I" formed in the mirror stage and the Other or "Name-of-the-Father"—is not identical to the Kantian aesthetic Subject, but it is similarly structured in a process of formalization. For Schema L, see Jacques Lacan, "D'une question préliminaire à tout traitement possible de la psychose," in *Écrits* 2 (Paris: Seuil, 1971), 63. Louis Althusser begins to sketch the relation between this subject, the ethical subject, and the ideological subject in "Ideology and Ideological State Apparatuses (Notes towards an Investigation)," in *Lenin and Philosophy and Other Essays*, trans. Ben Brewster (New York: Monthly Review, 1971), 127–86. On the temporality of subject formation and interpellation in Althusser, see Judith Butler, *The Psychic Life of Power: Theories in Subjection* (Stanford, Calif.: Stanford University Press, 1997).

30. The considerable anxiety aroused in many racist societies by miscegenation is a mark of the loss of verisimilitude in appeals to immediate visual discrimination. Miscegenation, as a metaphor for different possible cultural formations, is in turn troublesome precisely insofar as it raises the question of the verisimilitude or canonicity of dominant cultural narratives and suggests the possibility of a limitless transformation of cultures. Unlike assimilation, it cannot be organized in terms of a developmental hierarchy and, in relation to the formation of national culture, must always be recast in the form of an *embranqueamento*, or "whitening," which restores both the developmental narrative and, at a quite literal level, its "residual" logic. I am indebted for these observations, and for much of my initial thinking on assimilation in this chapter, to Zita Nunes's work on Brazilian modernism and anthropology in relation to the formation of national culture; see her *Cannibal Democracy: Race*

and Representation in the Literature of the Americas (Minneapolis: University of Minnesota Press, 2008). See also Jean Bernabé, Patrick Chamoiseau, and Raphael Confiant, *Éloge de la creolité* (Paris: Gallimard, 1989), 27–28: "*Du fait de sa mosaïque constitutive, la Créolité est une spécificité ouverte . . . L'exprimer c'est exprimer non une synthèse, pas simplement un métissage, où n'importe qu'elle autre unicité. C'est exprimer une totalité kaléidoscopique, c'est à dire la conscience non totalitaire d'une diversité preservée.*" On the social issues raised by miscegenation under slavery in the US South and the West Indies, see Robert J. C. Young, *Colonial Desire: Hybridity in Theory, Culture and Race* (New York: Routledge, 1995), chapter 6. On the displacement of anxious discourses on miscegenation by a celebratory language of "multiracialism," see Jared Sexton, *Amalgamation Schemes: Antiblackness and the Critique of Multiracialism* (Minneapolis: University of Minnesota Press, 2008).

31. Though in most respects this essay is profoundly indebted to Frantz Fanon's analysis of racism in *Black Skin, White Masks*, at this point I would depart somewhat from the emphasis he places on projection as the psychic mechanism of racism. See Fanon, "The Negro and Psychopathology," chap. 6 in *Black Skin, White Masks*, foreword Homi Bhabha, trans. Charles Lam Markmann (London: Pluto, 1986), esp. 190–94. As I shall argue below, Fanon very rapidly moves beyond and complicates the notion of projection, not least by invoking what he terms "cultural imposition" (193). Cited in the text hereafter as *BSWM*.

32. Charles Kingsley, *Charles Kingsley: His Letters and Memories of His Life*, vol. 3, ed. Frances E. Kingsley (London: Macmillan, 1901), 111, cited in L. P. Curtis, *Anglo-Saxons and Celts: A Study of Anti-Irish Prejudice in Victorian England* (Bridgeport, Conn.: University of Bridgeport, 1968), 84. Thomas Carlyle's oxymoron is to be found in his extended essay, *Sartor Resartus*, in *Sartor Resartus and On Heroes, Hero Worship and the Heroic in History* (London: Dent, 1908), 210. I discuss its implications for understanding the ascription of inauthenticity to the colonized in *Nationalism and Minor Literature*, 206–7. Carlyle and Kingsley, along with many other nineteenth-century British commentators, reproduce constantly the unstable slippage between metaphor and metonymy in their characterizations of the Irish as racial others. See my *Irish Culture and Colonial Modernity, 1800–2000: The Transformation of Oral Space* (Cambridge: Cambridge University Press, 2011), 31–48.

33. On the relation between "whiteness" as a metaphor and the identitarian structure of metaphor for which it is a metaphor, see Jacques Derrida's "White Mythology: Metaphor in the Text of Philosophy," in *Margins of Philosophy*, trans. Alan Bass (Chicago: University of Chicago Press, 1982), 207–71. In a more historical work than this, it would be necessary to supply here some account of the history and contradictory logic of imperial

practices of assimilation and their national varieties. Suffice it to say here that racism is at once the structure of and limit to assimilation insofar as it is predicated on a hierarchy of cultural differences yet universal in its claims and aims. Nunes's work, cited above, is very suggestive in this respect, as are the comparative studies in Patrick Wolfe's *Traces of History: Elementary Structures of Race* (London: Verso, 2016).

34. For some comments on the differences between British and French colonialism, see Renate Zahar, *Colonialism and Alienation: Concerning Frantz Fanon's Political Theory* (Benin City, Nigeria: Ethiope, 1974), xxi–xxii. Though differences of intensity may appear, the structure of assimilation remains largely the same where applied by either regime.

35. See, for example, Benedict Anderson's discussion of what he calls "colonial pilgrimages," *Imagined Communities: Reflections on the Origin and Spread of Nationalism* (London: Verso, 2006), 114–40. This phenomenon is crucial to the dialectic of decolonization outlined throughout Fanon's writings, especially in "Concerning Violence" and "The Pitfalls of National Consciousness," chaps. 1 and 3, respectively, in *Wretched of the Earth*.

36. Wynter, "Unsettling the Coloniality of Being," 271.

37. Samir Seikaly, "*Season of Migration to the North*: History in the Novel," in *Tayeb Salih's Season of Migration to the North: A Casebook*, ed. Mona Takieddine Amyuni (Beirut: American University of Beirut, 1985), 137–38. The implication here that the "primordial identity" sought by the colonized is an essential category stands in need of correction by Fanon's dialectical grasp of the turn of the colonized to a revalorization of cultures termed primitive or primordial by the colonizer. See especially "Racism and Culture," *Toward the African Revolution*, 41–43. Saree Makdisi, "The Empire Renarrated: *Season of Migration to the North* and the Reinvention of the Present," *Critical Inquiry* 18 (Summer 1992): 804–20, notes this divide of the main characters, "trapped between cultures" and as a result embodying the contradictions of the rest of society (814). His conclusion, however, invokes a Fanonian sense of dialectic. It is also worth referencing, in order not to overemphasize the "tragic" quality of the colonial divide, Dipesh Chakrabarty's more sanguine account of living a dual cultural identity in "Reason and the Critique of Historicism" in *Provincializing Europe*, 240–43.

38. Tayeb Salih, *Season of Migration to the North*, trans. Denys Johnson-Davies (London: Heinemann, 1976), 1–4. Page numbers cited in the text hereafter. The narrator will, in the course of the novel, come to realize the rather different valence of a European saying that a man of color is "just like a white man": just like but never quite.

39. Salih himself remarks on how he first intended to write a straightforward thriller but became gradually more interested in figures "who showed a

strange attraction to the Arab world, the type of romanticism which I started to challenge in the novel." Unpublished lecture to American University of Beirut, quoted by Mona Takieddine Amyuni in the introduction to *Tayeb Salih's Season of Migration to the North: A Casebook*, ed. Mona Takieddine Amyuni (Beirut: American University of Beirut, 1985), 15. The critique of romantic orientalism entails a critique also of its formal vehicles.

40. Though he does not invoke the *Bildungsroman*, Makdisi, in "The Empire Renarrated," explores the European "formal inspiration" of the novel and remarks on its sources in Arabic literary traditions, resulting in a text that is "an unstable synthesis of European and Arabic forms and traditions" (815).

41. Carmen Torres has pointed out that the destructive, and often disturbing, relations between Mustafa Sa'eed and English women could be attributable to the contradictory relation between gender and colonialism: White women are, as white, dominant subjects but, as women, dominated objects. The reverse is true for the African man; see her "Colonialism and Gender in *A Season of Migration to the North*" (master's thesis, University of California, Berkeley, May 1990), 11–23. I am also indebted to Kadiatu Kanneh's reminder of the hilariousness with which these relations can be perceived: Both colonial history and interracial sexual relations can be perceived alternately as tragedy or farce. In the latter case, what is perhaps emphasized is the element of performative masquerade and the ease with which characters can take one another's places; see "Place, Time, and the Black Body: Myth and Resistance," *Oxford Literary Review* 13, no. 1 (1991): 140–63.

42. From an interview with Salih, quoted in Ali Abdallah Abbas, "The Father of Lies: The Role of Mustafa Sa'eed as Second Self in *Season of Migration to the North*," in *Tayeb Salih's Season of Migration to the North: A Casebook*, ed. Mona Takieddine Amyuni (Beirut: American University of Beirut, 1985), 30. Since Abbas argues that Sa'eed is not a "representative" character but "a fragment of the human psyche" (27) and that the novel is a confrontation between two halves of the human psyche rather than between East and West (29), I would comment that such readings, though failing to give sufficient due to the novel's exploration of colonialism, do draw attention properly to the impossibility of integration that it dramatizes. The tantalizing "incompleteness" of the novel itself is matched by incompleteness within its characters.

43. It is perhaps superfluous to highlight Fanon's masculinist pronouns and perspective, though on the question of Fanon's contradictory position in relation to his colonized manhood, see Chapter 2. Charles Lam Markmann's translation perhaps aptly introduces the verb-form *slave*, where the French *s'acharne* is perhaps more accurately translated as "is bent on." For the French, see Frantz Fanon, *Peau Noire, Masques Blancs* (Paris: Éditions du Seuil, 1952), 7.

44. The French is "L'Expérience vécue du Noir" (The lived experience of the black), a more phenomenological twist than the English conveys. See Fred Moten, "The Case of Blackness," *Criticism* 50, no. 2 (Spring 2008): 177–218.

45. For discussion of Fanon's ambivalence toward *négritude* and his rejection of Sartre's effort in "Black Orpheus" to negate blackness by subsuming it into the dialectic of humanity, see Robert Bernasconi, "The Assumption of Negritude: Aimé Césaire, Frantz Fanon, and the Vicious Circle of Racial Politics," *Parallax* 8, no. 2 (2002): 69–83, and "Identity and Agency in Frantz Fanon," in *Sartre Studies International* 10, no. 2 (2004): 106–7; and Kelly Oliver, "Alienation and Its Double; or, The Secretion of Race," in *Race and Racism in Continental Philosophy*, ed. Robert Bernasconi (Bloomington: Indiana University Press, 2003), 190.

46. For the "demon of comparison," see Alexander G. Weheliye, *Habeas Viscus: Racializing Assemblages, Biopolitics, and Black Feminist Theories of the Human* (Durham, N.C.: Duke University Press, 2014), 72. Elsewhere he comments that the "grammar of comparison . . . will merely reaffirm Man's existent hierarchies rather than design novel assemblages of relation" (13).

47. Lewis R. Gordon, "Lived Experience, Embodying Impossibility," chap. 3 in *What Fanon Said: A Philosophical Introduction to His Life and Thought* (New York: Fordham University Press, 2015), 68.

48. Zahar comments that "there can be no doubt that by the very fact of idealizing assimilation, while at the same time brutally preventing its realization, the officially proclaimed policy of French colonialism contributed in no small measure to the specific phenomena of alienation and frustration analyzed [in her study]" (*Colonialism and Alienation*, xxii).

49. Weheliye, *Habeas Viscus*, 3.

50. Sylvia Wynter has gone furthest in registering and elaborating the force of Fanon's remark that "Beside phylogeny and ontogeny stands sociogeny" (*BSWM*, 13). Walter Mignolo comments: "Put differently, the sociogenic principle reveals what the ontogenesis principle hides: that race is not in the body but rather is built in the social imaginary grounded on colonial difference. Wynter follows Fanon by setting the limits of ontogenesis: ontogenesis is an imperial category while sociogenesis introduces the perspective of the subject that ontogenesis classifies as object." See Walter D. Mignolo, "Sylvia Wynter: What Does It Mean to Be Human?," in *Sylvia Wynter: On Being Human as Praxis*, ed. Katherine McKittrick (Durham, N.C.: Duke University Press, 2015), 116, and also Demetrius L. Eudell, "'Come on Kid, Let's Go Get the Thing': The Sociogenic Principle and the Being of Being Black / Human," in McKittrick, *Sylvia Wynter*.

51. See Omi and Winant, *Racial Formation*, 61; on the "racial state," see 76–77. We could remark that this structural requirement determined the necessity for Obama to represent himself as a "postracial" president.

52. Omi and Winant, 62.

53. Althusser, "Ideology and Ideological State Apparatuses," *Lenin and Philosophy*, 127–86.

54. Walter Benjamin, "On the Concept of History," in *Selected Writings*, vol. 4, *1938–1940*, ed. Howard Eiland and Michael W. Jennings, trans. Edmund Jephcott et al. (Cambridge, Mass.: Belknap, 2003), 392; Antonio Gramsci, *Selections from the Prison Notebooks*, ed. and trans. Quintin Hoare and Geoffrey Nowell Smith (New York: International, 1971), 52–55. My own effort to engage in such a project, impossible to achieve in the present theoretical framework, is in *Irish Culture and Colonial Modernity*.

55. Cedric J. Robinson, *Forgeries of Meaning: Blacks and the Regimes of Race in American Theater and Film before World War II* (Chapel Hill: University of North Carolina Press, 2007), xii.

4. REPRESENTATION'S COUP

1. Frantz Fanon, "Concerning Violence," chap. 1 in *The Wretched of the Earth*, preface by Jean-Paul Sartre, trans. Constance Farrington (New York: Grove, 1968), 51–52.

2. Gayatri Chakravorty Spivak, "Can the Subaltern Speak?," in *Marxism and the Interpretation of Culture*, ed. Cary Nelson and Lawrence Grossberg (Urbana: University of Illinois Press, 1988). I am using this version rather than that which now makes part of chapter 3 ("History") of *A Critique of Postcolonial Reason: Toward a History of the Vanishing Present* (Cambridge, Mass.: Harvard University Press, 1999) because it is reproduced there with little significant alteration and the prior published essay continues to be the text used in teaching and the one most frequently cited.

3. For this distinction, see Walter Benjamin, "Critique of Violence," in *Selected Writings*, vol. 1, *1913-1926* (Cambridge, MA: Belknap Press, 1996), 243.

4. Gayatri Chakravorty Spivak, "Supplementing Marxism," in *Whither Marxism? Global Crisis in the International Context*, ed. Bernard Magnus and Stephen Cullenberg (London: Routledge, 1995), 115. I am grateful to Heather Laird for drawing my attention to this essay in *Subversive Law in Ireland, 1879–1920: From 'Unwritten Law' to the Dail Courts* (Dublin: Four Courts, 2005), 136.

5. Homi Bhabha, in *The Location of Culture* (London: Routledge, 1994), is the postcolonial critic who has worked the terrains of hybridity and ambivalence most exhaustively. Alfred Arteaga draws together the concepts of

hybridity and *mestizaje* in "An Other Tongue," in *An Other Tongue: Nation and Ethnicity in the Linguistic Borderlands*, ed. Alfred Arteaga (Durham, N.C.: Duke University Press, 1994).

6. Laird, *Subversive Law*, 134.

7. For an elaboration of this point, see Lisa Lowe and David Lloyd, *The Politics of Culture in the Shadow of Culture* (Durham, N.C.: Duke University Press, 1997), 23–25.

8. Shahid Amin's *Event, Metaphor, Memory: Chauri Chaura, 1922–1992* (Berkeley: University of California Press, 1995) remains for me the most compelling study of the disjunction between subaltern and nationalist practice and ideology, though there are many such instances in the archives of subaltern studies.

9. Elsewhere, I argue that certain nationalist Marxist thinkers like James Connolly in Ireland and José Carlos Mariátegui in Peru envisage a different potentiality for radical resistance that did not have to pass through the stages of capitalist development but instead could draw on what we now term subaltern cultural formations. The recent resurgence of radical indigenous politics in Latin America may bear out their thinking. David Lloyd, "Rethinking National Marxism: James Connolly and 'Celtic Communism,'" in *Irish Times: Temporalities of Modernity* (Dublin: Field Day, 2008), 101–26.

10. Gayatri Chakravorty Spivak, "Subaltern Studies: Deconstructing Historiography," in *Selected Subaltern Studies*, ed. Ranajit Guha and Gayatri Chakravorty Spivak (New York: Oxford University Press, 1988), 16. See also Dipesh Chakrabarty, "Translating Life-worlds into Labor and History," in *Provincializing Europe: Postcolonial Thought and Historical Difference* (Princeton, N.J.: Princeton University Press, 2000), 72–96.

11. Spivak, "Can the Subaltern Speak?," 287.

12. Spivak, "Deconstructing Historiography," 11.

13. Spivak, 16.

14. Karl Marx, *The Eighteenth Brumaire of Louis Bonaparte* (Moscow: Foreign Languages, 1954), 106; cited hereafter in-text as *Brumaire*.

15. For the German, see Karl Marx and Friedrich Engels, *Der Achtzehnte Brumaire des Louis Bonaparte, Werke*, vol. 8 (Berlin: Dietz, 1960), 198–99.

16. As Marx notes, their support for the state had already been won by the uncle, Napoleon Bonaparte, who parceled out land among the peasants, transforming virtual serfs into smallholders and winning their allegiance to the state and to himself (*Brumaire*, 108).

17. Spivak, "Can the Subaltern Speak?," 279.

18. Spivak, 275.

19. Karl Marx, *Das Kapital: Kritik der politischen Oekonomie*, ed. B. Kautsky (Stuttgart, Germany: Kröner, 1957), 51; translated by S. Moore and E. Ave-

ling as *Capital: A Critique of Political Economy*, vol. 1, ed. F. Engels (London: Lawrence and Wishart, 1954), 77 (translation slightly modified).

20. Immanuel Kant, *The Critique of Judgement*, trans. James Creed Meredith (Oxford: Clarendon, 1952), 151; for the German text, see Immanuel Kant, *Kritik der Urteilskraft*, vol. 10 of *Werkausgabe*, ed. Wilhelm Weischedel (Frankfurt, Germany: Suhrkamp, 1974), 225–26.

21. See Chapter 1 for an elaboration of this passage and its relation to the very possibility of the political.

22. Georg Wilhelm Friedrich Hegel, introduction to *Aesthetics: Lectures on Fine Art*, 2 vols., trans. T. M. Knox (Oxford: Oxford University Press, 1975), 1:31; for the German text, see Georg Wilhelm Friedrich Hegel, *Vorlesungen über die Philosophie der Kunst*, ed. A. Gethmann-Siefert (1823; repr., Berlin: Meiner Felix, 1998), 13.

23. Hegel, introduction to *Aesthetics*, 31.

24. David Lloyd and Paul Thomas, *Culture and the State* (London: Routledge, 1997).

25. Nowhere is this more apparent than in recent debates over the Palestinian call for a boycott of Israeli academic institutions. Defenders of the racial state of Israel insist that the individual academic, who is not subject to boycott as such, cannot be distinguished from the state institutions that employ her or him. This assertion always implies an accusation of the immorality of the boycott, even as it immorally denies equivalent rights to Palestinians, which it can do precisely because they are denied a state.

26. Odo Marquard elaborates on Kant's *strikt vertretbare Erkenntnisubjekt* in "Kant und die Wende zur Aesthetik," in *Zur Kantforschung der Gegenwart*, ed. Peter Heintel and Ludwig Nagl (Darmstadt, Germany: Wissenschaftliche Buchgesellschaft, 1981), 244. See Chapter 1 for further discussion of the *vertretbares Subjekt* of the aesthetic.

27. Friedrich Schiller, *On the Aesthetic Education of Man, in a Series of Letters*, ed. and trans. Elizabeth M. Wilkinson and L. A. Willoughby (Oxford: Clarendon, 1967), 17; Matthew Arnold, *Culture and Anarchy, with Friendship's Garland and Some Literary Essays*, ed. R. H. Super (Ann Arbor: University of Michigan Press, 1965), 111.

28. Lloyd and Thomas, *Culture and the State*, 81–90. Here, we show that it was by no means the case that British radical writers of the 1820s and 1830s accepted the generalization of representative structures across the spheres of their practice. Representation needed to be inculcated and made self-evident.

29. Jacques Derrida, "Force of Law: The 'Mystical Foundation of Authority,'" in *Deconstruction and the Possibility of Justice*, ed. Drucilla Cornell, Michael Rosenfeld, and David Grey Carlson (London: Routledge, 1992), 47.

30. Peter Stallybrass, "'Well Grubbed, Old Mole': Marx, Hamlet, and the (Un)Fixing of Representation," *Cultural Studies* 12, no. 1 (1998): 3–14.

31. Louis Althusser, "Ideology and Ideological State Apparatuses: Notes towards an Investigation," in *Lenin and Philosophy and Other Essays*, trans. Ben Brewster (New York: Verso, 1971), 164.

32. Marx claims that "the Bonaparte dynasty represents not the revolutionary but the conservative peasant" (*Brumaire*, 107).

33. Sylvia Wynter, "Unsettling the Coloniality of Being/Power/Truth/Freedom: Towards the Human, After Man, Its Overrepresentation—An Argument," *CR: The New Centennial Review* 3, no. 3 (Fall 2003): 271.

34. Rosa Luxemburg, in *The Accumulation of Capital* (London: Routledge, 2003), was among the first extensively to critique Marx for failing to appreciate the impact of imperialism on the capacity of capitalism to survive and expand. More recent studies of the impact of imperialism on ideology and popular identification with nation and colonialism include Patrick Brantlinger, *Bread and Circuses: Theories of Mass Culture as Social Decay* (Ithaca, N.Y.: Cornell University Press, 1983); Peter H. Hoffenberg, *An Empire on Display: English, Indian, and Australian Exhibitions from the Crystal Palace to the Great War* (Berkeley: University of California Press, 2001); and Thomas Richards, *The Imperial Archive: Knowledge and the Fantasy of Empire* (London: Verso, 1993).

35. Catherine Hall, "Rethinking Imperial Histories: The Reform Act of 1867," *New Left Review* 208 (1994): 3–29.

36. See Lloyd and Thomas, *Culture and the State*, especially chapter 4.

37. John Stuart Mill, "Considerations on Representative Government," in *The Collected Works of John Stuart Mill*, vol. 19, ed. J. M. Robson (Toronto: University of Toronto Press, 1977), 396.

38. For all these terms see Frantz Fanon, *Black Skin, White Masks*, foreword Homi Bhabha, trans. C. L. Markmann (London: Pluto, 1986), chapter 1, "The Negro and Language," 17–40. Fanon's "Racism and Culture" is his most succinct and painstaking exploration of this dilemma of the colonized intellectual. Frantz Fanon, "Racism and Culture," in *Toward the African Revolution: Political Essays*, trans. Haakon Chevalier (New York: Grove Press, 1988), 29–44. Kelly Oliver refers to his analysis of a "double alienation" in "Alienation and Its Double; or, The Secretion of Race," in *Race and Racism in Continental Philosophy*, ed. Robert Bernasconi (Bloomington: Indiana University Press, 2003).

39. Thomas Babington Macaulay, "Minute on Indian Education," in *Speeches by Lord Macaulay, with his Minute on Indian Education*, ed. G. M. Young (1835; repr., Oxford: Oxford University Press, 1935).

40. "The postcolonial intellectuals learn that their privilege is their loss.

In this they are a paradigm of the intellectuals." Spivak, "Can the Subaltern Speak?," 287.

41. On this logic of translation, see Chakrabarty, "Translating Life-Worlds," in *Provincializing Europe*.

42. Mark Quigley, "Modernity's Edge: Speaking Silence on the Blaskets," chap. 1 in *Empire's Wake: Postcolonial Irish Writing and the Politics of Modern Literary Form* (New York: Fordham University Press, 2013), explores this problem in the context of transcribed oral autobiography. My own effort to engage with the ways in which modernity seeks to seize hold of and transform subaltern practices that exceed its mode of representation is in *Irish Culture and Colonial Modernity, 1800–2000: The Transformation of Oral Space* (Cambridge: Cambridge University Press, 2011).

43. Ranajit Guha, "The Prose of Counterinsurgency," in *Selected Subaltern Studies*, ed. Ranajit Guha and Gayatri Chakravorty Spivak (New York: Oxford University Press, 1988). In "Subaltern Studies: Deconstructing Historiography" (12–20) Spivak proves able to turn that dilemma back on the subaltern historian while maintaining sight nonetheless of the necessity of the task, making that essay for me a more critically political work than "Can the Subaltern Speak?."

44. Again, the reaction may also express itself as an insistent identification with—that is, as—the subaltern, with a corresponding affect of smugness. But identifying as the subaltern produces an impossible contradiction. As Spivak puts it, "No one can say 'I am a subaltern' in whatever language." Gayatri Chakravorty Spivak, "Scattered Speculations on the Subaltern and the Popular," *Postcolonial Studies* 8, no. 4 (2005): 476.

45. I would emphasize that this is the melancholy affect of the intellectual, not that of the Subaltern onto which Ranjana Khanna projects it. See Khanna, *Dark Continents: Psychoanalysis and Colonialism* (Durham, N.C.: Duke University Press, 2003), 19–21.

46. Albert Memmi, *The Colonizer and the Colonized*, introduction by Jean-Paul Sartre, trans. H. Greenfield (Boston: Beacon, 1967), 32. I comment elsewhere on a similar "constitutive ignorance" by which the university intellectual is rendered incapable of teaching difference in the classroom, a condition that produced much of the rage against "multiculturalism" when it still had some as yet unrecuperated political potential; see David Lloyd, "Foundations of Diversity," in *"Culture" and the Problem of the Disciplines*, ed. John Carlos Rowe (New York: Columbia University Press, 1998), 24–25.

47. Victor Li, in his powerful critique of subaltern theory, ties the problem that "the ideal subaltern other must be seen as a figure who is inaccessible to and inappropriable by statist, hegemonic and academic knowledge" to the pattern that "the subaltern dies or remains silent (a form of verbal

death) in order that the concept or theory of subaltern singularity or alterity may live on." As he puts it, "Dead subalterns, in their very unrepresentability, make ideal representatives of utopian decolonized space" (277, 280). This may capture the residual epistemological violence of subaltern historiography and theory, but it does not address sufficiently the problem that this is a structural rather than an ethical problem for the intellectual and, accordingly, is one that raises the ethical stance of the theorist as a problem in itself. Li's essay still unwittingly participates, therefore, in the ethical dismay that Spivak's essay constantly provokes. See Victor Li, "Necroidealism, or the Subaltern's Sacrificial Death," *Interventions* 11, no. 3 (2009): 275–92.

48. "Neither the groups celebrated by the early subalternists nor Bhubaneswari Bhaduri, in so far as they had burst their bonds into resistance, were in the position of subalternity" (Spivak, "Scattered Speculations," 476). I would, however, reserve the possibility that the groups in resistance as recorded by subaltern and related histories may yet be subaltern, strictly speaking: The differential of subalternity lies not in the fact of resisting but in the irrepresentability to the intellectual of the cultural formation or structure of resistance. Spivak's peculiarly defensive parenthetical response to the original version of this chapter seems to mistake the vocational standing of certain intellectuals for the structural position the term designates. Insofar as she was called on to represent the nation, and insofar as she is the daughter of even a "lower-middle-class schoolmaster," Bhaduri was, in relation to the subaltern, positioned as an intellectual. None of this in any way obviates the ways in which readings of "Can the Subaltern Speak?" have tended to appropriate Bhaduri as a figure of the subaltern. See Gayatri Chakravorty Spivak, "Response," *PMLA* 129, no. 3 (2014): 520.

49. Cf. Spivak, "Scattered Speculations," 477.

50. Fanon, *Wretched of the Earth*, 36.

51. I am here riffing off Spivak in "Scattered Speculations," 481.

52. Jean Rhys, *Wide Sargasso Sea: A Novel* (New York: Norton, 1982).

53. I discuss the parodic critique enacted by *Wide Sargasso Sea* and other "minor" works on the major canon in *Nationalism and Minor Literature: James Clarence Mangan and the Emergence of Irish Cultural Nationalism* (Berkeley: University of California Press, 1987), 21–23.

54. Rhys, *Wide Sargasso Sea*, 18, 23, 24, 26.

55. Rhys, 45.

56. Fanon, *Black Skin, White Masks*, 160–61, 161n. See my discussion of this passage in Chapter 2.

57. Rhys, *Wide Sargasso Sea*, 47.

58. Rhys, 60.

59. Rhys, 26. That Christophene rather than Tia is generally taken as the

instance of the Subaltern in the novel only marks the double disappearance of Tia from representation, in the novel and in the commentary, despite the fact that she is the object of Antoinette's desperate identificatory desire.

60. In *Critique of Postcolonial Reason*, Spivak reads this sequence of dreams rather in relation to *Jane Eyre* "as an allegory of the general epistemic violence of imperialism, the construction of a self-immolating colonial subject [Bertha] for the glorification of the social mission of the colonizer" (126–27).

61. Rhys, *Wide Sargasso Sea*, 189–90.

5. THE AESTHETIC TABOO: AURA, MAGIC, AND THE PRIMITIVE

1. Immanuel Kant, *Anthropology from a Pragmatic Point of View*, trans. Mary J. Gregor (The Hague, Netherlands: Nijhoff, 1974), 3.

2. For a discussion of the degree to which Kant's aesthetics serves as "the key to anthropology," insofar as anthropology is thought not as the accumulation of empirical data but as concerning the ends of man, see John Zammito's *The Genesis of Kant's Critique of Judgment* (Chicago: University of Chicago Press, 1992), 292–305. As we have seen in earlier chapters, most philosophical accounts of Kant's racism, and that of other Enlightenment philosophers, focus on his empirical anthropological writings. For an excellent account of Kant's *Anthropology* that links its racial and political schemata to his final concern with human *Bildung*, and consequently with the ends of whiteness, see J. Kameron Carter, *Race: A Theological Account* (Oxford: Oxford University Press, 2008), 96–108.

3. The gradual historical transition of judgments of taste and of moral censure that were the concern of the initial bourgeois public sphere into the political critique is compellingly presented by Reinhardt Kosellek in *Kritik and Krise: Ein Beitrag zur Pathogenese der bürgerlichen Welt* (Freiburg, Germany: Alber, 1959).

4. In *The Philosophy of History* Hegel states: "Negroes are enslaved by the Europeans and sold to America. Nevertheless, their lot in their own country, where slavery is equally absolute, is almost worse than this; for the basic principle of all slavery is that man is not yet consciousness of his freedom, and consequently sinks to the level of a mere object or worthless article." See Georg Wilhelm Friedrich Hegel, "Geographical Basis of World History," chap. 10 in *Race and the Enlightenment: A Reader*, ed. Emmanuel Chukwudi Eze (Oxford: Blackwell, 1997), 134–35.

5. Denise Ferreira da Silva, *Toward a Global Idea of Race* (Minneapolis: University of Minnesota Press, 2007), and "No Bodies," *Griffith Law Review* 18, no. 2 (2009): 213–36. On the normality of the state of exception, see Walter Benjamin, "On the Concept of History," in *Selected Writings*, vol. 4, *1938–1940*, ed. Howard Eiland and Michael W. Jennings, trans.

Edmund Jephcott et al. (Cambridge, Mass.: Belknap, 2003), 392. Nasser Hussain's *The Jurisprudence of Emergency: Colonialism and the Rule of Law* (Ann Arbor: University of Michigan Press, 2003) is the indispensable account of the relationship between colonial rule and the state of exception.

6. I discuss Schiller's elaboration of the pedagogical logic implicit in Kant's *Critique of Judgement* in "Kant's Examples," *Representations* 28 (Autumn 1989): 34–54.

7. Georg Wilhelm Friedrich Hegel, *Aesthetics: Lectures on Fine Art*, 2 vols., trans. T. M. Knox (Oxford: Oxford University Press, 1975), 1:31. It should be noted that in exemplifying the barbarian origins of the reflexive will to alter the self, Hegel replaces Kant's Iroquois and Carib with the Chinese practice of female foot-binding, a no less recurrent topos in the Western racial imagination.

8. Edward Burnett Tylor, *The Origins of Culture* (New York: Harper, 1958); Franz Boas, *The Mind of Primitive Man*, rev. ed. (New York: Macmillan/Free Press, 1965).

9. For an outline of the transformations of the meaning and reference of the word *culture* from its agricultural and ritual roots to its aesthetic, sociological, and anthropological usages, see Raymond Williams, *Keywords: A Vocabulary of Culture and Society*, rev. ed. (New York: Oxford University Press, 1985), 87–93.

10. On the relation between symbolism in aesthetics and nationalist ideas of political representation, see David Lloyd, "Counterparts," chap. 3 in *Irish Culture and Colonial Modernity, 1800–2000: The Transformation of Oral Space* (Cambridge: Cambridge University Press, 2011).

11. See Thomas Babington Macaulay, "Minute on Indian Education," in *Speeches by Lord Macaulay, with His Minute on Indian Education*, ed. G. M. Young (1835; repr., Oxford: Oxford University Press, 1935). John Stuart Mill, "What Is Poetry?," in *The Broadview Anthology of Victorian Poetry and Poetics*, ed. Thomas J. Collins and Vivienne J. Rundle (Peterborough, Ontario: Broadview, 1999), 1213.

12. On the initial affinity between aesthetic and anthropological conceptions of culture, see George W. Stocking Jr., "Mathew Arnold, E. B. Tylor, and the Uses of Invention," in *Race, Culture and Evolution: Essays in the History of Anthropology* (New York: Macmillan/Free Press, 1968), 69–90.

13. See Immanuel Kant, *The Critique of Judgement*, trans. James Creed Meredith (Oxford: Clarendon, 1952), 75–80.

14. T. S. Eliot, "The Wasteland," in *Collected Poems 1909–1962* (London: Faber and Faber, 1963), 80; Suzanne Marchand, "Leo Frobenius and the Revolt against the West," *Journal of Contemporary History* 32, no. 2 (April 1997): 153–70; Gregory Castle, *Modernism and the Celtic Revival* (Cambridge:

Cambridge University Press, 2001), 99. Even the epistemologically skeptical Samuel Beckett was not immune to the impact of ethnographic thinking. See Patrick Bixby's discussion of Beckett's wonderful parody of ethnography and the *Mathematical Intuitions of the Visicelts* in his novel *Watt* in Bixby, *Samuel Beckett and the Postcolonial Novel* (Cambridge: Cambridge University Press, 2009), 135–40. The classic study of primitivism and modernism is Marianna Torgovnick, *Gone Primitive: Savage Intellects, Modern Lives* (Chicago: University of Chicago Press, 1991).

15. On this French intellectual milieu, see Simonetta Falasca-Zamponi, *Rethinking the Political: The Sacred, Aesthetic Politics, and the Collège de Sociologie* (Montréal: McGill-Queen's University Press, 2011). There is not scope in this chapter to explore further the French modernist nexus of aesthetics, psychoanalysis, and ethnography that corresponds to that of the contemporaneous German critical theory that is my focus here.

16. On Bachofen and his influence on German thought, see Peter Davies, *Myth, Matriarchy and Modernity: Johann Jakob Bachofen in German Culture, 1860–1945* (New York: De Gruyter, 2010). On the German anthropological tradition see John H. Zammito, *Kant, Herder and the Birth of Anthropology* (Chicago: University of Chicago Press, 2002), and Andrew Zimmerman, ed., *Volksgeist as Method and Ethic: Essays on Boasian Ethnography and the German Anthropological Tradition* (Madison: University of Wisconsin Press, 1996). Zimmerman also shows the relation between the German anthropological tradition and German engagement in colonial projects in Africa and the Pacific in *Anthropology and Antihumanism in Imperial Germany* (Chicago: University of Chicago Press, 2001). For a direct instance of the influence of colonial experience and anthropological thought on German modernism, see Andrew Zimmerman, "Primitive Art, Primitive Accumulation, and the Origin of the Work of Art in German New Guinea," *History of the Present* 1, no. 1 (Summer 2011): 5–30.

17. Sigmund Freud, *Totem and Taboo: Some Points of Agreement between the Mental Lives of Savages and Neurotics*, vol. 13 of *Standard Edition of the Complete Psychological Works*, trans. James Strachey (London: Hogarth, 1957), viii–162. Cited in the text hereafter as *TT*.

18. Peter Fitzpatrick, *Modernism and the Grounds of Law* (Cambridge: Cambridge University Press, 2001), 36.

19. See Marcel Mauss, *A General Theory of Magic*, trans. Robert Brain (1950; repr., London: Routledge and Kegan Paul, 1972), 11–12, for a summary of Tylor's and Frazer's contributions to the general theory of "sympathetic magic."

20. Benjamin was particularly, even at times perilously, interested in Bachofen and the later mythologist, Ludwig Klages, while Adorno and

Horkheimer footnote their readings in cultural anthropology, including Marcel Mauss, Émile Durkheim, and Robert Lowie. On Benjamin's reading of Bachofen and Klages, and on Gershom Scholem's disapproval, see Beatrice Hanssen, *Walter Benjamin's Other History: Of Stones, Animals, Human Beings, and Angels* (Berkeley: University of California Press, 1998), 93–94. Adorno and Horkheimer's references to anthropology and psychoanalysis are more carefully documented in their texts and are not similarly subject to speculation.

21. While Benjamin read some of Freud's later writings, his reading in psychoanalysis was limited and somewhat idiosyncratic: "His study of Freud was, rather like his move to Palestine and study of Hebrew, always planned and promised, but never carried out." See Peter Buse, Ken Hirschkop, Scott McCracken, and Bertrand Taithe, eds., *Benjamin's Arcades: An unGuided Tour* (Manchester: Manchester University Press, 2005), 160. Regarding Klages as a rival source for Benjamin's interest in the unconscious (164), these writers take the view that Benjamin's readings in psychoanalysis were very limited. Others find less interest in the documentable, direct citations of Freud in Benjamin's work than in the correspondences that establish a "constellation" between the two thinkers. See Sarah Ley Roff, "Benjamin and Psychoanalysis," in *The Cambridge Companion to Walter Benjamin*, ed. David S. Ferris (Cambridge: Cambridge University Press, 2004), and Elizabeth Stewart, *Catastrophe and Survival: Walter Benjamin and Psychoanalysis* (New York: Continuum, 2010).

22. Walter Benjamin, "The Work of Art in the Age of Its Technological Reproducibility," in *Selected Writings*, 4:251–83. Translated previously as "The Work of Art in the Age of Mechanical Reproduction," this essay, which incorporates material on aura almost verbatim from "Little History of Photography" (1931) went through several drafts from 1936 to 1939; for the first version, see *Selected Writings*, vol. 2, *1931–1934*, ed. Michael W. Jennings, Howard Eiland, and Gary Smith, trans. Rodney Livingstone et al. (Cambridge, Mass.: Belknap, 1999), 507–30. The second version is reproduced in *Selected Writings*, vol. 3, *1935–1938*, ed. Howard Eiland and M. W. Jennings, trans. Edmund Jephcott (Cambridge, Mass.: Belknap, 2006), 101–33. I work from the third and quasi-definitive version, cited in the text as WATR.

23. Benjamin, "On Some Motifs in Baudelaire," *Selected Writings*, 4:338.

24. The correspondence is striking even in the absence of direct evidence that Benjamin had read *Totem and Taboo*. Hanssen, however, believes that he "undoubtedly was familiar" with the text and finds its trace, for example, in the essay on Kafka and in the theoretical outlines of the *Arcades Project*. See *Walter Benjamin's Other History*, 147.

25. Benjamin, "On Some Motifs in Baudelaire," *Selected Writings*, 4:343.

26. Theodor W. Adorno, "On Jazz," in *Essays on Music*, ed. Richard Leppert, trans. Susan H. Gillespie (Berkeley: California University Press, 2002), 474.

27. Benjamin's assumptions about the relationship between authority and contact in the laying-on of hands may be derived from Freud's discussion of the ruler's capacity to heal the sick by touch even while remaining a strictly taboo object himself (Freud, *Totem and Taboo*, 41–42).

28. The term *Zerstreuung*, which Benjamin uses throughout §XV of the essay, where he develops his theory of reception, has a semantic range that includes scattering, dispersal, or diffusion, as well as "absent-mindedness," and may imply "diversion" in the quite Pascalian sense that critics of popular culture use the term (Benjamin cites Georges Duhamel in this sense). Another term translated as distraction, *Ablenkung*, which Benjamin uses in relation to the reception of Dada in §XIV (WATR, 267), is in some ways more suggestive, even more precise. It embraces the idea of diversion or distraction figuratively, but it also describes the effects of a refraction (of light or magnets) or of diversion from a goal, deflection, or digression.

29. Adorno, indeed, refers to Benjamin's treatment of aura as an "inverse taboo": "You have startled art out of every one of its tabooed hiding places—but it is as though you feared a sudden irruption of barbarism as a result (and who could share that fear more than I do?) and protected yourself by elevating the feared object with a kind of inverse taboo." See Theodor W. Adorno and Walter Benjamin, *The Complete Correspondence, 1928–1940*, ed. Henri Lonitz, trans. Nicholas Walker (Cambridge, Mass.: Harvard University Press, 1999), 130.

30. See, for example, his claim in "Hashish, Beginning of March 1930" that "genuine aura appears in all things, not just in certain kinds of things, as people imagine" (*Selected Writings*, 2:328). Consider also "Benjamin's eventual definition of aura as the inanimate object's ability to return the gaze," on which Rebecca Comay comments in "Materialist Mutations of the *Bilderverbot*," in *Walter Benjamin and Art*, ed. Andrew Benjamin (New York: Continuum, 2005), 45. See Benjamin, "On Some Motifs in Baudelaire," *Selected Writings*, 4:338 for this observation.

31. See Benjamin, "Little History of Photography," *Selected Writings*, 2:518–19.

32. See Benjamin, "On the Concept of History," *Selected Writings*, 4:389–400. Especially germane is §XI, where he critiques the Social Democratic faith in progress and technology, attacking "the illusion that factory work ostensibly furthering technological progress constituted a political achievement" (393). The remarks on dialectical materialism are from "Convolute N: On the Theory of Knowledge, Theory of Progress," in *The Arcades Project*,

ed. Rolf Tiedemann, trans. Howard Eiland and Kevin McLaughlin (Cambridge, Mass.: Belknap, 1999), 460.

33. Adorno and Benjamin, *Complete Correspondence*, 128.

34. Adorno and Benjamin, 129.

35. Theodor W. Adorno, *Aesthetic Theory*, ed. Gretel Adorno and Rolf Tiedemann, trans. Robert Hullot-Kentor (Minneapolis: University of Minnesota Press, 1997), 56; cited in the text hereafter as *AT*.

36. Adorno and Benjamin, *Complete Correspondence*, 131.

37. Theodor W. Adorno and Max Horkheimer, *Dialectic of Enlightenment*, trans. John Cumming (New York: Continuum, 1972), 19.

38. I draw both these definitions of the *nomos* and the play on *Urteil* and *ur-teilen* from Carl Schmitt's *The Nomos of the Earth in the International Law of the Jus Publicum Europaeum*, trans. G. L. Ulmen (New York: Telos, 2003), 70–71, 326. This is, of course, neither to endorse the Nazi legal theorist's historical framework nor to accuse Adorno and Horkheimer of unwitting fascist leanings. It is, however, to recall how profoundly the aesthetic since Kant—who was concerned in the Critiques with the regulation of distinct domains of human practice—has been normative in its ends, not least in its production of the idea of the human.

39. Only Marcel Mauss remarks on the practice, and then as an incidental and by no means customary part of magic rituals: "If the spot has no special characteristic the magician may draw a magical circle or square, a *templum*, around him and he performs his magic inside this." Mauss, *General Theory of Magic*, 47. On the sorcerer's circle in Renaissance Europe, which seems to have shaped Adorno's conception of magical practice, see Eugene Thacker, *In the Dust of This Planet*, Horror of Philosophy, vol. I (Winchester, England: Zero, 2011), 55–81.

40. Theodor W. Adorno, "The Handle, the Pot, and Early Experience," in *Notes to Literature*, vol. 2, trans. Shierry Weber Nicholson (New York: Columbia University Press, 1992), 211.

41. Adorno, 217.

42. See, for example, the first spell in the supplement, *Das sogenannte Grimorium oder der grosse Grimoir des Papsts Honorius*, in Johannes Staricius, *Geheimnisvoller Heldenschatz oder Vollständiger Egyptische Magische Schild* (1750; repr., Freiburg, Germany: Aurum Verlag, 1978), 459–63.

43. Mauss, *General Theory of Magic*, 19.

44. Adorno and Horkheimer, *Dialectic of Enlightenment*, 18–19.

45. Adorno and Horkheimer, 11.

46. Adorno and Horkheimer, 10.

47. Adorno and Horkheimer, 27.

48. Adorno and Horkheimer, 28.

49. Theodor W. Adorno, *Negative Dialectics*, trans. E. B. Ashton (New York: Continuum, 1973), 344.

50. Adorno, 347.

51. Adorno and Benjamin, *Complete Correspondence*, 283. For comments on this letter of November 10, 1938, see Gerhard Richter, "Adorno and the Excessive Politics of Aura," in *Benjamin's Blind Spot: Walter Benjamin and the Premature Death of Aura and The Manual of Lost Ideas*, ed. Lise Patt (Topanga, Calif.: Institute of Cultural Inquiry, 2001), 30–31.

52. Benjamin, "On Some Motifs in Baudelaire," *Selected Writings*, 4: 338–39.

53. Adorno, "On Jazz," 478.

54. Da Silva, "No Bodies," 220–24.

55. Adorno, "On Jazz," 474. The ahistoricity of jazz is made explicit in "Perennial Fashion—Jazz," where it is explicitly connected with its lack of immanent formal development and to economic domination: "Just as no piece of jazz can, in a musical sense, be said to have a history, just as all its components can be moved about at will, just as no single measure follows from the logic of the musical progression—so the perennial fashion becomes the likeness of a planned congealed society." Theodor W. Adorno, "Perennial Fashion—Jazz," in *Prisms*, trans. Shierry Weber Nicholson and Samuel Weber (Cambridge, Mass.: MIT Press, 1983), 124–25.

56. Adorno, "On Jazz," 491. See also "Perennial Fashion—Jazz," 127: "Regression is not origin, but origin is the ideology of regression."

57. Frantz Fanon, *Black Skin, White Masks*, foreword by Homi Bhabha, trans. Charles Lam Markmann (London: Pluto, 1986), 123.

58. Da Silva describes this condition of "incorporation as the excluded" as the definition of the Savage: "It becomes the negative but interior ground on which the force of law stands" ("No Bodies," 216).

59. This argument is more fully elaborated in David Lloyd and Paul Thomas, *Culture and the State* (London: Routledge, 1997), and in my "Foundations of Diversity," in *"Culture" and the Problem of the Disciplines*, ed. John Carlos Rowe (New York: Columbia University Press, 1998). On Kant's *Conflict of the Faculties* and the retreat of philosophy from revolution into the aesthetic, see Rebecca Comay, *Mourning Sickness: Hegel and the French Revolution* (Stanford, Calif.: Stanford University Press, 2011), 20–21, 26–50.

60. Adorno, "Perennial Fashion—Jazz," 132.

61. Adorno, "On Jazz," 491. Benjamin, "On the Concept of History," *Selected Writings*, 4:392.

62. Adorno and Horkheimer, *Dialectic of Enlightenment*, 10. See David Kaufmann, "Beyond Gnosticism and Magic," *New German Critique* 118

(Winter 2013): 30–31, for a related commentary on Adorno and Horkheimer's account of the transition from magic through myth to exchange, in which magic is seen as "a first step toward the sovereignty of the subject."

63. Mauss, *General Theory of Magic*, 58, 11.

64. Adorno, *Negative Dialectics*, 150. Kaufmann considers this state to be "'something outside' second nature" ("Beyond Gnosticism and Magic," 35).

65. For the notion of the "vestige" as an alternative to the "sensuous presentation of the idea," see Jean-Luc Nancy, "The Vestige of Art," in *The Muses*, trans. Peggy Kamuf (Stanford, Calif.: Stanford University Press, 1996), 81–100. This essay would be a fundamental suggestion to any further rethinking of the aesthetic.

66. Frantz Fanon, "Concerning Violence," in *The Wretched of the Earth*, preface by Jean-Paul Sartre, trans. Constance Farrington (New York: Grove, 1968), 55.

67. Fanon, 56.

68. Alexander G. Weheliye, *Habeas Viscus: Racializing Assemblages, Biopolitics, and Black Feminist Theories of the Human* (Durham, N.C.: Duke University Press, 2014).

69. Fanon, "Concerning Violence," *Wretched of the Earth*, 55.

70. Fred Moten, "The Case of Blackness," *Criticism* 50, no. 2 (Spring 2008): 203.

71. Moten, 209.

Abbas, Ali Abdallah. "The Father of Lies: The Role of Mustafa Sa'eed as Second Self in *Season of Migration to the North*." In *Tayeb Salih's Season of Migration to the North: A Casebook*, edited by Mona Takieddine Amyuni, 27–38. Beirut: American University of Beirut, 1985.

Adorno, Theodor W. *Aesthetic Theory*. Edited by Gretel Adorno and Rolf Tiedemann. Translated by Robert Hullot-Kentor. Minneapolis: University of Minnesota Press, 1997.

———. "The Handle, the Pot, and Early Experience." In *Notes to Literature*, translated by Shierry Weber Nicholson, 211–19. Vol. 2. New York: Columbia University Press, 1992.

———. *Negative Dialectics*. Translated by E. B. Ashton. New York: Continuum, 1973.

———. "On Jazz." In *Essays on Music*, edited by Richard Leppert, translated by Susan H. Gillespie, 470–95. Berkeley: University of California Press, 2002.

———. "Perennial Fashion—Jazz." In *Prisms*. Translated by Shierry Weber Nicholson and Samuel Weber. Cambridge, Mass.: MIT Press, 1983.

Adorno, Theodor W., and Walter Benjamin. *The Complete Correspondence, 1928–1940*. Edited by Henri Lonitz. Translated by Nicholas Walker. Cambridge, Mass.: Harvard University Press, 1999.

Adorno, Theodor W., and Max Horkheimer. *Dialectic of Enlightenment*. Translated by John Cumming. New York: Continuum, 1972.

Althusser, Louis. *Lenin and Philosophy and Other Essays*. Translated by Ben Brewster. New York: Monthly Review, 1971.

Amin, Shahid. *Event, Metaphor, Memory: Chauri Chaura, 1922–1992*. Berkeley: University of California Press, 1995.

Amyuni, Mona Takieddine, ed. *Tayeb Salih's Season of Migration to the North: A Casebook*. Beirut: American University of Beirut, 1985.

Anderson, Benedict. *Imagined Communities: Reflections on the Origin and Spread of Nationalism*. London: Verso, 2006.

Aquila, Richard E. "A New Look at Kant's Aesthetic Judgments." In *Essays in*

Kant's Aesthetics, edited by Ted Cohen and Paul Guyer, 87–114. Chicago: University of Chicago Press, 1982.

Aravamudan, Srinivas. *Tropicopolitans: Colonialism and Agency*. Durham, N.C.: Duke University Press, 1999.

Arendt, Hannah. *Between Past and Future: Six Exercises in Political Thought*. New York: Viking, 1961.

———. *Lectures on Kant's Political Philosophy*. Edited by Ronald Beiner. Chicago: University of Chicago Press, 1982.

Armstrong, Meg. "'The Effects of Blackness': Gender, Race and the Sublime in Aesthetic Theories of Kant and Burke." *Journal of Aesthetics and Art Criticism* 54, no. 3 (Summer 1996): 221–26.

Arnold, Matthew. *Culture and Anarchy, with Friendship's Garland and Some Literary Essays*. Edited by R. H. Super. Ann Arbor: University of Michigan Press, 1965.

Arteaga, Alfred. *Chicano Poetics: Heterotexts and Hybridities*. Cambridge: Cambridge University Press, 1997.

———. "An Other Tongue." In *An Other Tongue: Nation and Ethnicity in the Linguistic Borderlands*, edited by Alfred Arteaga. Durham, N.C.: Duke University Press, 1994.

Badiou, Alain. *The Age of the Poets and Other Writings on Twentieth-Century Poetry and Prose*. Edited and translated by Bruno Bosteels. London: Verso, 2014.

———. *Handbook of Inaesthetics*. Translated by Alberto Toscano. Stanford, Calif.: Stanford University Press, 2005.

Bakhtin, Mikhail. *The Dialogic Imagination: Four Essays*. Edited by Michael Holquist. Translated by Caryl Emerson and Michael Holquist. Austin: University of Texas Press, 1981.

Banton, Michael. *Racial Theories*. Cambridge: Cambridge University Press, 1987.

Benjamin, Walter. *The Arcades Project*. Edited by Rolf Tiedemann. Translated by Howard Eiland and Kevin McLaughlin. Cambridge, Mass.: Belknap, 1999.

———. *Selected Writings*. Vol. 1, *1913–1926*, edited by Marcus Bullock and Michael W. Jennings, translated by Edmund Jephcott. Cambridge, Mass.: Belknap, 1996.

———. *Selected Writings*. Vol. 2, *1931–1934*, edited by Michael W. Jennings, Howard Eiland, and Gary Smith, translated by Rodney Livingstone et al. Cambridge, Mass.: Belknap, 1999.

———. *Selected Writings*. Vol. 3, *1935–1938*, edited by Howard Eiland and M. W. Jennings, translated by Edmund Jephcott. Cambridge, Mass.: Belknap, 2006.

———. *Selected Writings.* Vol. 4, *1938–1940*, edited by Howard Eiland and Michael W. Jennings, translated by Edmund Jephcott et al. Cambridge, Mass.: Belknap, 2003.

Bernabé, Jean, Patrick Chamoiseau, and Raphael Confiant. *Éloge de la creolité.* Paris: Gallimard, 1989.

Bernasconi, Robert. "The Assumption of Negritude: Aimé Césaire, Frantz Fanon, and the Vicious Circle of Racial Politics." *Parallax* 8, no. 2 (2002): 69–83.

———. "Identity and Agency in Frantz Fanon." *Sartre Studies International* 10, no. 2 (2004): 106–9.

———. "Kant and Blumenbach's Polyps: A Neglected Chapter in the History of the Concept of Race." In *The German Invention of Race*, edited by Sara Eigen, 73–90. Binghamton: SUNY Press, 2006.

———. "Kant's Third Thoughts on Race." In *Reading Kant's Geography*, edited by Stuart Elden and Eduardo Mendieta, 291–318. Albany: SUNY Press, 2011.

———. "Will the Real Kant Please Stand Up: The Challenge of Enlightenment Racism to the Study of the History of Philosophy." *Radical Philosophy* 117 (2003): 13–22.

Bhabha, Homi. *The Location of Culture.* London: Routledge, 1994.

Bhandar, Brenna. *Colonial Lives of Property: Regimes of Ownership.* Durham, N.C.: Duke University Press, 2018.

———. "The Other Question." *Screen* 24 (November/December 1983): 18–36.

Bixby, Patrick. *Samuel Beckett and the Postcolonial Novel.* Cambridge: Cambridge University Press, 2009.

Bloch, Ernst, Georg Lukács, Bertolt Brecht, Walter Benjamin, and Theodor Adorno. *Aesthetics and Politics.* Afterword by Frederic Jameson. London: New Left, 1977.

Boas, Franz. *The Mind of Primitive Man.* Rev. ed. New York: Macmillan/Free Press, 1965.

Brantlinger, Patrick. *Bread and Circuses: Theories of Mass Culture as Social Decay.* Ithaca, N.Y.: Cornell University Press, 1983.

Bruford, W. H. *The German Tradition of Self-Cultivation: "Bildung" from Humboldt to Thomas Mann.* Cambridge: Cambridge University Press, 1975.

———. *Germany in the Eighteenth Century: The Social Background of the Literary Revival.* 1935. Reprint, Cambridge: Cambridge University Press, 1959.

Burke, Edmund. *A Philosophical Enquiry into the Origin of Our Ideas of the Sublime and Beautiful.* 1759. Facsimile of the second edition. Menston, England: Scholar, 1970.

———. *Reflections on the Revolution in France.* Edited by Conor Cruise O'Brien. 1790. Reprint, Harmondsworth, England: Penguin, 1968.

Buse, Peter, Ken Hirschkop, Scott McCracken, and Bertrand Taithe, eds. *Benjamin's Arcades: An unGuided Tour*. Manchester: Manchester University Press, 2005.

Butler, Judith. *The Psychic Life of Power: Theories in Subjection*. Stanford, Calif.: Stanford University Press, 1997.

Carey, Daniel. *Locke, Shaftesbury, and Hutcheson: Contesting Diversity in the Enlightenment and Beyond*. Cambridge: Cambridge University Press, 2006.

Carey, Daniel, and Lynn Festa, eds. *Postcolonial Enlightenment: Eighteenth-Century Colonialism and Postcolonial Theory*. Oxford: Oxford University Press, 2009.

Carlyle, Thomas. *Sartor Resartus and On Heroes, Hero Worship and the Heroic in History*. London: Dent, 1908.

Carter, J. Kameron. *Race: A Theological Account*. Oxford: Oxford University Press, 2008.

Castle, Gregory. *Modernism and the Celtic Revival*. Cambridge: Cambridge University Press, 2001.

Chakrabarty, Dipesh. *Habitations of Modernity: Essays in the Wake of Subaltern Studies*. Princeton, N.J.: Princeton University Press, 2002.

———. *Provincializing Europe: Postcolonial Thought and Historical Difference*. Princeton, N.J.: Princeton University Press, 2000.

Chandler, Nahum Dimitri. *X: The Problem of the Negro as a Problem for Thought*. New York: Fordham University Press, 2014.

Chatterjee, Partha. *Nationalist Thought and the Colonial World: A Derivative Discourse*. London: Zed, 1986.

Chow, Rey. *Ethics after Idealism: Theory, Culture, Ethnicity, Reading*. Bloomington: Indiana University Press, 1998.

Comay, Rebecca. "Materialist Mutations of the *Bilderverbot*." In *Walter Benjamin and Art*, edited by Andrew Benjamin, 32–59. New York: Continuum, 2005.

———. *Mourning Sickness: Hegel and the French Revolution*. Stanford, Calif.: Stanford University Press, 2011.

Curtis, L. P. *Anglo-Saxons and Celts: A Study of Anti-Irish Prejudice in Victorian England*. Bridgeport, Conn.: University of Bridgeport, 1968.

Davies, Peter. *Myth, Matriarchy and Modernity: Johann Jakob Bachofen in German Culture, 1860–1945*. New York: De Gruyter, 2010.

Deane, Seamus. *Foreign Affections: Essays on Edmund Burke*. Cork: Cork University Press, 2005.

de Bolla, Peter. *Art Matters*. Cambridge, Mass.: Harvard University Press, 2001.

de Man, Paul. *Aesthetic Ideology*. Edited by Andrzej Warminski. Minneapolis: University of Minnesota Press, 1996.

———. "The Epistemology of Metaphor." In *On Metaphor*, edited by Sheldon Sacks, 11–28. Chicago: University of Chicago Press, 1979.

Derrida, Jacques. "Force of Law: The 'Mystical Foundation of Authority.'" In *Deconstruction and the Possibility of Justice*, edited by Drucilla Cornell, Michael Rosenfeld, and David Grey Carlson, 3–67. London: Routledge, 1992.

———. *La vérité en peinture*. Paris: Flammarion, 1978.

———. *Margins of Philosophy*. Translated by Alan Bass. Chicago: University of Chicago Press, 1982.

———. *Otobiographies: l'enseignement de Nietzsche et la politique du nom propre*. Paris: Galilée, 1986.

Donoghue, Denis. *Speaking of Beauty*. New Haven, Conn.: Yale University Press, 2003.

Eagleton, Terry. *The Function of Criticism: From* The Spectator *to Post-Structuralism*. London: Verso, 1984.

———. *The Ideology of the Aesthetic*. Oxford: Blackwell, 1990.

Elia, Nada et al. *Critical Ethnic Studies: A Reader*. Durham, N.C.: Duke University Press, 2016.

Eliot, T. S. "The Wasteland." In *Collected Poems 1909–1962*. London: Faber and Faber, 1963.

Engell, James. *The Creative Imagination: Enlightenment to Romanticism*. Cambridge, Mass.: Harvard University Press, 1981.

Escobar, Arturo. *Encountering Development: The Making and Unmaking of the Third World*. Princeton, N.J.: Princeton University Press, 1995.

Eudell, Demetrius L. "'Come on Kid, Let's Go Get the Thing': The Sociogenic Principle and the Being of Being Black / Human." In *Sylvia Wynter: On Being Human as Praxis*, edited by Katherine McKittrick, 226–48. Durham, N.C.: Duke University Press, 2015.

Eze, Emmanuel Chukwudi, ed. *Race and the Enlightenment: A Reader*. Oxford: Blackwell, 1997.

Fabian, Johannes. *Time and the Other: How Anthropology Makes Its Object*. New York: Columbia University Press, 1983.

Falasca-Zamponi, Simonetta. *Rethinking the Political: The Sacred, Aesthetic Politics, and the Collège de Sociologie*. Montréal: McGill-Queen's University Press, 2011.

Fanon, Frantz. *Black Skin, White Masks*. Foreword by Homi Bhabha. Translated by Charles Lam Markmann. London: Pluto, 1986.

———. *Peau Noire, Masques Blancs*. Paris: Éditions du Seuil, 1952.

———. *Toward the African Revolution: Political Essays*. Translated by Haakon Chevalier. 1964. Reprint, New York: Grove, 1988.

———. *The Wretched of the Earth*. Preface by Jean-Paul Sartre. Translated by Constance Farrington. New York: Grove, 1968.

Fehér, Ference, and Agnes Heller. "The Necessity and Irreformability of Aesthetics." In *Reconstructing Aesthetics: Writings of the Budapest School*, edited by Agnes Heller and Ference Fehér, 1–22. Oxford: Blackwell, 1986.

Ferguson, Roderick A. *The Reorder of Things: The University and Its Pedagogies of Minority Difference*. Minneapolis: University of Minnesota Press, 2012.

Fitzpatrick, Peter. *Modernism and the Grounds of Law*. Cambridge: Cambridge University Press, 2001.

Frank, Andre Gunder. *On Capitalist Underdevelopment*. Bombay: Oxford University Press, 1975.

Freud, Sigmund. *On Sexuality: Three Essays on the Theory of Sexuality and Other Works*. Harmondsworth, England: Penguin, 1977.

———. *Totem and Taboo: Some Points of Agreement between the Mental Lives of Savages and Neurotics*. Translated by James Strachey. Vol. 13 of *Standard Edition of the Complete Psychological Works*. London: Hogarth, 1957.

Fuss, Diana. *Identification Papers*. New York: Routledge, 1995.

Gibbons, Luke. *Burke and Colonial Ireland: Aesthetics, Politics and the Colonial Sublime*. Cambridge: Cambridge University Press, 2003.

Gikandi, Simon. "Race and the Idea of the Aesthetic." *Michigan Quarterly Review* 40, no. 2 (2001): http://quod.lib.umich.edu/cgi/t/text/text-idx?cc =mqr;c=mqr;c=mqrarchive;idno=act2080.0040.208;g=mqrg;rgn=main;view =text;xc=1.

Gilroy, Paul. *Against Race: Imagining Political Culture beyond the Color Line*. Cambridge, Mass.: Belknap, 2000.

Gintis, Herbert, and Samuel Bowles. "Structure and Practice in the Labor Theory of Value." *Review of Radical Political Economics* 12, no. 4 (Winter 1981): 1–26.

Godwin, William. *Enquiry Concerning Political Justice*. Edited by Isaac Kramnick. Harmondsworth, England: Penguin, 1976.

Goldberg, David T. *The Racial State*. Malden, Mass.: Blackwell, 2002.

Gooding-Williams, Robert. *Look, A Negro! Philosophical Essays on Race, Culture and Politics*. New York: Routledge, 2006.

Gordon, Lewis R. *What Fanon Said: A Philosophical Introduction to His Life and Thought*. New York: Fordham University Press, 2015.

Gramsci, Antonio. *Selections from the Prison Notebooks*. Edited and translated by Quintin Hoare and Geoffrey Nowell Smith. New York: International, 1971.

Grimm. *Deutsches Wörterbuch*. 33 vols. Munich: Deutscher Taschenbuchverlag, 1984.

Guha, Ranajit. "The Prose of Counter-Insurgency." In *Selected Subaltern Studies*, edited by Ranajit Guha and Gayatri Chakravorty Spivak, 45–86. New York: Oxford University Press, 1988.

Guillaumin, Colette. "Race and Nature: The System of Marks. The Idea of a Natural Group and Social Relationships." *Feminist Issues* 8, no. 2 (Fall 1988): 25–43.

Habermas, Jürgen. "Modernity—An Incomplete Project." In *The Anti-Aesthetic: Essays on Post-Modern Culture*, edited by Hall Foster, 3–15. Port Townsend, Wash.: Bay, 1983.

Hall, Catherine. "Rethinking Imperial Histories: The Reform Act of 1867." *New Left Review* 208 (1994): 3–29.

Hall, Stuart. "Race, Articulation and Societies Structured in Dominance." In *Sociological Theories: Race and Colonialism*. Paris: UNESCO, 1980.

Hamlin, Cyrus. "The Temporality of Selfhood: Metaphor and Romantic Poetry." *NLH* 6, no. 1 (Autumn 1974): 169–93.

Hanssen, Beatrice. *Walter Benjamin's Other History: Of Stones, Animals, Human Beings, and Angels*. Berkeley: University of California Press, 1998.

Hartley, George. *The Abyss of Representation: Marxism and the Postmodern Sublime*. Durham, N.C.: Duke University Press, 2003.

Hartman, Saidiya. *Scenes of Subjection: Terror, Slavery, and Self-Making in Nineteenth-Century America*. Oxford: Oxford University Press, 1997.

Hegel, Georg Wilhelm Friedrich. *Aesthetics: Lectures on Fine Art*. 2 vols. Translated by T. M. Knox. Oxford: Oxford University Press, 1975.

———. *Vorlesungen über die Philosophie der Kunst*. Edited by A. Gethmann-Siefert. 1823. Reprint, Berlin: Meiner Felix, 1998.

Hoffenberg, Peter H. *An Empire on Display: English, Indian, and Australian Exhibitions from the Crystal Palace to the Great War*. Berkeley: University of California Press, 2001.

Hussain, Nasser. *The Jurisprudence of Emergency: Colonialism and the Rule of Law*. Ann Arbor: University of Michigan Press, 2003.

Jäger, Hans-Wolf. *Politische Kategorien in Poetik und Rhetorik der zweiten Hälfte des 18. Jahrhunderts*. Stuttgart, Germany: J. B. Metzler, 1970.

Jameson, Frederic. *Aesthetics and Politics*. London: New Left, 1977.

Judy, Ronald A. T. "Fanon's Body of Black Experience." In *Fanon: A Critical Reader*, edited by Lewis R. Gordon, T. Denean Sharpley-Whiting, and Renée T. White, 53–73. Oxford: Blackwell, 1996.

———. "Kant and the Negro." *Surfaces* 1, no. 8 (1991): 4–70.

———. "Beside the Two Camps: Paul Gilroy and the Critique of Raciology." *boundary 2* 28, no. 3 (2001): 207–16.

Kanneh, Kadiatu. "Place, Time, and the Black Body: Myth and Resistance." *Oxford Literary Review* 13, no. 1 (1991): 140–63.

Kant, Immanuel. *Anthropology from a Pragmatic Point of View*. Translated by Mary J. Gregor. The Hague, Netherlands: Nijhoff, 1974.

———. *Critique of Judgement*. Translated by James Creed Meredith. Oxford: Clarendon Press, 1952.

———. *Critique of Pure Reason*. Translated by Norman Kemp Smith. London: Macmillan, 1978.

———. *Kritik der Urteilskraft*. Vol. 10 of *Werkausgabe*. Edited by Wilhelm Weischedel. Frankfurt, Germany: Suhrkamp, 1974.

Kaufmann, David. "Beyond Gnosticism and Magic." *New German Critique* 118 (Winter 2013): 29–41.

Kelly, Michael, ed. *Encyclopedia of Aesthetics*. 2nd ed. Oxford: Oxford University Press, 2014.

Khanna, Ranjana. *Dark Continents: Psychoanalysis and Colonialism*. Durham, N.C.: Duke University Press, 2003.

Koselleck, Reinhardt. *Kritik and Krise: Ein Beitrag zur Pathogenese der bürgerlichen Welt*. Freiburg, Germany: Alber, 1959.

Lacan, Jacques. *Ecrits 2*. Paris: Seuil, 1971.

Laird, Heather. *Subversive Law in Ireland, 1879–1920: From 'Unwritten Law' to the Dail Courts*. Dublin: Four Courts, 2005.

Land, Nick. *Fanged Noumena: Collected Writings, 1987–2007*. Edited by Robin MacKay and Ray Brassier. New York: Sequence, 2011.

Lazarus, Neil. *The Postcolonial Unconscious*. Cambridge: Cambridge University Press, 2011.

Li, Victor. "Necroidealism, or the Subaltern's Sacrificial Death." *Interventions* 11, no. 3 (2009): 275–92.

Lloyd, David. "Foundations of Diversity." In *"Culture" and the Problem of the Disciplines*, edited by John Carlos Rowe, 15–44. New York: Columbia University Press, 1998.

———. "Genet's Genealogy: European Minorities and the Ends of the Canon." *Cultural Critique* 6 (Spring 1987): 161–85.

———. *Irish Times: Temporalities of Modernity*. Dublin: Field Day, 2008.

———. *Irish Culture and Colonial Modernity, 1800–2000: The Transformation of Oral Space*. Cambridge: Cambridge University Press, 2011.

———. "Kant's Examples." *Representations* 28 (Autumn 1989): 34–54.

———. *Nationalism and Minor Literature: James Clarence Mangan and the Emergence of Irish Cultural Nationalism*. Berkeley: University of California Press, 1987.

Lloyd, David, and Paul Thomas. *Culture and the State*. London: Routledge, 1997.

Loesberg, Jonathan. *A Return to Aesthetics: Autonomy, Indifference, and Postmodernism*. Stanford, Calif.: Stanford University Press, 2005.

Lott, Tommy L. *The Invention of Race: Black Culture and the Politics of Representation*. Oxford: Blackwell, 1999.

Lowe, Lisa. *Immigrant Acts: On Asian American Cultural Politics*. Durham, N.C.: Duke University Press, 1997.

Lowe, Lisa, and David Lloyd. *The Politics of Culture in the Shadow of Culture.* Durham, N.C.: Duke University Press, 1997.

Lukács, Georg. *Probleme der Ästhetik, Werke.* Vol. 10. Berlin: Luchterhand, 1969.

———. *Theory of the Novel.* Translated by Anna Bostock. Cambridge, Mass.: MIT Press, 1971.

Luxemburg, Rosa. *The Accumulation of Capital.* London: Routledge, 2003.

Lyotard, Jean-François. *The Postmodern Condition: A Report on Knowledge.* Foreword by Frederic Jameson. Translated by Geoff Bennington and Brian Massumi. Minneapolis: University of Minnesota Press, 1984.

Macaulay, Thomas Babington. "Minute on Indian Education." In *Speeches by Lord Macaulay, with His Minute on Indian Education*, edited by G. M. Young, 345–61. 1835. Reprint, Oxford: Oxford University Press, 1935.

Makdisi, Saree. "The Empire Renarrated: *Season of Migration to the North* and the Reinvention of the Present." *Critical Inquiry* 18 (Summer 1992): 804–20.

Marchand, Suzanne. "Leo Frobenius and the Revolt against the West." *Journal of Contemporary History* 32, no. 2 (April 1997): 153–70.

Marcuse, Herbert. *The Aesthetic Dimension: Toward a Critique of Marxist Aesthetics.* Boston: Beacon, 1978.

———. *An Essay on Liberation.* Boston: Beacon, 1968.

———. *Negations: Essays in Critical Theory.* Translated by Jeremy J. Schapiro. Boston: Beacon, 1968.

Marquard, Odo. "Kant und die Wende zur Ästhetik." In *Zeitschrift für philosophische Forschung* 16 (1962). Reprint in *Zur Kantforschung der Gegenwart*, edited by Peter Heintel and Ludwig Nagl, 237–70. Darmstadt, Germany: Wissenschaftliche Buchgesellschaft, 1981.

Martens, Wolfgang. *Die Botschaft der Tugend. Die Aufklärung im Spiegel der deutschen moralischen Wochenschriften.* Stuttgart, Germany: J. B. Metzler, 1968.

Marx, Karl. *Capital: A Critique of Political Economy.* Vol. 1. Edited by F. Engels. Translated by S. Moore and E. Aveling. London: Lawrence and Wishart, 1954.

———. *A Contribution to the Critique of Political Economy.* Edited by Maurice Dobb. Translated by S. W. Ryazanskaya. Moscow: Progress, 1970.

———. *Das Kapital: Kritik der politischen Oekonomie.* Edited by B. Kautsky. Stuttgart, Germany: Kröner, 1957.

———. *Early Writings.* Introduction by Lucio Colletti. Edited by Quintin Hoare. Translated by Rodney Livingstone and Gregor Benton. New York: Vintage, 1975.

———. *The Eighteenth Brumaire of Louis Bonaparte.* Moscow: Foreign Languages, 1954.

————. *Grundrisse: Foundations of the Critique of Political Economy.* Translated and foreword by Martin Nicolaus. Harmondsworth, England: Penguin, 1973.

Marx, Karl. *Der Achtzehnte Brumaire des Louis Bonaparte.* In Karl Marx and Friedrich Engels, *Werke.* Vol. 8. Berlin: Dietz, 1960.

Mauss, Marcel. *A General Theory of Magic.* Translated by Robert Brain. 1950. Reprint, London: Routledge and Kegan Paul, 1972.

McKeon, Michael. "The Origins of Aesthetic Value." *Telos* 57 (Fall 1983): 63–82.

McKittrick, Katherine. "Yours in the Intellectual Struggle: Sylvia Wynter and the Realization of the Living." In *Sylvia Wynter: On Being Human as Praxis,* edited by Katherine McKittrick, 1–8. Durham, N.C.: Duke University Press, 2015.

McKittrick, Katherine, ed. *Sylvia Wynter: On Being Human as Praxis.* Durham, N.C.: Duke University Press, 2015.

Melamed, Jodi. *Represent and Destroy: Rationalizing Violence in the New Racial Capitalism.* Minneapolis: University of Minnesota Press, 2011.

Memmi, Albert. *The Colonizer and the Colonized.* Introduction by Jean-Paul Sartre. Translated by H. Greenfield. Boston: Beacon, 1967.

Merker, Nicolao. *An den Ursprüngen der deutschen Ideologie: Revolution und Utopie im Jakobinismus.* Edited and translated by Manfred Buhr. Berlin: Akademie-Verlag, 1984.

Mignolo, Walter D. "Sylvia Wynter: What Does It Mean to Be Human?" In *Sylvia Wynter: On Being Human as Praxis,* edited by Katherine McKittrick, 106–23. Durham, N.C.: Duke University Press, 2015.

Mikkelsen, Jon M. *Kant and the Concept of Race: Late Eighteenth-Century Writings.* Binghamton: State University of New York Press, 2004.

Mill, John Stuart. "Considerations on Representative Government." In *The Collected Works of John Stuart Mill.* Vol. 19. Edited by J. M. Robson, 572–73. Toronto: University of Toronto Press, 1977.

————. "What Is Poetry?" In *The Broadview Anthology of Victorian Poetry and Poetics,* edited by Thomas J. Collins and Vivienne J. Rundle, 1212–20. Peterborough, Ontario: Broadview, 1999.

Močnik, Rastko. "Towards a Materialist Concept of Literature." *Cultural Critique* 4 (Fall 1986): 171–89.

Mohanty, Satya P. "Kipling's Children and the Colour Line." *Race and Class* 31, no. 1 (July/September 1989): 21–40.

Morrison, Toni. *Playing in the Dark: Whiteness and the Literary Imagination.* Cambridge, Mass.: Harvard University Press, 1992.

Moten, Fred. "The Case of Blackness." *Criticism* 50, no. 2 (Spring 2008): 177–218.

———. *In the Break: The Aesthetics of the Black Radical Tradition.* Minneapolis: University of Minnesota Press, 2003.

Muñoz, José Esteban. *Cruising Utopia: The Then and There of Queer Futurity.* New York: New York University Press, 2009.

Nancy, Jean-Luc. *Listening.* Translated by Charlotte Mandell. New York: Fordham University Press, 2007.

———. *The Muses.* Translated by Peggy Kamuf. Stanford, Calif.: Stanford University Press, 1996.

Ngai, Sianne. *Our Aesthetic Categories: Zany, Cute, Interesting.* Cambridge, Mass.: Harvard University Press, 2012.

———. *Ugly Feelings.* Cambridge, Mass.: Harvard University Press, 2005.

Nunes, Zita. *Cannibal Democracy: Race and Representation in the Literature of the Americas.* Minneapolis: University of Minnesota Press, 2008.

Oliver, Kelly. "Alienation and Its Double; or, The Secretion of Race." In *Race and Racism in Continental Philosophy*, edited by Robert Bernasconi, 176–95. Bloomington: Indiana University Press, 2003.

Omi, Michael, and Howard Winant. *Racial Formation in the United States: From the 1960s to the 1990s.* 2nd ed. New York: Routledge, 1994.

Paine, Thomas. *Rights of Man.* Edited by Henry Collins. Harmondsworth, England: Penguin, 1969.

Pettit, Philip. *Republicanism: A Theory of Freedom and Government.* Oxford: Oxford University Press, 1997.

Purcell, Richard. "Trayvon, Postblackness, and the Postrace Dilemma," *boundary 2* 40, no. 3 (2013): 139–61.

Quigley, Mark. *Empire's Wake: Postcolonial Irish Writing and the Politics of Modern Literary Form.* New York: Fordham University Press, 2013.

Quijano, Anibal. "Coloniality of Power, Eurocentrism, and Latin America." *Nepantla* 1, no. 3 (2000): 533–80.

Rahnema, Majid. "Under the Banner of Development." *Seeds of Change* 1–2 (1986): 37–46.

Rancière, Jacques. *Dissensus: On Politics and Aesthetics.* Translated by Steven Corcoran. London: Bloomsbury Academic, 2015.

———. *Malaise dans l'esthétique.* Paris: Éditions Galilée, 2004.

———. *The Politics of Aesthetics.* Translated by Gabriel Rockhill. London: Verso, 2004.

Rhys, Jean. *Wide Sargasso Sea: A Novel.* New York: Norton, 1982.

Richards, Thomas. *The Imperial Archive: Knowledge and the Fantasy of Empire.* London: Verso, 1993.

Richter, Gerhard. "Adorno and the Excessive Politics of Aura." In *Benjamin's Blind Spot: Walter Benjamin and the Premature Death of Aura and The Manual of Lost Ideas*, edited by Lise Patt, 25–36. Topanga, Calif.: Institute of Cultural Inquiry, 2001.

Ricoeur, Paul. "Metaphor and the Main Problem of Hermeneutics." *NLH* 6, no. 1 (Autumn 1974): 95–110.

———. "The Metaphorical Process as Cognition, Imagination, and Feeling." In *On Metaphor*, edited by Sheldon Sacks, 141–57. Chicago: University of Chicago Press, 1979.

Robinson, Cedric. *Black Marxism: The Making of the Black Radical Tradition.* 2nd ed. 1983. Reprint, Raleigh: University of North Carolina Press, 2000.

———. *Forgeries of Memory and Meaning: Blacks and the Regimes of Race in American Theater and Film before World War II.* Chapel Hill: University of North Carolina Press, 2007.

Roff, Sarah Ley. "Benjamin and Psychoanalysis." In *The Cambridge Companion to Walter Benjamin*, edited by David S. Ferris, 115–33. Cambridge: Cambridge University Press, 2004.

Ryan, Alan. *Property and Political Theory.* Oxford: Blackwell, 1984.

Ryan, Vanessa L. "The Physiological Sublime: Burke's Critique of Reason." *Journal of the History of Ideas* 62, no. 2 (2001): 265–79.

Salih, Tayeb. *Season of Migration to the North.* Translated by Denys Johnson-Davies. London: Heinemann, 1976.

Sangari, Kumkum. *Politics of the Possible: Essays on Gender, History, Narratives, Colonial English.* London: Anthem, 2002.

Scarry, Elaine. *On Beauty and Being Just.* Princeton, N.J.: Princeton University Press, 2001.

Schiller, Friedrich. *On the Aesthetic Education of Man, in a Series of Letters.* Edited and translated by Elizabeth M. Wilkinson and L. A. Willoughby. Oxford: Clarendon, 1967.

Schmitt, Carl. *The Nomos of the Earth in the International Law of the Jus Publicum Europaeum.* Translated by G. L. Ulmen. New York: Telos, 2003.

Schrempp, Gregory. "Aristotle's Other Self: On the Boundless Subject of Anthropological Discourse." In *Romantic Motives: Essays on Anthropological Sensibility*, edited by George W. Stocking Jr., 10–43. Madison: University of Wisconsin Press, 1989.

See, Sarita Echavez. *The Decolonized Eye: Filipino American Art and Performance.* Minneapolis: University of Minnesota Press, 2009.

Seikaly, Samir. "*Season of Migration to the North*: History in the Novel." In *Tayeb Salih's Season of Migration to the North: A Casebook*, edited by Mona Takieddine Amyuni, 135–41. Beirut: American University of Beirut, 1985.

Sexton, Jared. *Amalgamation Schemes: Antiblackness and the Critique of Multiracialism.* Minneapolis: University of Minnesota Press, 2008.

Silliman, Ron. "Disappearance of the Word, Appearance of the World." In *The L=A=N=G=U=A=G=E Book*, edited by Bruce Andrews and Charles

Bernstein, 121–32. Carbondale: Southern Illinois University Press, 1984.

da Silva, Denise Ferreira. "Extraordinary Times: A Preface." *Cultural Dynamics* 26, no. 1 (2014): 3–8.

———. *Toward a Global Idea of Race.* Minneapolis: University of Minnesota Press, 2007.

———. "No Bodies." *Griffith Law Review* 18, no. 2 (2009): 213–36.

Spillers, Hortense J. *Black, White and in Color: Essays on American Literature and Culture.* Chicago: University of Chicago Press, 2003.

Spivak, Gayatri Charkravorty. "Can the Subaltern Speak?" In *Marxism and the Interpretation of Culture*, edited by Cary Nelson and Lawrence Grossberg, 271–313. Urbana: University of Illinois Press, 1988.

———. *A Critique of Postcolonial Reason: Toward a History of the Vanishing Present.* Cambridge, Mass.: Harvard University Press, 1999.

———. "Response." *PMLA* 129, no. 3 (2014): 518–21.

———. "Scattered Speculations on the Subaltern and the Popular." *Postcolonial Studies* 8, no. 4 (2005): 475–86.

———. "Subaltern Studies: Deconstructing Historiography." In *Selected Subaltern Studies*, edited by Ranajit Guha and Gayatri Chakravorty Spivak, 3–33. New York: Oxford University Press, 1988.

———. "Supplementing Marxism." In *Whither Marxism? Global Crisis in the International Context*, edited by Bernard Magnus and Stephen Cullenberg, 109–19. London: Routledge, 1995.

Sprinker, Michael. *Imaginary Relations: Aesthetics and Ideology in the Theory of Historical Materialism.* London: Verso, 1987.

Stallybrass, Peter. "'Well Grubbed, Old Mole': Marx, Hamlet, and the (Un)Fixing of Representation." *Cultural Studies* 12, no. 1 (1998): 3–14.

Staricius, Johannes. *Geheimnisvoller Heldenschatz oder Vollständiger Egyptische Magische Schild.* 1750. Facsimile reprint. Freiburg, Germany: Aurum Verlag, 1978.

Stewart, Elizabeth. *Catastrophe and Survival: Walter Benjamin and Psychoanalysis.* New York: Continuum, 2010.

Stocking, George W. Jr. *Race, Culture and Evolution: Essays in the History of Anthropology.* New York: Macmillan/Free Press, 1968.

Streeby, Shelley. *American Sensations: Class, Empire, and the Production of Popular Culture.* Berkeley: University of California Press, 2002.

Terada, Rei. "The Racial Grammar of Kantian Time." *European Romantic Review* 28, no. 3 (2017): 267–78.

Thacker, Eugene. *In the Dust of This Planet.* Horror of Philosophy, vol. I. Winchester, England: Zero, 2011.

Thomas, Paul. "Alien Politics: A Marxian Perspective on Citizenship and

Theory." In *After Marx*, edited by Terence Ball and James Farr, 124–40. Cambridge: Cambridge University Press, 1984.

Torgovnick, Marianna. *Gone Primitive: Savage Intellects, Modern Lives*. Chicago: University of Chicago Press, 1991.

Torres, Carmen. "Colonialism and Gender in *A Season of Migration to the North*." Master's thesis, University of California, Berkeley, May 1990.

Tylor, Edward Burnett. *The Origins of Culture*. New York: Harper, 1958.

Varadharajan, Asha. *Exotic Parodies: Subjectivity in Adorno, Said, and Spivak*. Minneapolis: University of Minnesota Press, 1995.

Vergès, Françoise. *Monsters and Revolutionaries: Colonial Family Romance and Métissage*. Durham, N.C.: Duke University Press, 1999.

Weheliye, Alexander G. *Habeas Viscus: Racializing Assemblages, Biopolitics, and Black Feminist Theories of the Human*. Durham, N.C.: Duke University Press, 2014.

Wilderson, Frank. "The Prison Slave as Hegemony's (Silent) Scandal." *Social Justice* 30, no. 2 (2003): 18–27.

Williams, Eric. *Capitalism and Slavery*. 1944. Reprint, Raleigh: University of North Carolina Press, 1994.

Williams, Raymond. *Keywords: A Vocabulary of Culture and Society*. Rev. ed. New York: Oxford University Press, 1985.

Wolfe, Patrick. *Traces of History: Elementary Structures of Race*. London: Verso, 2016.

Woodmansee, Martha. "Towards a Genealogy of the Aesthetic: The German Reading Debate of the 1790s." *Cultural Critique* 11 (Winter 1988–1989): 203–21.

Wynter, Sylvia. "On Disenchanting Discourse: 'Minority' Literary Criticism and Beyond." In *The Nature and Context of Minority Discourse*, edited by Abdul JanMohamed and David Lloyd, 432–69. Oxford: Oxford University Press, 1990.

———. "Unsettling the Coloniality of Being/Power/Truth/Freedom: Towards the Human, After Man, Its Overrepresentation—An Argument." *CR: The New Centennial Review* 3, no. 3 (Fall 2003): 257–337.

Young, Robert J. C. *Colonial Desire: Hybridity in Theory, Culture and Race*. New York: Routledge, 1995.

Zahar, Renate. *Colonialism and Alienation: Concerning Frantz Fanon's Political Theory*. Benin City, Nigeria: Ethiope, 1974.

Zammito, John H. *The Genesis of Kant's Critique of Judgment*. Chicago: University of Chicago Press, 1992.

———. *Kant, Herder and the Birth of Anthropology*. Chicago: University of Chicago Press, 2002.

Zimmerman, Andrew. *Anthropology and Antihumanism in Imperial Germany*. Chicago: University of Chicago Press, 2001.

———. "Primitive Art, Primitive Accumulation, and the Origin of the Work of Art in German New Guinea." *History of the Present* 1, no. 1 (Summer 2011): 5–30.

Zimmerman, Andrew, ed. *Volksgeist as Method and Ethic: Essays on Boasian Ethnography and the German Anthropological Tradition.* Madison: University of Wisconsin Press, 1996.

Printed and bound by CPI Group (UK) Ltd, Croydon, CR0 4YY

09/06/2025

14685656-0002